CREATING VISUAL SCHEDULES

CREATING VISUAL SCHEDULES

The Schedule Evaluation Tool (SET) for People with Autism Spectrum Disorder and Intellectual Disabilities

Johanne Mainville, Sonia Di Lillo, Nathalie Poirier, and Nathalie Plante

English translation directed by Nathalie Poirier

Translated by Tanina Drvar

University of Ottawa Press
2024

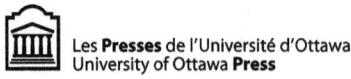

Les **Presses** de l'Université d'Ottawa
University of Ottawa **Press**

The University of Ottawa Press (UOP) is proud to be the oldest of the francophone university presses in Canada and the oldest bilingual university publisher in North America. Since 1936, UOP has been enriching intellectual and cultural discourse by producing peer-reviewed and award-winning books in the humanities and social sciences, in French and in English.

www.press.uOttawa.ca

Library and Archives Canada Cataloguing in Publication

Title: Creating visual schedules : the schedule evaluation tool (SET) for people with autism spectrum disorder and intellectual disabilities / by Johanne Mainville, Sonia Di Lillo, Nathalie Poirier, and Nathalie Plante ; preface by Dr. Guy Sabourin, psychologist ; translated by Tanina Drvar.
Other titles: Outil d'évaluation des structures du temps. English
Names: Mainville, Johanne, 1973- author. | Di Lillo, Sonia, author. | Poirier, Nathalie, 1969- author. | Plante, Nathalie, 1967- author.
Description: Translation of: Outil d'évaluation des structures du temps : pour les personnes présentant un trouble du spectre de l'autisme. | Includes bibliographical references.
Identifiers: Canadiana (print) 20220452520 | Canadiana (ebook) 20220452563 | ISBN 9780776639758 (hardcover) | ISBN 9780776639727 (softcover) | ISBN 9780776639734 (PDF) | ISBN 9780776639741 (EPUB)
Subjects: LCSH: Autistic people—Life skills guides. | LCSH: Autistic people—Time management—Handbooks, manuals, etc.
Classification: LCC RC553.A88 M34 2023 | DDC 616.85/882—dc23

Legal Deposit: First Quarter 2024 Library and Archives Canada		© Presses de l'Université du Québec, 2021, for the original edition. Original title: Outil d'évaluation des structures de temps : pour les personnes présentant un trouble du spectre de l'autisme. Translated from the French language. © University of Ottawa Press 2024, for the English edition. All rights reserved. No part of this publication may be reproduced or transmitted in any form or by any means, or stored in a database and retrieval system, without prior permission.
Production Team		
Copy editing	Crystal Chan	
Proofreading	Justine Hart	
Typesetting	Transforma	
Cover design	Lefrançois, agence marketing B2B	

Cover Image
Jean Lee, *Mind Meeting Heart*, acrylic on canvas, 91.44 cm x 91.44 cm

This book has been published with the financial support of the Université du Québec à Montréal.

The University of Ottawa Press gratefully acknowledges the support extended to its publishing list by the Government of Canada, the Canada Council for the Arts, the Ontario Arts Council, Ontario Creates, the Social Sciences and Humanities Research Council, the Canadian Federation for the Humanities and Social Sciences through the Scholarly Book Awards (ASPP), and by the University of Ottawa.

The painting featured on the cover of this book, reproduced here in black and white, is *Mind Meeting Heart* by Canadian artist Jean Lee. Using expressive, richly textured brushstrokes, Lee captures her exploration of her own self-awareness—an inquiry that requires deep introspection and inevitably strengthens the communication between mind and heart.

Lee is a Canadian contemporary painter who uses maps, the natural world, and the subconscious to envision landscapes from an aerial perspective. She currently works with a variety of media, including painting, collage, and digital photography. She has a diploma in Studio Arts from Capilano University and has studied at the Emily Carr Institute of Art and Design in Vancouver.

Table of Contents

List of Figures xi
List of Excerpts xiii
Description of Supplementary Material xv
Foreword xvii
Acknowledgements xix

Presentation A1
    The Importance of a Schedule A2
    The SET's Main Objectives A3
    Target Population A3
    Examiner Training A3

EVALUATING SCHEDULE CHARACTERISTICS
Introduction A7
    The Eight Schedule Characteristics
    Evaluated Using the SET A7
    Schedule Evaluation Sequence A8
    Required Material A8
        Overview of the Schedule Evaluation Protocol A9
        Symbol Meaning A10
    Information on the Visual Supports Used During
    the Evaluation A10

Part 1 .... A13
    Goal A13
    Duration A13
    Administration A13
    Sequence A14
        1. Prepare the Material for Evaluating Part 1 .... A14
        2. Identify Where to Start the Evaluation A15
        3. Use the Stop Standards to Identify Which
            Section or Subsection to Evaluate Next A15
        4. Demonstrations, Evaluation, and Scoring A16
            4.1. Detailed Procedure for 1A Subsections A21
            4.2. Detailed Procedure for 1B Subsections A23
            4.3. Detailed Procedure for 1C Subsections A29
        5. Scoring Part 1 in the Schedule Evaluation
            Protocol A36

Part 2 .... A45
    Goal A45
    Duration.. A45
    Administration A45
    Sequence A46
        1. Fill in the Required Information in the
           Schedule Evaluation Protocol A46
        2. Choose the Visual Support Category
           to Evaluate.. A47
        3. Determine Where the Matching Boxes Will
           Be Installed A47
        4. Prepare the Material for Part 2 .... A50
        5. Prepare the Material for the Visual Support
           Form to Evaluate A52
        6. Demonstrations, Evaluation, and Scoring............. A53
              6.1. Detailed Procedure for Visual Support
                  Form 1.. A56
              6.2. Detailed Procedure for Visual Support
                  Form 2 .... A60
              6.3. Detailed Procedure for Visual Support
                  Form 3.. A63
        7. Scoring Part 2 of the Evaluation in the
           Schedule Evaluation Protocol A66

Part 3 .... A71
    Goal A71
    Duration.. A71
    Administration A71
    Sequence for Section 3A A72
        1. Prepare the Material for Evaluating
           Section 3A A73
              1.1. For a Visual Support in OBJ Form................... A73
              1.2. For Other Visual Support Forms..................... A75
        2. Demonstrations, Evaluation, and Scoring............. A78
              2.1. Detailed Procedure for Subsection 3A.1 .... A80
              2.2. Detailed Procedure for Subsection 3A.2 .... A84
              2.3. Detailed Procedure for Subsection 3A.3 .... A88
    Sequence for Section 3B A90
        1. Identify the Visual Support Form, the Category,
           and the Type of Schedule Being Evaluated........... A92

  2. Prepare the Material for Evaluating Section 3B ...A92
  3. Demonstrations, Evaluation, and Scoring.............A97
   3.1. Detailed Procedure for Subsection 3B.1 ....A100
   3.2. Detailed Procedure for Subsection 3B.2 ....A102
  4. Scoring Part 3 in the Evaluation Protocol A104

Part 4 ....A107
 Goal A107
 Duration..A107
 Administration A107
 Sequence A108
  1. Detailed Procedure for Section 4A: Identifying the Schedule with a Cue That Relates to the User's Interests A108
  2. Detailed Procedure for Section 4B: Finding an Individualized Location A109
  3. Detailed Procedure for Section 4C: Schedule Content (Activities and Representative Visual Supports) A110

RECOMMENDATIONS REPORT
 Schedule Characteristics.. A117
 Schedule Content... A119
 Procedures to Follow..A121
 Comments and Signature..A121

SCHEDULE ADJUSTMENT PROTOCOL
 Use the Adjustment Protocol to Modify These Seven Characteristics A126
 Schedule Adjustment Sequence...................................A127
 Material Required for the Adjustment........................A127
 Administration A127
  Part 1...A127
   A. Identify If the Adjustment's Prerequisites Are Met A128
   B. Evaluate the Level of Independence for the Current Schedule A128
   C. Identify the Characteristics to Adjust A128
  Part 2... A131
   Adjustment Prerequisites A131

    Adjustment Benefits A132
    Pre-Evaluation A132
    Introduction and Evaluation Phases A132
    Recommendations Report A134

Pre-Experimental Results A137

Bibliography A141

SUPPLEMENTARY MATERIAL: SCHEDULE EVALUATION TOOL

List of Figures

Figure 1.1.	Matching boxes mounted on corrugated plastic sheet panels used for Part 1 of the evaluation	A14
Figure 1.2.	Basket labelled "Bag 1C"	A30
Figure 2.1.	How to use the examiner's tray while moving around (form of visual support evaluated: OBJ)	A51
Figure 2.2.	Organization of examiner's tray for the PIC visual support form	A52
Figure 2.3.	Matching box stuck to the bathroom door with toothbrush visual support in OBJ form	A53
Figure 3.1.	Examiner's tray arranged for the evaluation of Section 3A, OBJ form	A74
Figure 3.2.	Piggy bank mounted on schedule strip	A75
Figure 3.3.	Examiner's tray assembled to evaluate Section 3A, visual support forms other than OBJ	A76
Figure 3.4.	Schedule cues box mounted on the schedule strip	A78
Figure 3.5.	Detailed actions for a token schedule, "Work/School" category, and the WWH visual support form	A91
Figure 3.6.	Examples for displaying the checkmark schedule	A93
Figure 3.7.	Examples for displaying the token schedule	A94
Figure 3.8.	Triage station for the "Work/School" category	A94
Figure 3.9.	Location identification using visual supports with names, WWH visual support form	A95
Figure 3.10.	Examiner's tray assembled for Subsection 3B	A96

List of Excerpts

Excerpt 1.	Schedule Evaluation Protocol, Subsection 1C.WTC	A18
Excerpt 2.	Schedule Evaluation Protocol, Subsection 1C.PHO	A31
Excerpt 3.	Schedule Evaluation Protocol, Table 2. Scoring Part 1	A47
Excerpt 4.	Schedule Evaluation Protocol, Visual Support Form 1	A49
Excerpt 5.	Schedule Evaluation Protocol, Table 3. Location of Visual Supports	A50
Excerpt 6.	Schedule Evaluation Protocol, Visual Support Form 1	A57
Excerpt 7.	Schedule Evaluation Protocol, Table 8. Location of 3B Baskets: Object Baskets (Different than in Section 3A)	A96
Excerpt 8.	Schedule Evaluation Protocol, Subsection 3B.1	A99
Excerpt 9.	Schedule Evaluation Protocol, Table 12. Scoring Part 3. "Identification" Characteristic + Section 4A	A108
Excerpt 10.	Schedule Evaluation Protocol, Section 4B	A111
Excerpt 11.	Schedule Evaluation Protocol, Section 4C, Home Setting	A113
Excerpt 12.	Completed Independence Evaluation Grid (One Day Out of Three Required)	A130
Excerpt 13.	Schedule Adjustment Protocol, Adjustment 9, Characteristic to Adjust: Schedule Manipulation	A133

Description of Supplementary Material

1. The Schedule Evaluation Protocol — B1
   To photocopy and use throughout the evaluation.*

2. The Recommendations Report — B47
   To photocopy and fill out after evaluating schedule characteristics or completing schedule adjustments.*

3. The Schedule Adjustment Protocol — B55
   Another tool to use once the schedule is well established and the user is comfortable using it. To photocopy.*

4. The Independence Evaluation Grid — B87
   To photocopy.*

   A1. Appendix 1: Material — B89
   Description of material to prepare for the SET kit.

   A2. Appendix 2: Token Schedule and Checkmark Schedule Sheets — B115
   Token schedule or checkmark schedule sheets to photocopy for Part 3 of the evaluation.*

*It is essential that these documents are photocopied on 8.5″ × 11″ sheets of paper. They will need to be enlarged.

Foreword

When the authors asked me to write the foreword for *Creating Visual Schedules*, I first thought to share the quite revealing story behind this tool. Emerging from a significant number of clinical observations made in the early 2000s, the project was developed in Montréal by the Regional Multidisciplinary Expertise Program for Persons with Severe Behavior Disorders (PREM-TGC). Johanne Mainville and Sonia Di Lillo were our specialists in autism spectrum disorders (ASD) at the time.

Most people who were referred to us back then had autism spectrum disorder with various mild to severe behavioural disorders. It became clear rather quickly in our clinical discussions that most of these individuals were lacking environmental adaptations to better mitigate the different deficits of their disorders. We postulated that a substantial part of their behavioural problems stemmed from the lack of visual supports and the great need for predictability in their environments.

During this time, the programs available in several rehabilitation centres and adapted to patients with ASD were not well known and poorly implemented. We also observed that even though some individuals did not have an ASD diagnosis in their files, many had cognitive and behavioural deficits similar to those of autism. These individuals responded very well to structured support and responsive means of communication, which were focused on time management through visual stimuli.

This was the specific clinical context that led to the development of the Schedule Evaluation Tool (SET). There was an absolute necessity to create a tool like this to support professionals who directly evaluate the needs of this clientele and to implement a time-management system, which was, of course, inspired by the TEACCH® approach. To develop the SET, two other ASD specialists, Nathalie Poirier and Nathalie Plante, collaborated with the PREM-TGC.

According to Siegel (2003), the TEACCH® approach focuses on the preferences and strengths of people with ASD, particularly their aptitude for using and processing visual information in the form of schedules to adapt to their environment. People with ASD require a lot of explicit rules to self-regulate and a highly predictable environment to function properly.

This may be largely explained by the fact that they have a different neurological and cognitive function and a very particular profile of associated deficits. Thus, if their environment has not been suitably adapted to compensate for their specific deficits, namely their difficulties with planning and behavioural flexibility, they will tend to behave in inappropriate, rather inflexible, and ineffective ways. Moreover, the greater a person's neurological impairment, the more present this particular way of functioning will be (Carbonneau et al. 2009). A 2009 study has also shown that if the autistic symptomatology is severe, then the problematic behaviour will be more extensive (Matson, Wilkins, and Macken 2009).

Since the Rehabilitation Centre for People with Intellectual Disabilities or a Pervasive Developmental Disorder (RCID-PDD) has been entrusted with the mandate to organize and provide services to clients with ASD, important work has been done in Quebec to develop expertise in this field under the aegis of the Fédération québécoise des CRDITED (Quebec federation of RCID-PDDs). These efforts have better equipped professionals who work directly with people with ASD and helped them develop programs that are better adapted to their clientele.

The authors are to be commended and thanked for their determination and dedication to this clientele. The result of their work in recent years has made it possible to create this most useful tool. I would also like to highlight their remarkable efforts to share their expertise, which is invaluable to professionals working directly with people with ASD, but more importantly to the people with ASD themselves.

Guy Sabourin
Psychologist and Director of the Service québécois d'expertise en troubles graves du comportement

Acknowledgements

We would like to express our gratitude to the Service québécois d'expertise en troubles graves du comportement (SQETGC) for their financial support and for participating in a substantial part of this work. Their support throughout the years has allowed us to create, adapt, and improve the Schedule Evaluation Tool (SET), and without them, this tool would not be available today. A special thank-you to Dr. Guy Sabourin, Psychologist and Director of the SQETGC, for his involvement and guidance, which helped us design and finalize the tool. Thank you as well for writing the foreword and for the pre-experimental results.

We would also like to say a very special thank-you to Tanina Drvar for the English translation; her professionalism and dedication allowed this project to become a reality. And we are very grateful to the University of Ottawa Press for their interest in making this important tool available to an English-speaking audience, and to Nathalie Poirier, the third author on this book, for her time and energy in coordinating the project.

A very big thank-you to the late Yves Desjardins from CCI Grafix for his invaluable design assistance and helping us lay out the graphics, photographs, and pictograms in the original version. Without his support and professionalism, this tool would not be functional.

We would also like to thank the students at Édouard-Montpetit High School of the Commission scolaire de Montréal, and the teachers who work with students with autism spectrum disorder, for helping us to build the very first version of the tool by cutting out photographs and pictograms, and sorting and assembling all the evaluation materials.

We are also very grateful to the educators who tested the SET in the field and provided us with data on the children, teenagers, and adults they work with. This allowed us to build a pre-experimental sample. For reviewing the evaluation, thank you to Éric Lauzon (Commission scolaire Marguerite-Bourgeoys), Johanne Rouleau (Commission scolaire de Montréal), Sophie Turcotte (Commission scolaire de Montréal), Lina Cloutier (Commission scolaire de la Pointe-de-l'Île), Lise Proulx (Client Services at CRDITED

Gabrielle-Major), Daniel Brisson (resources manager at Deux-Rives), Isabelle Lehouillier (guidance counselor specialized in autism spectrum disorders), and Mélanie Lamoureux-Hébert (psychologist at CRDITED Services de réadaptation du Sud-Ouest et du Renfort).

And most importantly, a very special thank-you to the children, teenagers, and adults with autism spectrum disorder who kindly took part in an evaluation using the SET. Their help was invaluable.

Presentation

Several studies highlight the importance for people with autism spectrum disorder (ASD) to have visual tools, a schedule, and guides to understand their environment and cope with everyday life (Missouri Autism Guidelines Initiative 2012; National Autism Center 2015; Virginia Department of Education 2011). These elements are part of the person's environmental structure and their effectiveness rests on individualization and adaptation. Educators who wish to implement such a structure must therefore determine each user's individual needs and understanding to ensure the structure's effectiveness.[1]

However, as there was no formal test available to do this, we created the Schedule Evaluation Tool (SET) specifically for this purpose. This tool aims to support educators in evaluating schedule characteristics, including whether the user will easily understand the visual supports and whether those visual supports will be appropriate to use in their individual schedule.

The goal of the SET is to help educators and anyone else working with people with ASD determine which type of schedule is best suited to the user and the most effective ways to use it. The schedule can then

---

1   In this context, the term "user" refers to the person with autism spectrum disorder (ASD) and "educator" to the person managing the user's schedule and helping them use it.

be implemented in the user's environment to develop their autonomy and ultimately improve their quality of life.

The Importance of a Schedule

Schedules are essential tools for people with ASD: they help them understand the activities they need to do and the sequence in which to do them. They thus represent an invaluable receptive communication tool for people with ASD. Educators can use the SET to choose visual supports (objects, photographs, pictograms, etc.) so they can develop tools that will help the person understand their environment (receptive communication) and express themselves (expressive communication). Additionally, the process of personalizing the schedule is closely related to the physical structure that, at times, must be set up in the environment where the activities will take place. The SET can thus also guide educators in determining which visual supports to use to identify places.

Over time, educators may need to modify a user's personalized schedule according to different considerations. For example, a user's environment may change (they may be integrating into a new workplace) or the educator may wish to make the structure more portable (if they are assisting a student who may travel more frequently between different environments when they transition from elementary school to high school). For assistance in this process, the educator can refer to the Schedule Adjustment Protocol, which provides guidelines for making these changes.[2]

In short, a schedule allows people with autism spectrum disorder to plan and understand the sequence of activities to carry out. Teaching a routine by using a visual schedule facilitates a user's concentration and their management of emotions, and can even reduce rigid behaviours when a user is faced with unforeseen events. It also promotes autonomy in completing tasks as well as a better understanding of instructions, and helps to mitigate mnestic deficits.

The schedule's purpose is to visually communicate what the person with ASD needs to do. The tool has several benefits:

1. Using a daily schedule reduces anxiety. Seeing the sequence of tasks to be done throughout the day puts the user more at ease.

---

[2] This document is hereafter referred to as the "Adjustment Protocol."

2. Viewing a sequence of activities allows the person with ASD to know what needs to be done and allows them to carry out a full series of activities on their own.
3. The schedule encourages active participation in activities, as after completing mandatory tasks, the users can devote themselves to the activities they prefer.
4. Implementing a schedule eases the anticipation of upcoming activities and helps manage the unexpected.

The SET's Main Objectives

The SET consists of two separate procedures: evaluating the schedule's characteristics and adjusting the schedule.

The first procedure is performed using the Schedule Evaluation Protocol.[3] The protocol evaluates a schedule's characteristics to identify components to include in a user's first schedule.

The second uses the Adjustment Protocol, which assists in adjusting a schedule's different characteristics to help the user reach a greater level of autonomy. The user can thus become more independent in managing their schedule, reducing the time the educator devotes to managing the schedule daily. This second procedure can be used both for a schedule that was created using the SET or one created through other means.

Target Population

- Children with autism spectrum disorder without an intellectual disability.
- Children, teenagers, and adults with autism spectrum disorder and an intellectual disability.
- Children, teenagers, and adults with an intellectual or developmental disability.

Examiner Training

Educators who administer, score, and interpret the results of the SET should be trained in the process. The training should include general guidelines on how to administer the evaluation, and how to score and

---

[3] This document is hereafter referred to as the "Evaluation Protocol."

interpret the results. There are different ways to participate in training, including evaluation courses taught at universities or colleges and usually offered by the psychology, psychoeducation, or special education departments. Additionally, it may be offered by school boards, social and health services, or private organizations.

Educators should also be familiar with the structured and individualized intervention principles of the TEACCH® model, and possess the knowledge required to evaluate people with ASD or developmental disabilities.

Educators with little to no evaluation experience should follow a specific SET training or conduct the evaluation using the SET at least three times under the direct supervision of an experienced examiner. For more information about SET training, please email formations.ouest@gmail.com.

EVALUATING SCHEDULE CHARACTERISTICS

Introduction

Evaluating a schedule's characteristics using the Evaluation Protocol identifies which components to include in a user's first schedule.

The Eight Schedule Characteristics Evaluated Using the SET[1]

Layout: The schedule can be arranged from top to bottom or from left to right.

Location: When the schedule is placed in a specific location (stationary schedule), it must be easily accessible. It can be put in a common area with other people's schedules (group transition area) or kept apart in a place specific to the user (individualized location).

Presentation: The schedule can be in a stationary format, such as a schedule displayed on a flat surface or mounted on a wall, or in a portable format, such as an agenda. In some instances, the examiner may need to present the visual support representing the next activity to the user before each transition, and in that case, the schedule will not be installed anywhere.

Length: Schedules can vary in length, ranging from one item at a time to a full day of activities (sometimes even a full week, organized in a binder).

---

1 Inspired by Dougherty (1995).

Forms of visual support: Depending on the user's developmental level, the schedule can use the following forms of visual support:

a) Objects
b) Photographs
c) Pictograms
d) Words (typed or handwritten)

Identification: For the user to identify their schedule, particularly when it is kept in a group transition area their name or picture, or even a visual support representing one of their interests, can be added.

Initiation: Initiation refers to the routine that helps the user disengage from an activity and engage with their schedule. If the user needs help identifying when it is time to consult their schedule, the educator can provide a schedule cue to let them know it is time to make the transition.

Manipulation: The user may need to manipulate the schedule's visual supports at the end of an activity to indicate that the activity has been completed and that it is time to transition to the next one. For example, they can remove the activity cue, carry it with them to where the activity will take place, remove the visual support once the activity is complete, and then put it in a box marked "Finished," flip the cue over, place a token over it, cross off the activity, or place a checkmark next to it on a written list.

Schedule Evaluation Sequence

The schedule evaluation is divided into four parts. The first part is undertaken in a formal evaluation setting, at a table. The second and third parts are conducted in the environment where the schedule will be used. The fourth part entails interviewing a person who knows the user well in the environment where the schedule will be implemented. The evaluation can vary in duration (see details for each part of the evaluation) and may be done over the course of one or more meetings.

Required Material

A schedule's characteristics are evaluated using this guide, the Evaluation Protocol, the SET kit (email trousse.ouest@gmail.com to find out how to obtain an entire SET kit or the materials required to create the kit on your own and see appendices 1 and 2 in the Supplementary

Material section for instructions on how to create the kit), and the Recommendations Report.

The Evaluation Guide contains detailed information for evaluating schedule characteristics.

The Evaluation Protocol, on the other hand, includes a summary of the important information needed to evaluate schedule characteristics. It outlines what materials to use from the kit, standards on when to stop the evaluation ("stop standards"), and other useful instructions.

The Recommendations Report must be filled in after the evaluation. This document contains all the relevant information identified during the evaluation.

The Evaluation Protocol and the Recommendations Report are included in the Supplementary Material. When photocopying, these documents must be enlarged to an 8.5" × 11" format; this will give the examiner enough space to write down all the necessary information during the evaluation.

CREATING VISUAL SCHEDULES

Overview of the Schedule Evaluation Protocol

① **SECTION 1A**

🚩 **START THE EVALUATION HERE**
Only if the user's skill level is unknown or they are unable to match two identical pictograms.

③
- 3 object bags: Home bag, Work/School bag, and Other bag
- Bottom panel and back panel
- 3 matching boxes

② **SUBSECTION 1A.OBJ (OBJECT–OBJECT)**

CATEGORY	DEMOS	ORDER OF VISUAL SUPPORTS ON MATCHING BOXES	SCORING	COMMENTS AND OBSERVATIONS
Home	2 opt. demos/ support	Toothbrush Sock Lego	/3	
Work/ School	2 opt. demos/ support	Spoon Pencil Disc	/3	
Other	2 opt. demos/ support	Ball Marker Sponge	/3	
		SUBTOTAL	/9	
		TOTAL **1A.OBJ** (SUBTOTAL X 2)	/18	☐ 1A.OBJ not evaluated (18/18)

① Section name
② Subsection name
③ Material to use for Section 1A

Symbol Meaning

For the examiner to quickly locate the information they need to proceed with the evaluation, several symbols are used in the Evaluation Protocol.

Legend of Symbols

SYMBOL	MEANING
🚩	Section or subsection where evaluation may directly begin (found in three locations).
🛠	Materials needed to evaluate a part, section, or subsection.
✋	Stop the evaluation here (stop standard) and follow the outlined procedure.
✏	Score the section or subsection indicated after this symbol.
▶	Continue the evaluation at the part, section, or subsection that directly follows the scoring indicated before the symbol.
⏩	Skip ahead several sections or subsections and continue the evaluation at the location indicated after this symbol.
↩	Return to the section or subsection indicated to the right of this symbol and proceed with the evaluation based on the results obtained by the user.
1 opt. demo	Number of optional demonstrations allowed.
1 mand. demo	Number of mandatory demonstrations.
≤	Less than or equal to…
≥	Greater than or equal to…
❷ PRESENTATION MODE	Relevant information for the Schedule Recommendations Report. The corresponding number and title can be found in the report.

Information on the Visual Supports Used During the Evaluation

Nine visual representations of objects are used in the evaluation, each in six different forms. They are grouped into three categories: Home, Work/School, and Other. Below is a list of the visual supports used in each category.

CATEGORIES	OBJECTS REPRESENTED BY VISUAL SUPPORTS
HOME	Toothbrush Sock Lego
WORK/SCHOOL	Spoon Pencil Disc
OTHER	Ball Marker Sponge

Each category's visual supports are used throughout the evaluation in different forms. These include:

1. Objects (OBJ)
2. Photographs (PHO)
3. Colour pictograms (PIC)
4. Black-and-white pictograms (BWP)
5. Words typed on the computer (WTC)
6. Words written by hand (WWH)

The visual supports in the "Other" category are all the same colour; this helps assess whether the user mainly relies on colour to match objects and images. Similarly, the colour of each pictogram (PIC) in all three categories differs from the colour of the same visual support in object form (OBJ). This helps gauge whether the user recognizes the representation of an object even when the physical features of the actual object are not identical to its image representation.

Part 1

Goal

The goal of Part 1 is to identify the different forms of visual supports that will be used in Part 2 to experiment with different types of schedules. To do this, the user will be asked to match different visual supports to corresponding boxes.

Duration

10 to 20 minutes.

Administration

Part 1 of the evaluation is conducted in a formal setting. The examiner and user are seated at a table. Three matching boxes, each identified with a visual support, are placed before the user. The examiner gives the user one visual support at a time. The user must then match each support to the corresponding box.

Part 1 of the evaluation is divided into three sections: 1A, 1B, and 1C. Each section is divided into subsections, for example 1A.OBJ, 1B.PHO, 1B.PIC. The alphanumeric characters to the left of the period refer to the section (e.g., 1A), and the letters to the right refer to the form of visual support used (e.g., OBJ = object, PHO = photograph, etc.).

Sequence

The evaluation sequence as presented here applies to all of Part 1. The steps to follow for the demonstration, evaluation, and scoring are explained in greater detail in each section of Part 1 (1A, 1B, 1C).

The evaluation should proceed as follows for all Part 1 subsections: the examiner hands the user one visual support at a time, and the user is then asked to match that support to the corresponding box.

1. Prepare the Material for Evaluating Part 1

First, we recommend always preparing the material required for the evaluation beforehand to ensure it can be accessed quickly when needed. To know which materials are necessary for Part 1, refer to the ✂ symbol (located on p. B8 of the Evaluation Protocol directly under the "Part 1" title). Material is typically labelled for easy identification.

For Part 1, mount the three matching boxes on the back and bottom corrugated plastic panels. Unfold the two panels, mount the three matching boxes to the bottom panel, then mount the back panel to the bottom of the boxes (see Figure 1.1).

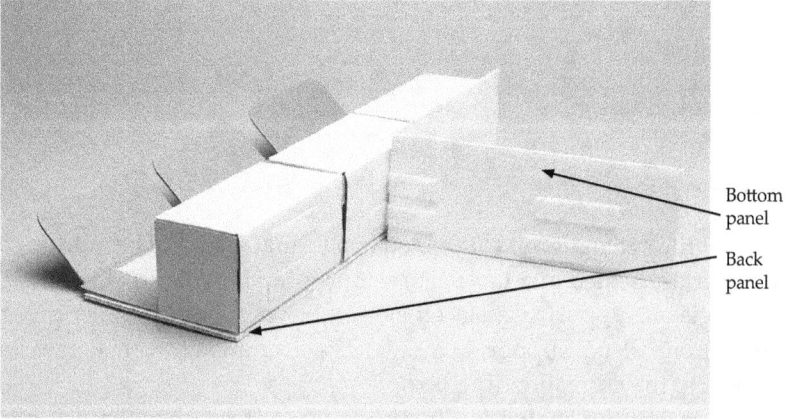

Figure 1.1. Matching boxes mounted on corrugated plastic sheet panels used for Part 1 of the evaluation.

Source: Artimage 2015.

To know what materials are required for each subsection, refer to the ✂ symbol at the beginning of each section in the Evaluation Protocol as well as the beginning of each subsection where the evaluation may begin.

2. Identify Where to Start the Evaluation

The evaluation can be personalized for each user. As individuals with ASD have very diverse functional skills, the evaluation may start at different sections or subsections.

To know where to start the evaluation, follow these instructions (the instructions can also be found next to the ▶ symbol in the Evaluation Protocol in Subsections 1A.OBJ, 1B.PIC, and 1C.WTC):

- Start the evaluation in Subsection 1A.OBJ if the user's skill level is unknown or they are unable to match two identical pictograms.
- Start the evaluation in Subsection 1B.PIC if the user can match two identical pictograms but they do not have functional reading skills.
- Start the evaluation in Subsection 1C.WTC only if the user has functional reading skills.

Therefore, the sequence of the evaluation may not necessarily follow the alphanumeric order of the subsections; this aims to reduce the time it takes to complete the evaluation based on the user's results.

3. Use the Stop Standards to Identify Which Section or Subsection to Evaluate Next

Once you have identified where to start the evaluation, proceed with material preparation, demonstrations, evaluation, and scoring of the subsection.

Then, identify the next subsection to evaluate. Generally, this would be the following subsection, unless, based on the user's results, the stop standards in the Evaluation Protocol suggest otherwise. The purpose of following this individualized sequence is to avoid having the user experience successive and unnecessary failures. Moreover, this will reduce the time it takes to complete the evaluation. The stop standards can be found at the beginning of certain subsections and should be applied to the entire subsection. Or, they may be included at the beginning of a section and should then be applied to that whole section. The instructions outline when to stop the evaluation for that subsection and explain how to proceed (i.e., where to record the results and where to continue the evaluation).

Symbols to Locate

SYMBOL	MEANING
✋	Stop the evaluation here (stop standard) and follow the outlined procedure.
✏️	Score the section or subsection indicated after this symbol.
▶	Continue the evaluation at the part, section, or subsection directly following the scoring indicated before this symbol.
⏩	Skip ahead several sections or subsections and continue the evaluation at the location indicated after this symbol.
↩	Return to the section or subsection indicated to the right of this symbol and proceed with the evaluation based on the results obtained by the user.
1 opt. demo	Number of optional demonstrations allowed.
1 mand. demo	Number of mandatory demonstrations.
≤	Less than or equal to…
≥	Greater than or equal to…

4. Demonstrations, Evaluation, and Scoring

Prepare the material required for the section (refer to the 🛠 symbol in the Evaluation Protocol located at the beginning of each section or subsection where the evaluation may begin).

Using different kinds of reinforcers (e.g., saying, "well done!" or giving treats or an object the user likes) is not only permitted but strongly recommended. This will help the user better understand the task during the demonstrations and encourage them to pay attention and stay motivated throughout the evaluation.

Demonstrations (Optional)

When indicated in the Evaluation Protocol, the examiner can demonstrate how to complete the task. This will be indicated either in the "Demos" column of the subsection (see ④ in the example of a Part 1 subsection on p. B6 of the Evaluation Protocol) or in the "Demos and Scoring—If Evaluation Starts Here" column in Subsections 1B.PIC and 1C.WTC (see ④ in Excerpt 1). The number of demonstrations allowed will be indicated. For example, in 1A.OBJ, the "Demos" column for each category states: "2 opt. demos/support." This means that these demonstrations are optional, and that two demonstrations are allowed per visual support, for a total of six.

When demonstrations are permitted, the examiner can choose to do them all at once. They can also hand the user a visual support and check whether they will be able to match it correctly before deciding to provide a demonstration. However, demonstrations for the three visual supports in a category must be done all at once. The examiner cannot demonstrate the task for the first visual support, ask the user to complete it on their own, then give a demonstration for the second visual support. Demonstrations for a single category must be done all at once before asking the user to match the three visual supports on their own.

The user's performance is not scored during demonstrations but is scored in all other instances. Thus, if there are no instructions indicating a mandatory or optional demonstration (as is the case for 1B.BWP, 1B.WTC, 1B.WWH, 1C.PIC, 1C.BWP, and 1C.WWH), the user is expected to match the visual supports on their own. If the user makes a mistake or if it appears they will make one, the examiner can use their clinical judgment and assist them to correct or prevent it. This may help the user better understand what is expected of them. It is important, however, to remember that the goal is to assess the user's skills and not teach new ones. Scoring these attempts is mandatory and the help provided will automatically impact the score.

It should also be noted that 1B.PIC and 1C.WTC include two scoring columns; demonstrations are only permitted when the evaluation starts at these subsections (i.e., in the "Demos and Scoring—If Evaluation Starts Here" column; see ④ in Excerpt 1). Demonstrations are therefore not permitted for 1B.PIC and 1C.WTC if the evaluation started in a previous subsection. As mentioned above, if the user made a mistake in the latter case and the examiner feels it is appropriate to assist them, then their score will be impacted.

Excerpt 1. Schedule Evaluation Protocol, Subsection 1C.WTC

- Bag 1C (visual supports mounted on matching boxes)
- Filing box 1B + 1C (visual supports handed to the user)
- Bottom panel and back panel
- 3 matching boxes

SUBSECTION 1C.WTC (WORDS TYPED ON THE COMPUTER–OBJECT)	
✋ If the evaluation starts here and during the first evaluation only	↪ 1B.PIC if 1C.WTC ≤ 8/9
✋ 1B.WTC = 0 **and** 1B.WWH = 0	✎ "Scoring Part 1: Table 1; Table 2 if required" ▸
✋ 1C.BWP = 0 **and** 1C.WTC = 0	✎ "Scoring Part 1: Table 1; Table 2 if required" ▸

CATEGORY	ORDER OF VISUAL SUPPORTS ON MATCHING BOXES	DEMOS AND SCORING—IF EVALUATION STARTS ④ HERE	SCORING— IF 1C.BWP WAS EVALUATED PREVIOUSLY	COMMENTS AND OBSERVATIONS
Home	Toothbrush Sock Lego	1 opt. demo/ support /3	/3	
Work/School	Spoon Pencil Disc	1 opt. demo/ support /3	/3	
Other	Ball Marker Sponge	1 opt. demo/ support /3	/3 ☐ Other not evaluated (3/3)	
	TOTAL	/9	/9	
	TOTAL 1C.WTC (highest score if subsection evaluated twice)	/9	☐ 1C.WTC not evaluated (0/9)	

④ Indication for demonstrations (not scored); this is the scoring column if the evaluation started at 1C.WTC.

Evaluation and Scoring

Proceed with the same material as in the demonstrations.

The general procedure is as follows: the examiner mounts a visual support to the top of each of the three boxes and gives the user a corresponding visual support. The user needs to match the visual support to the correct box. Once matched, the examiner removes the visual support from the box and repeats the procedure for the other two visual supports in that category, and for the other three supports in the next two categories.

The user must drop the visual support into the box. If the user tries to stick the support on or beside the matching box's visual support, the examiner should help them place the support into the box.

If the examiner feels as though the user matched a visual support by chance, they can retest that same visual support but only after asking the user to match one or two others beforehand. If they are asked to do it again right away, the user may think they made a mistake, which is in fact not the case, and this may then lead to a mistake on the second attempt.

Removing each visual support from the box after it is matched, as described in the procedure, is key to avoid giving hints on where to match the next visual support.

In the "Scoring" column of each subsection, assign one point for every visual support in each category that the user matches correctly on their own (without any form of help). If help was provided, excluding during demonstrations, assign a score of 0 for that visual support. Any attempts made during the demonstration are not scored. If the user matches a support before the demonstration is given and a demonstration is then required, the first attempt and demonstration are not scored.

As stated in the Evaluation Protocol, the evaluation should start with the "Home" category, then continue with the "Work/School" category, and end with the "Other" category. Evaluating all three categories is generally required. However, if the user has correctly matched the three visual supports in the first two categories (receiving a score of 3/3 for each category), then the examiner can decide not to proceed with the third category. They must then check "Other not evaluated" in the "Comments and Observations" column (see ⑧ in the example of a Part 1 subsection on p. B6 of the Evaluation Protocol) and assign a grade of 3/3 for this category. The examiner can nonetheless choose to test the third category. In all other cases, the three categories must be evaluated. Please note that all three categories must be evaluated for the first evaluated subsection in Part 1, regardless of where the evaluation starts for that user (whether 1A.OBJ, 1B.PIC, or 1C.WTC).

Additional Scoring Information

Subsections 1B.PIC and 1C.WTC each have two columns where the examiner can record the user's performance as these subsections may need to be tested twice. This will occur if the evaluation started at one of these subsections and the user did not get a perfect score. In this case, the ↶ symbol will instruct the examiner to go back to a previous section, specified to the right of the symbol. As such, the user will be asked to redo the subsection where their evaluation initially began (unless a stop standard is reached before then). Thus, if the evaluation started at 1B.PIC or 1C.WTC, the results are recorded in the "Demos and Scoring—If Evaluation Starts Here" column. Moreover, if the evaluation started at 1C.WTC and the user did not get a perfect score on this subsection, the ↶ symbol will instruct the examiner to return to Subsection 1B.PIC. In this case, the examiner should proceed as if they started the evaluation at 1B.PIC, and record the results in the "Demos and Scoring—If Evaluation Starts Here (or If 1C.WTC Was Evaluated Previously)" column. In all other cases, use the other column (i.e., "Scoring—If 1X.XXX Was Evaluated Previously").

Once the evaluation of Part 1 is complete, proceed with scoring the subsections that were not evaluated.

a) If the evaluation started at 1B.PIC or 1C.WTC, and the user obtained a perfect score for this subsection, the previous subsections do not need to be evaluated. Check "1X.XXX not evaluated (X/X or X/X)" at the bottom of the "Comments and Observations" column of the non-evaluated subsection (see ⑩ in the example of a Part 1 subsection on p. B6 of the Evaluation Protocol) and give the maximum number of points for each subsection.

b) If subsections are not evaluated because the user's results point to a stop standard, a score of 0 should be given to every subsequent subsection that will not be evaluated only if the stop standard instructs the examiner to jump ahead to Section 1C or to immediately proceed with the scoring of Part 1. However, if the stop standard indicates anything other than ▶ 1C or ✐ "Scoring Part 1: Table 1; Table 2, if required" or ✐ "Scoring Part 1: Tables 1 and 2," then it is important not to score the non-evaluated subsections.

c) If 1B.PIC and 1C.WTC have been evaluated twice, record the highest score obtained.

4.1. Detailed Procedure for 1A Subsections

Section 1A has only one subsection, 1A.OBJ. Here, the user is asked to match objects. The visual supports, both the ones mounted on the top of the boxes and the ones given to the user, are in object form. In the detailed procedure for this section, the word "object" is often used over "visual support" for the sake of clarity. However, it is important to understand that the objects are in fact visual supports.

Prepare the required material for Section 1A (refer to the ✂ symbol at the beginning of Section 1A on p. B8 of the Evaluation Protocol).

Demonstrations

As mentioned above, demonstrations are optional. In Section 1A, the "Demos" column states "2 opt. demos/support" for each category, which means that the examiner can give two demonstrations for each visual support, for a total of six demonstrations per category (or a total of 18 for the section).

The detailed procedure below provides an example with two sets of three demonstrations for each category. However, the examiner can also give the first object in a category to the user to see if they can match it correctly before deciding if a demonstration for this category is in fact necessary. They may as well choose to do a single set of three demonstrations rather than two sets for a given category or for all categories.

a) **E (Examiner):** Take the "Home" bag of objects.
b) **E:** Mount a first version of the three objects in this category to the top of the matching boxes (see Figure 5 on p. B100 and Figure 12 on p. B104 in Appendix 1 to the Supplementary Material), following the order indicated in the "Order of Visual Supports on Matching Boxes" column in Subsection 1A.OBJ, on p. B8 of the Evaluation Protocol. This order is also written on the label of each category bag to ensure the evaluation runs smoothly. Then, place the boxes in front of the user.
c) **E:** Give the user one object from this category.
In Section 1A, there is no strict order to follow on how the objects are handed to the user. However, it is important for the examiner to switch up the order and avoid handing the user the objects in the same order as they appear on the boxes. The order will obviously vary from one category to another.

In the object bag, there are several similar visual supports; not all the objects from each category bag will be used in Section 1A. Several versions of the same visual support have been included, as they may be used in Parts 2 and 3.

U (User): Take the object.
E: Communicate[1] to the user that they must drop the object in the corresponding box.
U: Place the object in the box.
d) **E:** Remove the object from the box.
e) **E and U:** Repeat steps c and d for a second object.
f) **E and U:** Repeat steps c and d for a third object.
g) **E and U:** Repeat steps c through f for a second round of demonstrations for the same category.
h) **E:** Remove the three objects from the top of the matching boxes.
i) **E and U:** Repeat steps a through h for the "Work/School" category.
j) **E and U:** Repeat steps a through h for the "Other" category.

Evaluation and Scoring

Use the same material as in the demonstrations.

a) **E (Examiner):** Take the "Home" bag of objects.
b) **E:** Mount a first version of the three objects in this category to the top of the matching boxes (see Figure 5 on p. B100 and Figure 12 on p. B104 in Appendix 1 to the Supplementary Material), following the order indicated in the "Order of Visual Supports on Matching Boxes" column in Subsection 1A.OBJ, on p. B8 of the Evaluation Protocol. The order is also written on the label of each category bag to ensure the evaluation runs smoothly. Then, place the boxes in front of the user.
c) **E:** Give the user one object from this category. As mentioned above, it is important for the examiner to switch up the order in

---

1. Here and in the following steps, the verb "communicate" is purposefully vague and refers to any means required, whether verbal, gestural, or physical, to help the user understand the task at hand. It is, however, important to choose carefully how you communicate what to do to the user so that they are more likely to be able to do it on their own after the demonstrations.

which they hand the objects to the user from the order used during demonstrations and from the order on the matching boxes.
U (User): Take the object and place it in the box.
d) E: Remove the object from the box.
e) **E and U:** Repeat steps c and d for a second object.
f) **E and U:** Repeat steps c and d for a third object.
g) E: Score the user's performance for this category.
Reminder: Give one point for every visual support in that category that the user matched correctly on their own (without any form of help). If help was provided (excluding during demonstrations), assign a score of 0 for that visual support.
h) E: Remove the three objects from the top of the matching boxes.
i) **E and U:** Repeat steps a through h for the "Work/School" category.
j) **E and U:** Repeat steps a through h for the "Other" category.
k) E: Record the score for Section 1A in the box provided ("Subtotal: /9").
l) E: Record the final score for Section 1A in the box provided ("Total 1A.OBJ: /18") by multiplying the subtotal by two.

Continue the evaluation at 1B.PHO.

4.2. Detailed Procedure for 1B Subsections

In Section 1B, the user is asked to match visual supports that are in the same form, specified in parentheses to the right of the subsection title (see ⑤ and ⑥ in the example of a Part 1 subsection on p. B6 of the Evaluation Protocol).

Prepare the material required for Section 1B (refer to the ✂ symbol at the beginning of Section 1B on p. B9 of the Evaluation Protocol). It is important to note that this step must be performed only once for all of Section 1B (i.e., at the first subsection where the evaluation of Section 1B begins).

Pick Up the Visual Supports for the Subsection Being Evaluated

In Section 1B, the visual support form required is indicated by the three letters to the right of the period in the subsection title (see ② and ⑤ in the example of a Part 1 subsection on p. B6 of the Evaluation Protocol). Generally, the filing box names correspond to the different sections to evaluate. For example, filing box 1B + 1C will be used in Sections 1B and 1C. Each filing box also contains dividers, which are labelled according to the subsection names. For example, the visual supports found behind divider 1B.PIC are required to evaluate Subsection 1B.PIC and have been numbered sequentially on the back to indicate the order to follow.

It is important to respect the order of visual supports in the filing box; this ensures visual supports are handed to the user in a varied order and that the evaluation runs smoothly. Visual supports should therefore be placed back in the filing box in the same order and according to the alphanumeric characters on the back. This must be done right after the demonstrations, and also after the evaluation. But in the latter case, this can be done in the absence of the user, after the evaluation is complete. The first three supports in the category have Velcro on the back so they can be mounted to the matching boxes, while the next three do not and are the ones intended for the user.

Demonstrations

As in Section 1A, demonstrations in Section 1B are optional. Although, demonstrations may only be given for the first subsection where the evaluation for 1B begins, either 1B.PHO or 1B.PIC. Additionally, if the evaluation started at 1B.PHO, once you reach 1B.PIC (if applicable), use the "Scoring—If 1B.PHO Was Evaluated Previously" column and do not give any demonstrations. However, if the evaluation of Part 1 begins at 1B.PIC or if it started at 1C.WTC and the stop standards indicate to return to 1B.PIC, demonstrations are allowed and the examiner must use the "Demos and Scoring—If Evaluation Starts Here (or if 1C.WTC Was Evaluated Previously)" column. In these two subsections (1B.PHO and 1B.PIC), it says, "1 opt. demo/support" for each category, meaning one demonstration per visual support is allowed, and three demonstrations are accepted per category (for a total of nine).

The detailed procedure described below provides an example of an evaluation with a set of three demonstrations for all three visual support categories. However, the examiner may also give a visual support to the user and see if they are able to match it correctly before deciding if demonstrations are required for that category.

  a) **E (Examiner):** Mount the first three visual supports to the top of the matching boxes (see Figure 5 on p. B100 and Figure 12 p. B104 in Appendix 1 to the Supplementary Material), from left to right and in the same order as they were placed in filing

box 1B + 1C (following the alphanumeric sequence on the back of the visual supports). Then, put the matching boxes in front of the user.
b) **E:** Give the user the next visual support following the numbered order.
U (User): Take the visual support.
E: Communicate[2] to the user that they must put the visual support in the corresponding box.
U: Place the visual support in the box.
c) **E:** Remove the visual support from the box.
d) **E and U:** Repeat steps b and c for a second visual support.
e) **E and U:** Repeat steps b and c for a third visual support.
f) **E:** Remove the three visual supports from the top of the boxes.
g) **E and U:** Repeat steps a through f for the next six visual supports (corresponding to the "Work/School" category).
h) **E and U:** Repeat steps a through f for the next six visual supports (corresponding to the "Other" category).
i) **E:** Return the visual supports to their original order and placement (follow the numbering on the back of each support).

As mentioned above, Subsection 1B.PIC includes two scoring columns: demonstrations are only permitted when the evaluation starts at this subsection, i.e., in the "Demos and Scoring—If Evaluation Starts Here (or If 1B.WTC Was Evaluated Previously)" column (see ④ in Excerpt 1).

Demonstrations are therefore not allowed for 1B.PIC if the evaluation started at 1A.OBJ. On the other hand, if the evaluation started at 1C.WTC and the user did not score perfectly on this subsection, the stop standard symbol will indicate a need to return to 1B.PIC; the examiner will then proceed as though the evaluation started at 1B.PIC, using the "Demos and Scoring—If Evaluation Starts Here (or If 1C.WTC Was Evaluated Previously)" column, and they are then allowed to give demonstrations.

---

2   Here and in the following steps, the verb "communicate" is purposefully vague and refers to any means required, whether verbal, gestural, or physical, to help the user understand the task at hand. It is, however, important to choose carefully how you communicate to the user what to do so that they are more likely to be able to do it on their own after the demonstrations.

Evaluation and Scoring

Proceed with the same material as in the demonstrations or, if demonstrations are not allowed, select the visual supports for the subsection being evaluated.

   a) **E (Examiner):** Mount the first three visual supports to the top of the matching boxes (see Figure 5 on p. B100 and Figure 12 on p. B104 in Appendix 1 to the Supplementary Material) from left to right and in the same order as they were placed in filing box 1B + 1C (following the alphanumeric sequence on the back of the visual supports). Then, place the matching boxes in front of the user.
   b) **E:** Give the user the next visual support following the numbered order.
   U (User): Take the visual support and place it in the corresponding box.
   c) **E:** Remove the visual support from the box.
   d) **E and U:** Repeat steps b and c for a second visual support.
   e) **E and U:** Repeat steps b and c for a third visual support.
   f) **E:** Score the user's performance for this category.
   Reminder: Give one point for every visual support in that category that the user matched correctly on their own (without any form of help). If help was provided (excluding during demonstrations), assign a score of 0 for that visual support.
   g) **E:** Remove the visual supports from the top of the matching boxes.
   h) **E and U:** Repeat steps a through g for the next six visual supports (corresponding to the "Work/School" category).
   If the user obtained a score of 3/3 for the first two visual support categories, evaluating the "Other" category is not mandatory. Check "Other not evaluated (3/3)" and, as indicated in parentheses, assign a score of 3/3 for this category.
   i) **E and U:** In all other instances, repeat steps a through g for the next six visual supports (corresponding to the "Other" category). Please note that if the evaluation started at 1B.PIC, it is mandatory to proceed with the evaluation of all three visual support categories the first time this subsection is evaluated.
   j) **E:** Record the score for the subsection evaluated in the box provided ("Total 1B.XXX: /9").
   k) **E:** Determine whether a stop standard in Section 1B is reached or whether the evaluation of Section 1B continues.

Evaluating Schedule Characteristics | Part 1   A27

STOP STANDARDS FOR SECTION 1B	
STOP STANDARD FOR SUBSECTION 1B.PHO	PROCEDURE TO FOLLOW IF THE STOP STANDARD IS REACHED
✋ 1A.OBJ = 0 **and** 1B.PHO = 0	✏️ "Scoring Part 2: Table 6" + "Scoring Part 3: Table 12" ▶ 4C If the user obtains a score of 0 at 1A.OBJ and at 1B.PHO: • Stop the evaluation of Part 1. • Score Part 2 by filling in Table 6 in the Evaluation Protocol (see scoring instructions for Part 2 on p. A66). • Score Part 3 by filling in Table 12 in the Evaluation Protocol (see scoring instructions for Part 3 on p. A104). • Then skip ahead to Part 4, Section 4C to complete the evaluation.
STOP STANDARD FOR SUBSECTION 1B.PIC	PROCEDURE TO FOLLOW IF THE STOP STANDARD IS REACHED
✋ If the evaluation starts here and only the first time this subsection is evaluated <u>or</u> if **1C.WTC** was evaluated previously	↩ 1A.OBJ if 1B.PIC ≤ 8/9 If the evaluation of Part 1 started at **1B.PIC** or if **1C.WTC** was evaluated previously and the user obtains a score less than or equal to 8/9 during this evaluation: • Go back to Subsection 1A.OBJ and evaluate this subsection. • Then evaluate the following subsections in order respecting the stop standards as if the evaluation started at 1A.OBJ. • If the evaluation continues to 1B.PIC (because the 1B.PHO stop standard is not reached) use the "Scoring—If 1B.PHO Was Evaluated Previously" column. • Record the highest score from both evaluations in the box provided: "Total 1B.PIC (highest score if subsection evaluated twice): /9."

(Continued)

✋ 1B.PHO = 0 **and** 1B.PIC = 0 **and** 1A.OBJ ≤ 8/18	✏️ "Scoring Part 2: Table 6" + "Scoring Part 3: Table 12" ▶ 4C
	If the user obtains a score of 0 at 1B.PHO and at 1B.PIC and if they obtain a score of less than or equal to 8/18 at 1A.OBJ: • Stop the evaluation of Part 1. • Score Part 2 by filling in Table 6 in the Evaluation Protocol (see scoring instructions for Part 2 on p. A66). • Score Part 3 by filling out Table 12 in the Evaluation Protocol (see scoring instructions for Part 3 on p. A104). • Then skip ahead to Part 4, Section 4C to complete the evaluation.
✋ 1B.PHO = 0 **and** 1B.PIC = 0 **and** 1A.OBJ ≥ 10/18	✏️ "Scoring Part 1: Tables 1 and 2" ▶
	If the user obtains a score of 0 at 1B.PHO and at 1B.PIC and they obtain a score greater than or equal to 10/18 at 1A.OBJ: • Check "1X.XXX not evaluated (0/9 or 9/9)" at the bottom of the "Comments and Observations" column in the subsections that follow 1B.PIC and that will not be evaluated, including all the 1C subsections, and assign a score of 0/9. • Score Part 1 by filling out Tables 1 and 2 (see scoring instructions for Part 1 on p. A36). • Continue the evaluation at Part 2.
STOP STANDARD FOR SUBSECTION 1B.BWP	**PROCEDURE TO FOLLOW IF THE STOP STANDARD IS REACHED**
✋ 1B.PIC = 0 **and** 1B.BWP = 0	▶ 1C
	If the user obtains a score of 0 at 1B.PIC and at 1B.BWP: • Check "1B.XXX not evaluated (0/9 or 9/9)" at the bottom of the "Comments and Observations" column in the 1B subsections that follow and assign a score of 0/9. • Then skip ahead to Part 1, Section 1C and continue the evaluation.

(Continued)

STOP STANDARD FOR SUBSECTION 1B.WTC	PROCEDURE TO FOLLOW IF THE STOP STANDARD IS REACHED
✋ 1B.WTC = 0	▶ 1C If the user obtains a score of 0 at 1B.WTC: • Check "1B.WWH not evaluated (0/9 or 9/9)" at the bottom of the "Comments and Observations" column in 1B.WWH and assign a score of 0/9. • Then skip ahead to Part 1, Section 1C and continue the evaluation.

If no stop standard is reached in Section 1B:

a) If the evaluation of Part 1 started at 1B.PIC and the result did not require going back, check "1X.XXX not evaluated (X/X)" at the bottom of the "Comments and Observations" column of 1A.OBJ and 1B.PHO, and assign a score of 18/18 and 9/9 respectively.
b) Continue the evaluation at the next subsection (or at Section 1C after evaluating 1B.WWH).

4.3. Detailed Procedure for 1C Subsections

In Section 1C, the user is asked to match visual supports in different forms. For each category, objects are mounted to the top of the matching boxes and the user is given the visual supports in different forms. The form of the support is specified in parentheses to the right of the subsection title (see ⑤ and ⑥ in Excerpt 2). Exceptionally, and for the sake of clarity, we distinguish two-dimensional visual supports from objects by using the terms "2D supports" and "objects" in the detailed procedure for this section.

Prepare the required material for the evaluation of Section 1C (refer to the ✂ symbol at the beginning of Section 1C on p. B13 in the Evaluation Protocol), including the basket labelled "Bag 1C."

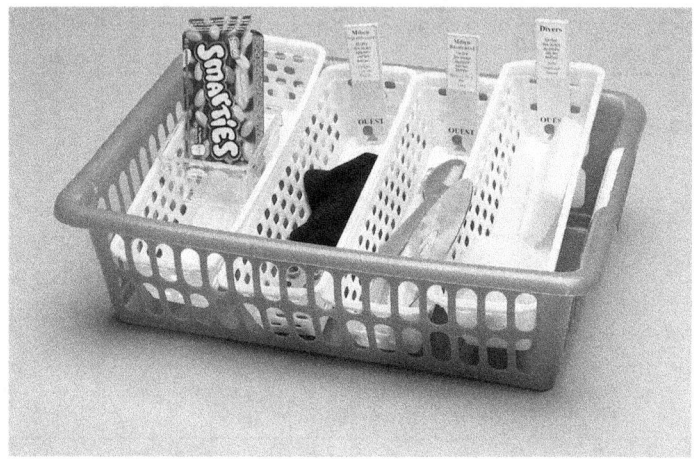

Figure 1.2. Basket labelled "Bag 1C."
Source: Artimage 2015.

Pick the Visual Supports Required to Evaluate the Subsection

In Section 1C, the form of the visual supports required for the evaluation is indicated in parentheses to the right of the subsection title (see ⑤ and ⑥ in Excerpt 2). Generally, the file names correspond to the different sections to evaluate. For example, filing box 1B + 1C will be used in Sections 1B and 1C. Each filing box also contains dividers, which are labelled according to the subsection names. For example, the visual supports found behind divider 1C.PHO are required to evaluate Subsection 1C.PHO and have been numbered sequentially on the back to indicate the order to follow.

It is important to respect the order in the filing box; this ensures visual supports are handed to the user in a varied order and that the evaluation runs smoothly. After demonstrations, visual supports should be placed back in the filing box in the same order and according to the alphanumeric characters on the back. This must be done after the demonstrations and also after the evaluation. In the latter case, this can be done in the absence of the user, after the evaluation has been completed.

To know which visual supports to mount to the top of the boxes and which ones to hand to the user, two visual support forms are written in parentheses to the right of each subsection title. The visual support form on the left (⑤ in Excerpt 2) specifies the one to give to the user, and the one on the right (⑥ in Excerpt 2) is the form the examiner mounts to the top of the matching boxes.

Excerpt 2. Schedule Evaluation Protocol, Subsection 1C.PHO

- Bag 1C (visual supports mounted on matching boxes)
- Filing box 1B + 1C (visual supports handed to user)
- Bottom panel and back panel
- 3 matching boxes

✋ 2 consecutive subsections = 0   ✏️ "Scoring Part 1: Table 1; Table 2 if required" ▶

CATEGORY	DEMOS	ORDER OF VISUAL SUPPORTS ON MATCHING BOXES	SCORING	COMMENTS AND OBSERVATIONS
Home	1 opt. demo/ support	Toothbrush Sock Lego	/3	
Work/School	1 opt. demo/ support	Spoon Pencil Disc	/3	
Other	1 opt. demo/ support	Ball Marker Sponge	/3	☐ Other not evaluated (3/3)
		TOTAL 1C.PHO	/9	☐ 1C.PHO not evaluated (0/9 or 9/9)

⑤ The first word, "Photo," indicates the form of visual support to give to the user. In this case, the photos should be taken from filing box 1B + 1C (as mentioned in the list of materials), behind the 1C.PHO divider.

⑥ The second word, "Object," indicates the form of visual support to mount to the top of the matching boxes. In this case, these objects should be taken from Bag 1C.

Demonstrations

As in the two previous sections, demonstrations are optional. In Section 1C, demonstrations may only be given for the first subsection where the evaluation for Section 1C begins, either 1C.PHO or 1C.WTC. Additionally, if the evaluation started at 1A.OBJ or 1B.PIC, once you reach 1C.WTC (if applicable), use the "Scoring—If 1C.BWP Was Evaluated Previously" column and do not give any demonstrations.

However, if the evaluation of Part 1 begins at 1C.WTC, demonstrations are allowed and the examiner must use the "Demos and Scoring—If Evaluation Starts Here" column. In these two subsections (1C.PHO and 1C.WTC), it states "1 opt. demo/support" for each category, meaning one demonstration per visual support is allowed, and three demonstrations are accepted per category (for a total of nine).

The detailed procedure described below provides an example of an evaluation with a series of three demonstrations for all three visual support categories. But the examiner may also give a visual support to the user and see if they are able to match it correctly before deciding if demonstrations are required for that category.

To proceed with the demonstrations, the examiner should have the basket labelled "Bag 1C" and the 2D supports from filing box 1B + 1C, which can be found behind the divider that corresponds to the title of the subsection being evaluated.

a) **E (Examiner):** Mount the three objects from the "Home" category to the top of the matching boxes (see Figure 5 on p. B100 and Figure 12 on p. B104 in Appendix 1 to the Supplementary Material) from left to right, and in the order indicated in the "Order of Visual Supports on Matching Boxes" column in the Evaluation Protocol. This order is also written on each label identifying the baskets in Bag 1C to ensure the evaluation runs smoothly (see Figure 1.2). Then, place the boxes in front of the user.

b) **E:** Give the user the first 2D support from this category.
U (User): Take the 2D support.
E: Communicate[3] to the user that they must place the 2D support in the corresponding box.
U: Place the 2D support in the box.

c) **E:** Remove the 2D support from the box.

d) **E and U:** Repeat steps b and c for a second 2D support.

e) **E and U:** Repeat steps b and c for a third 2D support.

---

3   Here and in the following steps, the verb "communicate" is purposefully vague and refers to any means required, whether verbal, gestural, or physical, to help the user understand the task at hand. It is, however, important to choose carefully how you communicate to the user what to do so that they are more likely to be able to do it on their own after the demonstrations.

f) **E:** Remove the three objects from the top of the boxes and place them back in the "Home" basket located in the bigger basket labelled "Bag 1C."
g) **E and U:** Repeat steps a through f for the "Work/School" category.
h) **E and U:** Repeat steps a through f for the "Other" category.
i) **E:** Place the visual supports back in their original order (see numbering on back).

Evaluation and Scoring

Proceed with the same material as in the demonstrations.

a) **E (Examiner):** Mount the three objects from the "Home" category to the top of the matching boxes (see Figure 5 on p. B100 and Figure 12 on p. B104 in Appendix 1 to the Supplementary Material) from left to right, and in the order indicated in the "Order of Visual Supports on Matching Boxes" column in the Evaluation Protocol. This order is also written on each label identifying the baskets in Bag 1C to ensure the evaluation runs smoothly (see Figure 1.2). Then, place the boxes in front of the user.
b) **E:** Give the user the first 2D support from this category.
   U (User): Take the 2D support and place it in the box.
c) **E:** Remove the 2D support from the box.
d) **E and U:** Repeat steps b and c for a second 2D support.
e) **E and U:** Repeat steps b and c for a third 2D support.
f) **E:** Score the user's performance for this category.
   Reminder: Give one point for every visual support in that category that the user matched correctly on their own (without any form of help). If help was provided (excluding during demonstrations), assign a score of 0 for that visual support.
g) **E:** Remove the three objects from the top of the boxes and place them back in the "Home" basket located in the bigger basket labelled "Bag 1C."
h) **E and U:** Repeat steps a through g for the "Work/School" category.
   If the user obtained a score of 3/3 for the first two categories, evaluating the "Other" category is not mandatory. Check "Other not evaluated (3/3)" and, as indicated in parentheses, assign a score of 3/3 for this category.

i) **E and U:** In all other instances, repeat steps a through g for the next six visual supports (corresponding to the "Other" category).
Please note that if the evaluation started at 1C.WTC, it is mandatory to proceed with the evaluation of all three visual support categories the first time this subsection is evaluated.
j) **E:** Record the score for the subsection in the box provided ("Total: 1C.XXX: /9").
k) **E:** Determine whether a stop standard in Section 1C was reached or whether the evaluation of Section 1C continues.

STOP STANDARDS FOR SECTION 1C	
STOP STANDARD FOR SECTION 1C	PROCEDURE TO FOLLOW IF THE STOP STANDARD IS REACHED
✋ 2 consecutive subsections = 0	✏️ "Scoring Part 1: Table 1; Table 2, if required" ▶ If the user obtains a score of 0 for 2 consecutive subsections: • Check "1C.XXX not evaluated (0/9 or 9/9)" at the bottom of the "Comments and Observations" column in the 1C subsections that follow and that will not be evaluated, and assign a score of 0/9. • Score Part 1 by filling in Table 1 and Table 2 if required, i.e., if the stop standard following Table 1 has not been reached in the Evaluation Protocol (see scoring instructions for Part 1 on p. A36). • Continue the evaluation at Part 2 if the stop standard for Part 1 has not been reached.
STOP STANDARD FOR SUBSECTION 1C.WTC	PROCEDURE TO FOLLOW IF A STOP STANDARD IS REACHED
✋ If the evaluation starts here and only the first time, this subsection is evaluated	↩ 1B.PIC if 1C.WTC ≤ 8/9 If the evaluation of Part 1 started at 1C.WTC and the user obtained a score less than or equal to 8/9 the first time this subsection is evaluated:

(Continued)

	• Go back to 1B.PIC and evaluate this subsection. • Then follow the procedure as if the evaluation started at 1B.PIC, i.e., use the "Demos and Scoring—If Evaluation Starts Here (or If 1C.WTC Was Evaluated Previously)" column; then proceed with the evaluation of the following subsections if the user obtained a score of 9/9 at 1B.PIC, otherwise go back to 1A.OBJ (1B.PIC stop standard was reached). • If going back to 1A.OBJ was required and 1B.PIC is evaluated a second time (because no stop standard was reached), use the "Scoring—If 1B.PHO Was Evaluated Previously" column. • Record the highest score in the box provided, "Total 1B.PIC (highest score if subsection evaluated twice): /9." • If the evaluation continues to 1C.WTC (because no stop standard is reached), use the "Scoring—If 1C.BWP Was Evaluated Previously" column. • Record the highest score in the box provided, "Total 1C.WTC (highest score if subsection evaluated twice): /9."
✋ 1B.WTC = 0 <u>and</u> 1B.WWH = 0	🖉 "Scoring Part 1: Table 1; Table 2 if required" ▶ If the user obtains a score of 0 at 1B.WTC and at 1B.WWH, do not evaluate 1C.WTC or 1C.WWH. Furthermore, it should be noted that the user obtained 0 at 1B.WWH because of their score of 0 at 1B.WTC. • Check "1C.XXX not evaluated (0/9)" at the bottom of the "Comments and Observations" column in 1C.WTC and in 1C.WWH and assign a score of 0.

(Continued)

	• Score Part 1 by filling in Table 1 and Table 2 if required, i.e., if the stop standard following Table 1 has not been reached in the Evaluation Protocol (see scoring instructions for Part 1 on p. A36). • Continue with the evaluation at Part 2 if the stop standard for Part 1 is not reached.
✋ 1C.BWP = 0 **and** 1C.WTC = 0	✏️ "Scoring Part 1: Table 1; Table 2 if required" ▶ If the user obtains a score of 0 at 1C.BWP and at 1C.WTC: • Check "1C.WWH not evaluated (0/9 or 9/9)" at the bottom of the "Comments and Observations" column (1C.WWH will not be evaluated) and assign a score of 0/9. • Score Part 1 by filling in Table 1 and Table 2 if required, i.e., if the stop standard following Table 1 has not been reached in the Evaluation Protocol (see scoring instructions for Part 1 on p. A36). • Continue with the evaluation at Part 2 if the stop standard for Part 1 is not reached.

If no stop standard is reached in Section 1C:

a) If the evaluation of Part 1 started at 1C.WTC and the result did not require going back, check "1X.XXX not evaluated (X/X)" at the bottom of the "Comments and Observations" column for all previous subsections in Part 1 (Sections 1A, 1B, and 1C) and assign a score of 18/18 (for 1A.OBJ) and 9/9 (for all other subsections).

b) Continue the evaluation at the next subsection. If this subsection is 1C.WWH then proceed with the scoring of Part 1.

5. Scoring Part 1 in the Schedule Evaluation Protocol

a) Write down the results of each subsection and for each visual support form in Table 1.

Add up the points for each visual support form and add up the results in the "Subtotal" column. Then divide the subtotal by three and write down the result, rounded off to the nearest whole number, in the "Total" column.

b) Determine whether the stop standard for Part 1 has been reached or if the evaluation should continue.

STOP STANDARDS FOR PART 1	
STOP STANDARD FOR PART 1	PROCEDURE TO FOLLOW IF THE STOP STANDARD IS REACHED
✋ 1A.OBJ ≤ 8/18 **and** all other subsections ≤ 4/9	✏️ "Scoring Part 2: Table 6" + "Scoring Part 3: Table 12" ▶ 4C
	If the user obtains a score less than or equal to 8/18 at 1A.OBJ and a score of less than or equal to 4/9 for all visual support forms evaluated in the other two sections (1B and 1C): • Stop the evaluation of Part 1. • Score Part 2 by filling in Table 6 in the Evaluation Protocol (see scoring instructions for Part 2 in on p. A66). • Score Part 3 by filling in Table 12 in the Evaluation Protocol (see scoring instructions for Part 3 on p. A104). • Skip ahead to 4C in Part 4 to complete the evaluation.

If the stop standard is not reached:

In all other instances and to identify the visual support forms that will be used in Part 2 (which is the whole purpose of Part 1), follow the scoring instructions below **from top to bottom** and fill in the "Visual Supports Selected for the Evaluation of Part 2" column in Table 2.

1. In Table 1, going **from bottom to top**, circle the first two highest scores in the "Total" column.
   Exception: If five scores out of six are 0, circle the one score greater than 0 as well as the visual support form located the **closest to the top** that received a score of 0.
2. From these two circled visual support forms, take the one closest to the top in the "Visual Support Form" column in Table 1 and enter it into the "Visual Support Form 1" box in the right hand column of Table 2.

3. From these two circled visual support forms, take the one closest to the bottom in the "Visual Support Form" column in Table 1 and enter it into the "Visual Support Form 2" box in the right hand column of Table 2.
4. If Visual Support Forms 1 and 2 are not located directly one above the other in the "Visual Support Form" column in Table 1, enter one of the following in the "Visual Support Form 3" box in the right hand column of Table 2:
   a) The visual support form located between the two if there is only one.
   b) The visual support form with the highest score if there is more than one.
   c) If the scores are the same, the visual support form located closest to Visual Support Form 1 in the "Visual Support Form" column of Table 1.

Scoring Examples and Visual Support Form Selection

Below are several scoring and visual support form selection examples to illustrate how to proceed moving forward. In these examples, only the "Subtotal" and "Total" columns have been filled in (not the three section columns).

Example 1

TABLE 1. RESULT FOR PART 1

Record the results obtained for each visual support form in the different subsections of Part 1, then fill in the "Subtotal" and "Total" columns.

	Visual Support Form	Section 1A	Section 1B	Section 1C	Subtotal	Divide by	Total (round off to the nearest whole number)
Top ↑ ↓ Bottom	OBJ	12/18			12/18	÷ 3	(4/6)
	PHO		8/9	2/9	10/18	÷ 3	(3/6)
	PIC		5/9	0/9	5/18	÷ 3	2/6
	BWP		0/9	0/9	0/18	÷ 3	0/6
	WTC		0/9	0/9	0/18	÷ 3	0/6
	WWH		0/9	0/9	0/18	÷ 3	0/6

Evaluating Schedule Characteristics | Part 1   A39

Visual support forms selected:

- Visual Support Form 1 (the closest to the top in the "Visual Support Form" column of Table 1): OBJ
- Visual Support Form 2 (the closest to the bottom in the "Visual Support Form" column of Table 1): PHO
- Visual Support Form 3 (between Support Form 1 and Support Form 2 in the "Visual Support Form" column of Table 1): none

Example 2

TABLE 1. RESULT FOR PART 1

Record the results obtained for each visual support form in the different subsections of Part 1, then fill in the "Subtotal" and "Total" columns.

	Visual Support Form	Section 1A	Section 1B	Section 1C	Subtotal	Divide by	Total (round off to the nearest whole number)
Top ↑	OBJ	18/18			18/18	÷3	6/6
	PHO		9/9	9/9	18/18	÷3	6/6
	PIC		9/9	8/9	17/18	÷3	⬚6/6⬚
	BWP		8/9	9/9	17/18	÷3	⬚6/6⬚
↓ Bottom	WTC		9/9	3/9	12/18	÷3	4/6
	WWH		5/9	0/9	5/18	÷3	2/6

Visual support forms selected:

- Visual Support Form 1 (the closest to the top in the "Visual Support Form" column of Table 1): PIC
- Visual Support Form 2 (the closest to the bottom in the "Visual Support Form" column of Table 1): BWP
- Visual Support Form 3 (between Support Form 1 and Support Form 2 in the "Visual Support Form" column of Table 1): none

Example 3

TABLE 1. RESULT FOR PART 1

Record the results obtained for each visual support form in the different subsections of Part 1, then fill in the "Subtotal" and "Total" columns.

	Visual Support Form	Section 1A	Section 1B	Section 1C	Subtotal	Divide by	Total (round off to the nearest whole number)
Top ↑	OBJ	18/18			18/18	÷3	⟨6/6⟩
	PHO		6/9	3/9	9/18	÷3	3/6
	PIC		9/9	4/9	13/18	÷3	4/6
	BWP		7/9	5/9	12/18	÷3	⟨4/6⟩
Bottom	WTC		1/9	0/9	1/18	÷3	0/6
	WWH		0/9	0/9	0/18	÷3	0/6

Visual support forms selected:

- Visual Support Form 1 (the closest to the top in the "Visual Support Form" column of Table 1): OBJ
- Visual Support Form 2 (the closest to the bottom in the "Visual Support Form" column of Table 1): BWP
- Visual Support Form 3 (between Support Form 1 and Support Form 2 in the "Visual Support Form" column of Table 1): PIC

Example 4

TABLE 1. RESULT FOR RESULT 1

Record the results obtained for each visual support form in the different subsections of Part 1, then fill in the "Subtotal" and "Total" columns.

	Visual Support Form	Section 1A	Section 1B	Section 1C	Subtotal	Divide by	Total (round off to the nearest whole number)
Top ↑	OBJ	18/18			18/18	÷3	6/6
	PHO		8/9	9/9	17/18	÷3	6/6
	PIC		9/9	9/9	18/18	÷3	⟨6/6⟩
	BWP		9/9	6/9	15/18	÷3	5/6
Bottom	WTC		9/9	5/9	14/18	÷3	5/6
	WWH		9/9	9/9	18/18	÷3	⟨6/6⟩

Visual support forms selected:

- Visual Support Form 1 (the closest to the top in the "Visual Support Form" column of Table 1): PIC
- Visual Support Form 2 (the closest to the bottom in the "Visual Support Form" column of Table 1): WWH
- Visual Support Form 3 (between Support Form 1 and Support Form 2 in the "Visual Support Form" column of Table 1): BWP

Example 5

TABLE 1. RESULT FOR PART 1

Record the results obtained for each visual support form in the different subsections of Part 1, then fill in the "Subtotal" and "Total" columns.

	Visual Support Form	Section 1A	Section 1B	Section 1C	Subtotal	Divide by	Total (round off to the nearest whole number)
Top ↑ Bottom	OBJ	10/18			10/18	÷ 3	(3/6)
	PHO		0/9	0/9	0/18	÷ 3	(0/6)
	PIC		1/9	0/9	1/18	÷ 3	0/6
	BWP		0/9	0/9	0/18	÷ 3	0/6
	WTC		0/9	0/9	0/18	÷ 3	0/6
	WWH		0/9	0/9	0/18	÷ 3	0/6

Visual support forms selected:

- Visual Support Form 1 (the closest to the top in the "Visual Support Form" column of Table 1): OBJ
- Visual Support Form 2 (the closest to the bottom in the "Visual Support Form" column of Table 1): PHO
- Visual Support Form 3 (between Support Form 1 and Support Form 2 in the "Visual Support Form" column of Table 1): none

Example 6

TABLE 1. RESULT FOR PART 1

Record the results obtained for each visual support form in the different subsections of Part 1, then fill in the "Subtotal" and "Total" columns.

	Visual Support Form	Section 1A	Section 1B	Section 1C	Subtotal	Divide by	Total (round off to the nearest whole number)
Top ↑	OBJ	12/18			12/18	÷3	4/6
	PHO		1/9	0/9	1/18	÷3	0/6
	PIC		2/9	0/9	2/18	÷3	1/6
	BWP		1/9	0/9	1/18	÷3	0/6
Bottom	WTC		0/9	0/9	0/18	÷3	0/6
	WWH		0/9	0/9	0/18	÷3	0/6

Visual support forms selected:

- Visual Support Form 1 (the closest to the top in the "Visual Support Form" column of Table 1): <u>OBJ</u>
- Visual Support Form 2 (the closest to the bottom in the "Visual Support Form" column of Table 1): <u>PIC</u>
- Visual Support Form 3 (between Support Form 1 and Support Form 2 in the "Visual Support Form" column of Table 1): <u>PHO</u>

Part 2

Goal

The goal of Part 2 is to establish the form of visual supports that will be selected in the implementation of the user's schedule.

Duration

10 to 20 minutes.

Administration

Part 2 of the evaluation takes place in the environment where the schedule will be implemented. It is divided into three sections, named after the visual support forms selected at the end of Part 1. These will be evaluated here: Visual Support Form 1, Visual Support Form 2, and Visual Support Form 3.

This part of the evaluation once again involves matching visual supports. It is thus similar to Part 1 in its execution. There are, however, some differences, the most obvious being that the user and examiner will move around matching visual supports in the environment where the schedule will ultimately be used.

Sequence

The evaluation sequence as presented here applies to all of Part 2. The steps to follow for the demonstration, evaluation, and scoring are explained in greater detail for each visual support form to evaluate.

Generally, the evaluation should proceed as follows: the user alternately goes to three different locations to drop visual supports into the matching boxes. The examiner will hand the user one visual support at a time, and the user must walk to the correct box and match each visual support.

For all users, the two or three visual support forms must be evaluated in the order listed in the Evaluation Protocol (contrary to Part 1 where a more individualized order was allowed). However, based on the user's results, the stop standards will determine a more individualized progression by indicating whether the evaluation should continue with the next visual support form or whether it should stop. As in Part 1, these stop standards reduce the number of potential failures and the time it takes to complete the evaluation.

Additionally, the help provided in Part 2 differs from what was allowed in Part 1. In Part 1, although it was not mandatory, the examiner could offer help, even when demonstrations were not indicated in the procedure. However, any assistance impacted the user's score. Based on their clinical judgment, the examiner could decide whether to help or not. In Part 2, the user must correctly match the visual supports to the boxes. It may therefore be necessary to assist them with physical, gestural, or verbal prompts (e.g., guiding them by hand and helping them place the visual support in the correct box) if required. As in Part 1, any assistance provided will consequently impact the score.

Finally, another difference is the collection of visual supports. In Part 2, the examiner should not systematically remove the visual supports from the boxes after the user matches them. They should only do so when specifically instructed in the Evaluation Protocol or if the user makes a mistake. In this case, the examiner should remove the incorrectly matched visual support, give it back to the user, and ensure they match it correctly by providing the required help as mentioned above.

1. Fill In the Required Information in the Schedule Evaluation Protocol

By first referring to Part 1, Table 2, on p. B17 of the Evaluation Protocol, write down the visual support forms selected in the "Visual Support

Form 1," "Visual Support Form 2," and "Visual Support Form 3" boxes (if applicable, i.e., if Visual Support Form 3 was selected in Part 1, Table 2) on pp. B21–B23 of the Evaluation Protocol.

Excerpts 3 and 4 (below) from the Evaluation Protocol present an example of Table 2 and Visual Support Form 1 respectively.

2. Choose the Visual Support Category to Evaluate

Next, the examiner should choose the category for Part 2 of the evaluation. Once again, there are three choices: "Home," "Work/School," or "Other." Choosing the category with most relevant visual supports for the environment where the evaluation is taking place is recommended (usually "Home" or "Work/School"). Check the visual support category being evaluated in Table 3 on p. B19 of the Evaluation Protocol (see Excerpt 5).

3. Determine Where the Matching Boxes Will Be Installed

Then determine where the matching boxes will be installed. The locations are generally chosen based on where the activity represented by the visual support will take place. For example, when evaluating the "Home" category, the toothbrush will typically be placed on the bathroom door or by the bathroom's entrance.

Excerpt 3. Schedule Evaluation Protocol, Table 2. Scoring Part 1

TABLE 2. SCORING PART 1	
Follow the scoring standards for Part 1 **from top to bottom** and fill in the "Visual Supports Selected for the Evaluation of Part 2" column	
SCORING STANDARDS FOR PART 1	**VISUAL SUPPORTS SELECTED FOR THE EVALUATION OF PART 2**
1. In Table 1, going **from bottom to top**, circle the first two highest scores in the "Total" column. Exception: If five scores out of six are 0, circle the one score greater than 0 as well as the visual support form located the **closest to the top** that received a score of 0.	Visual Support Form 1 (the **closest to the top** in the "Visual Support Form" column in Table 1): OBJ
	Visual Support Form 2 (the **closest to the bottom** in the "Visual Support Form" column of Table 1): BWP

*See remaining instructions (2, 3, and 4) on the next page.

2. From these two circled visual support forms, take the one closest to the top in the "Visual Support Form" column in Table 1 and enter it into the "Visual Support Form 1" box in the right hand column of this table.	Visual Support Form 3 (**between** Support Form 1 and Support Form 2 in the "Visual Support Form" column of Table 1): PIC
3. From these two circled visual support forms, take the one closest to the bottom in the "Visual Support Form" column in Table 1 and enter it into the "Visual Support Form 2" box in the right hand column of this table.	
4. If Visual Support Forms 1 and 2 are not located directly one above the other in the "Visual Support Form" column in Table 1, enter one of the following in the "Visual Support Form 3" box in the right hand column of this table: a) The visual support form located **between** the two if there is only one b) The visual support form with the highest score if there is more than one c) If the scores are the same, the visual support form located closest to Visual Support Form 1 in the "Visual Support Form" column of Table 1	

Certain parameters must be respected when selecting locations: the distance between matching boxes should vary between 12 and 40 feet, and ideally the three boxes should be easy for the user to see as they move around matching the visual supports. Boxes could be placed on flat surfaces (e.g., shelves, tables, counters) or mounted on vertical surfaces (e.g., walls, doors).

It is possible that a visual support does not correspond to a user's daily activity or that the activity represented by the visual support takes place in a room that is too far away from the other visual supports. This visual support should then be installed in the best location possible, respecting the distance guidelines even if that visual support does not mean anything for the user or refer to the location where it is installed.

Write the locations of the visual supports down in Table 3 on p. B19 of the Evaluation Protocol. Excerpt 5 (on p. A50) presents an example of Table 3, filled in for an evaluation taking place in the user's home.

Evaluating Schedule Characteristics | Part 2   A49

Excerpt 4. Schedule Evaluation Protocol, Visual Support Form 1

VISUAL SUPPORT FORM 1   OBJ

✋ Subtotal for attempts 1 to 6 for Visual Support Form 1 = 0/6	✏️ "Subtotal attempts 7 to 9" + "Total Visual Support Form 1" + "Scoring Part 2: Tables 4, 5, and 6" + "Scoring Part 3: Table 12" ▶ 4C
✋ Total for Visual Support Form 1 ≤ 3/9	✏️ "Scoring Part 2: Tables 4, 5, and 6" + "Scoring Part 3: Table 12" ▶ 4C

ACTIONS DONE BY USER (6 attempts, 2 trips per location)	DEMOS	①1	2	3	4	5	6	SUBTOTAL ATTEMPTS 1 TO 6
The user takes the visual support.	② 2 demos/ location 1 mand. + 1 opt.							④ Not scored
The user walks and drops the visual support in the correct box.	2 demos/ location 1 mand. + 1 opt.	③ 0/1	/1	/1	/1	/1	/1	/6

⚠ **Note:** *Visual Support Form 1 is the only one for which a second demonstration is allowed.*

⚠ **Note:** *Collect the visual supports from the matching boxes and put them back in order before continuing with attempts 7 to 9 (if required).*

ACTIONS DONE BY USER (3 attempts, 1 trip per location)	7	8	9	SUBTOTAL ATTEMPTS 7 TO 9	TOTAL VISUAL SUPPORT FORM 1
The user takes the visual support.				④ Not scored	④ Not scored
The user walks and drops the visual support in the correct box.	/1	/1	/1	/3 ☐ Not evaluated (0/3 or 3/3)	/9

① Attempt number.

② Indication for demonstrations (not scored).

③ User's performance; in this case, the user received a score of 0 on attempt 1 as they needed help to complete the match correctly.

④ The action "User takes the visual support" is not scored.

Excerpt 5. Schedule Evaluation Protocol, Table 3. Location of Visual Supports

TABLE 3. LOCATION OF VISUAL SUPPORTS		
CHECK THE CATEGORY BEING EVALUATED	VISUAL SUPPORTS	WRITE DOWN THE VISUAL SUPPORT LOCATIONS (only for the category being evaluated)
☑ Home	Toothbrush	L1: On the counter by the entrance of the bathroom.
	Sock	L2: On the dresser by the entrance of the bedroom.
	Lego	L3: On the small table by the entrance of the living room.
☐ Work/School	Spoon	L1:
	Pencil	L2:
	Disc	L3:
☐ Other	Ball	L1:
	Marker	L2:
	Sponge	L3:

4. Prepare the Material for Part 2

  a) To know what materials are required for Part 2, refer to the ✂ symbol located after Table 3 on p. B19 in the Evaluation Protocol. For example, if you are evaluating the "Home" category and one of the visual support forms to evaluate is OBJ, then prepare the object bag for the "Home" category, among others. Also prepare the three matching boxes (without the bottom and back panels), filing box 2–3 + 3H for the category being evaluated (e.g., "Home"), the examiner's tray (if desired), and the blue mounting putty as you may need it to mount the matching boxes.

  b) Place the matching boxes in the three designated locations written down in Table 3 on p. B19 of the Evaluation Protocol. If a vertical surface has been chosen (e.g., a door or a wall), use the blue mounting putty or another adhesive to mount the boxes.

c) Using the examiner's tray is recommended even though it is listed as optional in the list of materials. It will ensure that the evaluation runs smoothly as the examiner will need to carry around a certain amount of material while scoring the performance at the same time.

Place the Evaluation Protocol and a pencil in the bottom of the large basket (i.e., the examiner's tray). As mentioned in Appendix 1, on p. B111 of the Supplementary Material section, place the smaller basket inside the large one and insert the small square basket. If using reinforcers, put those into the small square basket. The visual supports to place in the examiner's tray will be identified in step 5.

Figure 2.1 illustrates how to conduct the evaluation and score results by using the tray (in this case, the visual supports are in OBJ form).

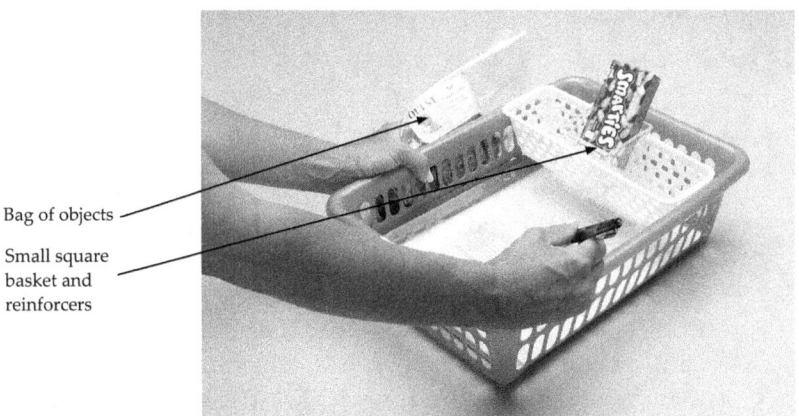

Figure 2.1. How to use the examiner's tray while moving around (form of visual support evaluated: OBJ).

Source: Artimage 2015.

Figure 2.2 illustrates how to organize the tray for the evaluation of the PIC visual support form.

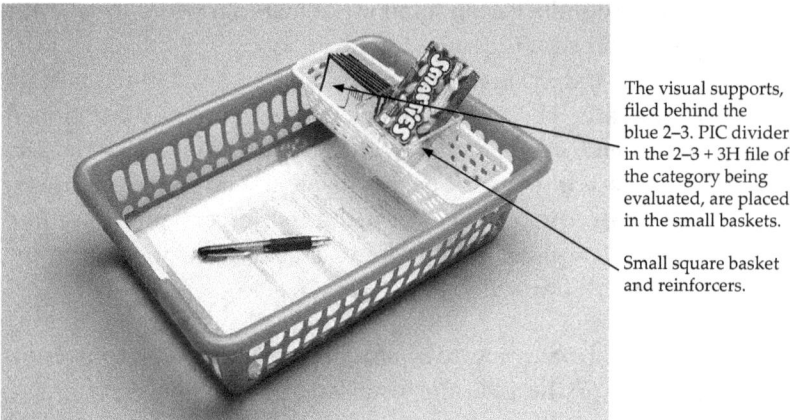

Figure 2.2. Organization of examiner's tray for the PIC visual support form.

Source: Artimage 2015.

5. Prepare the Material for the Visual Support Form to Evaluate

a) Among the materials prepared in step 4, take the material for the visual support form and category you will evaluate. If evaluating the OBJ visual support form, take the object bag from the category chosen beforehand; in all other cases, take filing box 2–3 + 3H for the category being evaluated and the corresponding visual supports (the supports are filed behind the blue dividers labelled "2–3.XXX," where "XXX" refers to the form of visual support to evaluate, as for example 2–3.PIC). If using the examiner's tray, place all the visual supports taken from behind the divider into the tray as shown in Figure 2.2. Make sure to place visual supports in the right order (refer to the numbers on the back).

b) Then mount an example of the visual support form being evaluated to the top of each of the three matching boxes (refer to Table 3 on p. B19 of the Evaluation Protocol to know which visual support to place where). If the OBJ form is being evaluated, use one example of each object from the bag of the category being evaluated. In all other cases, use the first three visual supports from filing box 2–3 + 3H of the category being evaluated following the numbered order.

Figure 2.3 shows a matching box stuck on the bathroom door with the blue mounting putty. A toothbrush in OBJ form has been mounted to the top of the box.

Figure 2.3. Matching box stuck to the bathroom door with toothbrush visual support in OBJ form.

Source: Artimage 2015.

6. Demonstrations, Evaluation, and Scoring

Generally, the evaluation for each visual support form in Part 2 will proceed as follows: the examiner hands the user a visual support; the user takes the visual support and walks and drops the support into the correct box.

As in Part 1, using reinforcers (e.g., saying, "well done!" or giving the user food or objects they like) is not only recommended but strongly encouraged; this will help them better understand the task to perform, pay attention, and stay motivated throughout the evaluation.

Throughout the evaluation of Part 2, the user must successfully complete the match. It is thus important to provide assistance if required; this can include physical, gestural, or verbal prompts (e.g., guiding them by the hand and helping them put the visual support in the correct box) both during the demonstrations and the evaluation. However, the help provided during demonstrations and the evaluation should not be the same.

Demonstrations

Contrary to Part 1, demonstrations in Part 2 are not all optional. In the "Demos" column in the Evaluation Protocol, "mand." will specify when a demonstration is mandatory and "opt." when it is optional (see ② in Excerpt 4).

Generally, a demonstration is mandatory to evaluate Visual Support Forms 1, 2, and 3, as at the beginning of the evaluation, the user does not know where to take the visual supports. A second optional demonstration is only allowed for the evaluation of Visual Support Form 1 (not for forms 2 and 3). For Visual Support Form 1, this is indicated as "2 demos/location 1 mand. + 1 opt." in the Evaluation Protocol, and for Visual Support Forms 2 and 3 as "1 mand. demo/location."

For the three locations, demonstrations must be done in a single series (one demonstration per location). The examiner cannot give a demonstration for the first location, hand a visual support to the user to match, and then give a demonstration for the second location.

For demonstrations for visual supports in OBJ form, the examiner should ensure that they give the user three visual supports from the category being evaluated (one example of each object in that category). They should vary the order in which they hand them to the user and ensure the user does not have to go to the same location twice in a row.

For demonstrations for visual support forms other than OBJ, the examiner should take one visual support at a time for that category, ensuring that they follow the order of the numbers on the back; as such, demonstrations will automatically be done all at once.

If it seems appropriate, the examiner can give a second demonstration for each location but only for Visual Support Form 1. First, give a demonstration for each location. Then choose whether to give a second round of demonstrations for each location or start the evaluation and check whether the user successfully matches the first three visual supports. If the user makes a mistake in one of the three locations on their first attempt, the examiner can then give a second round of demonstrations, meaning the demonstrations for all three locations are done all at once. Start the evaluation over and only record the results of the second attempt (discard the results of the first attempt before the second round of demonstrations). For the OBJ visual support form, make sure the order differs from that used in the first round of demonstrations.

As in Part 1, demonstrations are not scored. During demonstrations, the help provided should be proactive so the user understands the task at hand and what is expected of them. The examiner should thus communicate to the user that they need to take the visual support, and the examiner should show them where to take it and where to put it.

Evaluation and Scoring

Continue with the same material as in the demonstrations.

If evaluating the OBJ visual support form, give the user a first visual support in a different order from that in the demonstrations. Additionally, as the examiner hands the user the three visual supports from the category being evaluated (one example of each object in the category), they should make sure to vary the order so the user never goes to the same location twice in a row.

If evaluating a visual support form other than OBJ, hand the user the next visual support, following the numbered order. As mentioned previously, the user must successfully make a match. Therefore, the examiner should provide whatever help is needed to achieve this. It is important to remember that the objective is to assess the user's skills and not teach new ones. As a rule, once the demonstrations are complete, wait until the user drops the visual support into a box before intervening, as they may correct themselves in the meantime. But, depending on the examiner's judgment, and if it is obvious that the user will make a mistake, the examiner can provide assistance before the user drops the visual support into the wrong box. The score will be impacted if any help is given.

If the examiner feels as though the user successfully made a match by chance, they can collect the visual support from the box and re-evaluate it a little later, after the user has matched another support in a different location at least once.

Score each attempt in the following way: if the user walked to the right location entirely on their own without any help (do not lead the way by walking ahead of them) and placed the visual support in the right box on their own, assign a score of 1. If they required even minimal help, assign a score of 0 for that attempt.

In the Evaluation Protocol, the action "The user takes the visual support" is not scored. While the user is required to perform this action, their performance will not be a determining factor in the selection of the visual support form.

6.1. Detailed Procedure for Visual Support Form 1

Prepare the material required for Visual Support Form 1.

Demonstrations

a) **E (Examiner):** Hand the user a visual support.
   U (User): Take the visual support.
b) **E:** Walk with the user, show[1] them where to go and that they need to drop the visual support into the correct box.
   U: Walk and drop the visual support into the correct box.
c) **E and U:** Repeat steps a and b for the two other locations.
d) **E and U:** Repeat steps a to c for the three locations a second time if it is deemed appropriate (optional demonstrations).

---

[1] Here and in the following steps, the verb "show" is purposefully vague and refers to any means required, whether verbal, gestural, or physical, to help the user understand the task at hand. It is, however, important to choose carefully how you show the user what to do so that they are more likely to be able to do it on their own after the demonstrations.

Evaluation and Scoring

Attempts 1 to 6

a) **E (Examiner):** Hand the user a visual support.
   U (User): Take the visual support.
b) **U:** Walk and drop the visual support into the correct box.
   E: Score the user's results.
   Reminder: Score each attempt as follows: if the user walked over to the correct location entirely on their own without any help (specifically do not walk in front of the user to lead the way), assign a score of 1. If they required even minimal help, assign a score of 0.
c) **E and U:** Repeat steps a and b for the next five visual supports (attempts 2 to 6).
d) **E:** Record the results for the first six attempts in the box provided ("Subtotal Attempts 1 to 6").

If the user scored 6/6 on their first six attempts, evaluating attempts 7 to 9 for Visual Support Form 1 is not mandatory. Check "Not evaluated (0/3 or 3/3)" in the "Subtotal Attempts 7 to 9" box and assign a score of 3/3 for attempts 7 to 9. Then add up the two subtotals in the "Total Visual Support Form 1" box, which will inevitably be 9/9. In this case, skip to the evaluation of Visual Support Form 2. Excerpt 6 presents an example of a user scoring 6/6 on their first six attempts and the examiner deciding not to evaluate attempts 7 to 9.

Excerpt 6. Schedule Evaluation Protocol, Visual Support Form 1

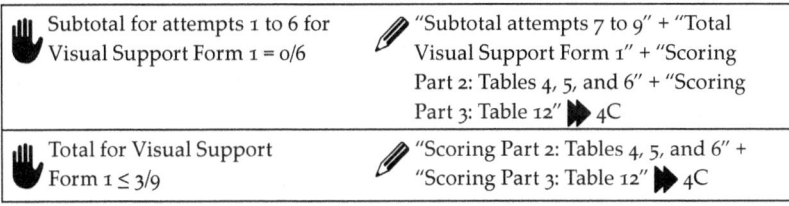

✋ Subtotal for attempts 1 to 6 for Visual Support Form 1 = 0/6	✏ "Subtotal attempts 7 to 9" + "Total Visual Support Form 1" + "Scoring Part 2: Tables 4, 5, and 6" + "Scoring Part 3: Table 12" ▶ 4C
✋ Total for Visual Support Form 1 ≤ 3/9	✏ "Scoring Part 2: Tables 4, 5, and 6" + "Scoring Part 3: Table 12" ▶ 4C

(Continued)

CREATING VISUAL SCHEDULES

ACTIONS DONE BY USER (6 attempts, 2 trips per location)	DEMOS	1	2	3	4	5	6	SUBTOTAL ATTEMPTS 1 TO 6
The user takes the visual support.	2 demos/ location 1 mand. + 1 opt.							Not scored
The user walks and drops the visual support in the correct box.	2 demos/ location 1 mand. + 1 opt.	1/1	1/1	1/1	1/1	1/1	1/1	6/6

⚠ *Note: Visual Support Form 1 is the only one for which a second demonstration is allowed.*

⚠ *Note: Collect the visual supports from the matching boxes and put them back in order before continuing with attempts 7 to 9 (if required).*

ACTIONS DONE BY USER (3 attempts, 1 trip per location)	7	8	9	SUBTOTAL ATTEMPTS 7 TO 9	TOTAL VISUAL SUPPORT FORM 1
The user takes the visual support.				Not scored	Not scored
The user walks and drops the visual support in the correct box.	/1	/1	/1	① 3/3 ☑ Not evaluated (0/3 or 3/3)	② 9/9

① The user obtained a score of 6/6 for attempts 1 to 6 and the examiner chose not to evaluate attempts 7 to 9. The examiner thus checked "Not evaluated (0/3 or 3/3)" and assigned a score of 3/3 for attempts 7 to 9.

② The total score for Visual Support Form 1 is 9/9 (6 points for the first six attempts and 3 points assigned by the examiner after choosing not to evaluate attempts 7 to 9).

 e) **E:** Determine whether the first stop standard for Visual Support Form 1 is reached or if the evaluation of Visual Support Form 1 continues with attempts 7 to 9.

Evaluating Schedule Characteristics | Part 2   A59

STOP STANDARDS FOR VISUAL SUPPORT FORM 1	
FIRST STOP STANDARD FOR VISUAL SUPPORT FORM 1	PROCEDURE TO FOLLOW IF THE STOP STANDARD IS REACHED
✋ Subtotal for attempts 1 to 6 for Visual Support Form 1 = 0/6	✏️ "Subtotal attempts 7 to 9" + "Total Visual Support Form 1" + "Scoring Part 2: Tables 4, 5, and 6" + "Scoring Part 3: Table 12" ▶ 4C If the user's subtotal is 0 for attempts 1 to 6 for Visual Support Form 1: • Stop the evaluation of Part 2. • Check "Not evaluated (0/3 or 3/3)" in the "Subtotal Attempts 7 to 9" box and assign a score of 0/3. • Add up both subtotals in the "Total for Visual Support Form 1" box, which will inevitably be 0/9. • Score Part 2 by filling in Tables 4, 5, and 6 of the Evaluation Protocol (see scoring instructions for Part 2 on p. A66). • Score Part 3 by filling in Table 12 of the Evaluation Protocol (see scoring instructions for Part 3 on p. A104). • Then skip ahead to Part 4, Section 4C to finish the evaluation.

If the first stop standard for Visual Support Form 1 is not reached, continue the evaluation with attempts 7 to 9.

Attempts 7 to 9

Collect the visual supports from the matching boxes. If using a form other than OBJ, put them back in order (see numbering on back).

a) **E (Examiner):** Hand the user a visual support.
   U (User): Take the visual support.
b) **U:** Walk and drop the visual support into the correct box.
   E: Score the user's performance.
c) **E and U:** Repeat steps a and b for the next two visual supports (attempts 8 and 9).

d) **E:** Record the results for attempts 7 to 9 in the box provided ("Subtotal Attempts 7 to 9"). Then add up the two subtotals in the "Total Visual Support Form 1" box.
e) **E:** Determine whether the second stop standard for Visual Support Form 1 was reached or whether the evaluation continues with Part 2.

STOP STANDARDS FOR VISUAL SUPPORT FORM 1	
SECOND STOP STANDARD FOR VISUAL SUPPORT FORM 1	PROCEDURE TO FOLLOW IF THE STOP STANDARD IS REACHED
✋ Total for Visual Support Form 1 ≤ 3/9	✏️ "Scoring Part 2: Tables 4, 5, and 6" + "Scoring Part 3: Table 12" ▶ 4C
	If the user's total for Visual Support Form 1 is less than or equal to 3/9: • Stop the evaluation of Part 2. • Score Part 2 by filling in Tables 4, 5, and 6 of the Evaluation Protocol (see scoring instructions for Part 2 on p. A66). • Score Part 3 by filling in Table 12 of the Evaluation Protocol (see scoring instructions for Part 3 on p. A104). • Then skip ahead to Part 4, Section 4C to finish the evaluation.

If the second stop standard for Visual Support Form 1 is not reached, continue the evaluation for Visual Support Form 2.

6.2. Detailed Procedure for Visual Support Form 2

Remove the three visual supports from the top of the matching boxes. Leave the boxes in their locations for Visual Support Forms 2 and 3 (if applicable), but also for the evaluation of Part 3, Section 3A, which will take place in the same area. If using a visual support form other than OBJ, put the visual supports representing the locations back in order (see numbers on back).

Demonstrations

Prepare the material required for Visual Support Form 2.

a) **E (Examiner):** Hand the user a visual support.
U (User): Take the visual support.

b) **E:** Walk with the user, show[2] them where to go and that they need to drop the visual support into the correct box.
U: Walk and drop the visual support into the correct box.
c) **E and U:** Repeat steps a and b for the two other locations.

Evaluation and Scoring

Attempts 1 to 6

a) **E (Examiner):** Hand the user a visual support.
U (User): Take the visual support.
b) **U:** Walk and drop the visual support into the correct box.
E: Score the user's results.
c) **E and U:** Repeat steps a and b for the next five visual supports (attempts 2 to 6).
d) **E:** Record the results for the first six attempts in the box provided ("Subtotal Attempts 1 to 6").

If the user scored 6/6 on their first six attempts, evaluating attempts 7 to 9 for Visual Support Form 2 is not mandatory. Check "Not evaluated (0/3 or 3/3)" in the "Subtotal Attempts 7 to 9" box and assign a score of 3/3 for attempts 7 to 9. Then add up the two subtotals in the "Total Visual Support Form 2" box, which will inevitably be 9/9. In this case, the second stop standard for Visual Support Form 2 has been reached; follow the procedure outlined in the Stop Standard.

e) **E:** Determine whether the first stop standard for Visual Support Form 2 is reached or whether the evaluation of Visual Support Form 2 continues with attempts 7 to 9.

---

2 Here and in the following steps, the verb "show" is purposefully vague and refers to any means required, whether verbal, gestural, or physical, to help the user understand the task at hand. It is, however, important to choose carefully how you show the user what to do so that they are more likely to be able to do it on their own after the demonstrations.

STOP STANDARDS FOR VISUAL SUPPORT FORM 2	
FIRST STOP STANDARD FOR VISUAL SUPPORT FORM 2	PROCEDURE TO FOLLOW IF THE STOP STANDARD IS REACHED
✋ Subtotal for attempts 1 to 6 for Visual Support Form 2 = 0/6	✏️ "Subtotal attempts 7 to 9" + "Total Visual Support Form 2" ▶ If no Visual Support Form 3 was selected "Scoring Part 2: Tables 4, 5, and 6" ▶ If the user's subtotal is 0 for attempts 1 to 6 for Visual Support Form 2: • Check "Not evaluated (0/3 or 3/3)" in the "Subtotal Attempts 7 to 9" box and assign a score of 0/3. • Add up both subtotals in the "Total for Visual Support Form 2" box, which will inevitably be 0/9. • Continue the evaluation for Visual Support Form 3 if this form was selected in Part 1, Table 2. • If no Visual Support Form 3 was selected in Part 1, Table 2, then score Part 2 by filling in Tables 4, 5, and 6 of the Evaluation Protocol (see scoring instructions for Part 2 on p. A66). Then continue the evaluation of Part 3 if no stop standards are reached for Part 2.

If the first stop standard for Visual Support Form 2 is not reached, continue the evaluation of Visual Support Form 2 with attempts 7 to 9.

Attempts 7 to 9

a) **E (Examiner):** Hand the user a visual support.
   U (User): Take the visual support.
b) **U:** Walk and drop the visual support into the correct box.
   E: Score the user's performance.
c) **E and U:** Repeat steps a and b for the next two visual supports (attempts 8 and 9).
d) **E:** Record the results for attempts 7 to 9 in the box provided ("Subtotal Attempts 7 to 9"). Then add up the two subtotals in the "Total Visual Support Form 2" box.

e) **E:** Determine whether the second stop standard for Visual Support Form 2 was reached or whether the evaluation of Part 2 continues.

STOP STANDARDS FOR VISUAL SUPPORT FORM 2	
SECOND STOP STANDARD FOR VISUAL SUPPORT FORM 2	PROCEDURE TO FOLLOW IF THE STOP STANDARD IS REACHED
✋ Total for Visual Support Form 2 ≥ 7/9	✏️ "Scoring Part 2: Tables 4, 5, and 6" ▶ If the user's total for Visual Support Form 2 is greater or equal to 7/9: • Stop the evaluation of Part 2. • Score Part 2 by filling in Tables 4, 5, and 6 of the Evaluation Protocol (see scoring instructions for Part 2 on p. A66). • Continue with evaluation at Part 3.

If the second stop standard for Visual Support Form 2 is not reached, continue the evaluation for Visual Support Form 3. However, if no Visual Support Form 3 was selected in Table 2 of Part 1 (p. B17 of the Evaluation Protocol), proceed with scoring Part 2 by filling in Tables 4, 5, and 6 on p. B23 of the Evaluation Protocol (see instructions on Part 2 scoring standards).

6.3. Detailed Procedure for Visual Support Form 3

Remove the three visual supports from the top of the matching boxes. Leave the boxes in their locations for the evaluation of Visual Support Form 3, but also for the evaluation of Part 3, Section 3A, which will take place in the same area. If using a visual support form other than OBJ, put the visual supports representing the locations back in order (see numbers on back).

Demonstrations

Prepare the material required for Visual Support Form 3.

a) **E (Examiner):** Hand the user a visual support.
U (User): Take the visual support.

b) **E:** Walk with the user, show[3] them where to go and that they need to drop the visual support into the correct box.
   U: Walk and drop the visual support into the correct box.
   c) **E and U:** Repeat steps a and b for the two other locations.

Evaluation and Scoring

Attempts 1 to 6

   a) **E (Examiner):** Hand the user a visual support.
   U (User): Take the visual support.
   b) **U:** Walk and drop the visual support into the correct box.
   E: Score the user's results.
   c) **E and U:** Repeat steps a and b for the next five visual supports (attempts 2 to 6).
   d) **E:** Record the results for the first six attempts in the box provided ("Subtotal Attempts 1 to 6").

If the user scored 6/6 on their first six attempts, evaluating attempts 7 to 9 for Visual Support Form 3 is not mandatory. Check "Not evaluated (0/3 or 3/3)" in the "Subtotal Attempts 7 to 9" box and assign a score of 3/3 for attempts 7 to 9. Then add up the two subtotals in the "Total Visual Support Form 3" box, which will inevitably be 9/9. In this case, proceed directly to scoring Part 2.

   e) **E:** Determine whether the stop standard for Visual Support Form 3 is reached or whether the evaluation of Visual Support Form 3 continues with attempts 7 to 9.

---

3   Here and in the following steps, the verb "show" is purposefully vague and refers to any means required, whether verbal, gestural, or physical, to help the user understand the task at hand. It is, however, important to choose carefully how you show the user what to do so that they are more likely to be able to do it on their own after the demonstrations.

STOP STANDARDS FOR VISUAL SUPPORT FORM 3	
STOP STANDARD FOR VISUAL SUPPORT FORM 3	PROCEDURE TO FOLLOW IF THE STOP STANDARD IS REACHED
✋ Subtotal for attempts 1 to 6 for Visual Support Form 3 = 0/6	✏ "Subtotal attempts 7 to 9" + "Total Visual Support Form 3" + "Scoring Part 2: Tables 4, 5, and 6" ▶ If the user's subtotal is 0 for attempts 1 to 6 for Visual Support Form 3: • Check "Not evaluated (0/3 or 3/3) in the "Subtotal Attempts 7 to 9" box and assign a score of 0/3. • Add up both subtotals in the "Total Visual Support Form 3" box, which will inevitably be 0/9. • Score Part 2 by filling in Tables 4, 5, and 6 of the Evaluation Protocol (see scoring instructions for Part 2 on p. A66). • Continue the evaluation at Part 3 if no stop standard is reached for Part 2.

If the stop standard for Visual Support Form 3 is not reached, continue the evaluation of Visual Support Form 3 with attempts 7 to 9.

Attempts 7 to 9

a) **E (Examiner):** Hand the user a visual support.
   U (User): Take the visual support.
b) **U:** Walk and drop the visual support into the correct box.
   E: Score the user's performance.
c) **E and U:** Repeat steps a and b for the next two visual supports (attempts 8 and 9).
d) **E:** Record the results for attempts 7 to 9 in the box provided ("Subtotal Attempts 7 to 9"). Then add up the two subtotals in the "Total Visual Support Form 3" box.
e) **E:** Score Part 2.

7. Scoring Part 2 of the Evaluation in the Schedule Evaluation Protocol

If Part 2 was not evaluated because a stop standard was reached in Part 1, only fill in Table 6. If this is the case, go directly to step c.

If Part 2 was evaluated, whether partially or completely, fill in Tables 4, 5, and 6 as follows:

a) **Table 4:** Copy results from Part 1 (Table 1 on p. B17 of the Evaluation Protocol) of the evaluation (only the "Total" column) into Table 4 (p. B23 of Evaluation Protocol).

b) **Table 5:** Copy the visual supports selected for the evaluation of Part 2 (Table 2 on p. B17 of the Evaluation Protocol) in the "Visual Support Form" column of Table 5 (p. B23 of Evaluation Protocol).

Then write down the results from Part 2 in Table 5 referring to each visual support form evaluated; check "not evaluated" for Visual Support Form 2 and Visual Support Form 3 if applicable.

Here is a more detailed explanation of how to fill in the "Total" column in Table 5. Record the result for Visual Support Form 1. If Visual Support Form 2 was not evaluated because a stop standard for Support Form 1 was reached, check "not evaluated." If it was evaluated, write down the result. If no form of visual support was selected for Part 2 of the evaluation (so no visual support form was written down in the "Visual Support Form" column) or if Visual Support Form 3 was not evaluated because a stop standard for Visual Support Form 1 or Visual Support Form 2 was reached, check "not evaluated." And if Visual Support Form 3 was selected and evaluated, then write down the score.

c) **Table 6:** To determine which visual support form to select for the user's schedule (the goal of Part 2), follow the scoring standards below **from top to bottom** (these are also provided in the Evaluation Protocol). The instructions for Table 6 are very important: Follow the scoring standards for Part 2 **from top to bottom**. The highest standard in the list corresponding to the user's results is the right one for the user; check it in the "Visual Support Form Selected ❶" column. This guideline must be fully respected to ensure that the visual support form selected is the most appropriate for the user, as the user's results may correspond to more than one scoring standard. As such, start with the first scoring standard; if it applies, check OBJ-U. Otherwise, move on to the next scoring standard and so on until the standard that corresponds to the user's results is reached.

1. If Part 2 was not evaluated because of stop standards, check OBJ-U.
2. Check the visual support form located closest to the bottom with a score of 7/9 or higher in Table 5.
3. Check the visual support form located closest to the bottom with a score of 5/6 or higher in Table 4.
4. Check OBJ-U in all other cases.

d) Indicate whether a stop standard for Part 2 is reached or whether the evaluation continues with Part 3.

STOP STANDARDS FOR PART 2	
STOP STANDARDS FOR PART 2	PROCEDURE TO FOLLOW IF THE STOP STANDARD IS REACHED
✋ Total (Table 5) Visual Support Forms 1, 2, <u>and</u> 3 (only visual support forms evaluated) ≤ 5/9	✏️ "Scoring Part 3: Table 12" ▶ 4C If the user obtains a score less than or equal to 5/9 for the visual support forms evaluated (1, 2, <u>and</u> 3) — do not take into account the forms checked "not evaluated": • Score Part 3 by filling in Table 12 of the Evaluation Protocol (see scoring instructions for Part 3 on p. A104). • Go to Part 4, Section 4C to finish the evaluation.
✋ Visual support forms selected = OBJ-U	✏️ "Scoring Part 3: Table 12" ▶ 4C If the visual support form selected after scoring Part 2 is OBJ-U: • Score Part 3 by filling in Table 12 of the Evaluation Protocol (see scoring instructions for Part 3 on p. A104). • Go to Part 4, Section 4C to finish the evaluation.

Scoring and Selection of Visual Support Form Example

Here is an example illustrating the steps for scoring and for visual support form selection.

Table 1 compiles the results from Part 1 of the evaluation.

TABLE 1. RESULTS FOR PART 1

Record the results obtained for each visual support form in the different subsections of Part 1, then fill in the "Subtotal" and "Total" columns.

	Visual Support Form	Section 1A	Section 1B	Section 1C	Subtotal	Divide by	Total (round off to the nearest whole number)
Top ↑	OBJ	18/18			18/18	÷ 3	ⓐ6/6
	PHO		6/9	3/9	9/18	÷ 3	3/6
	PIC		9/9	4/9	13/18	÷ 3	4/6
	BWP		7/9	5/9	12/18	÷ 3	ⓐ4/6
Bottom	WTC		1/9	0/9	1/18	÷ 3	0/6
	WWH		0/9	0/9	0/18	÷ 3	0/6

Visual support forms selected:

- Visual Support Form 1 (the closest to the top in the "Visual Support Form" column of Table 1): OBJ
- Visual Support Form 2 (the closest to the bottom in the "Visual Support Form" column of Table 1): BWP
- Visual Support Form 3 (between Support Form 1 and Support Form 2 in the "Visual Support Form" column of Table 1): PIC

To score Part 2, the examiner must copy the results from Part 1 into Table 4, but only the "Total" column.

TABLE 4. RESULTS FOR PART 1 (TOTALS ONLY)

Copy results from Part 1, Table 1 on page 17 ("Total" column only)

	VISUAL SUPPORT FORM	TOTAL (round off to the nearest whole number)
Top ↑	OBJ	6/6
	PHO	3/6
	PIC	4/6
	BWP	4/6
Bottom	WTC	0/6
	WWH	0/6

Part 2 was evaluated for the same user, and their results are compiled in Table 5.

TABLE 5. RESULTS FOR PART 2

Copy the visual support forms selected for the evaluation of Part 2 (Table 2, p. B17) in the "Visual Support Forms" column. Then, write down the results of Part 2 referring to each form of visual support evaluated and check "not evaluated" if applicable.

	VISUAL SUPPORT FORMS	TOTAL
VISUAL SUPPORT FORM 1	OBJ	6/9
VISUAL SUPPORT FORM 2	BWP	3/9 or ☐ not evaluated
VISUAL SUPPORT FORM 3 (IF APPLICABLE)	PIC	4/9 or ☐ not evaluated

By complying with the scoring standards **from top to bottom** (the highest standard in the list corresponding to the user's results is the right one for the user) the recommended visual support form for this user is OBJ (owing to scoring standard 3).

TABLE 6. SCORING PART 2

Follow the scoring standards for Part 2 **from top to bottom**. The highest standard in the list corresponding to the user's results is the right one for the user; check it in the "Visual Support Form Selected ❶" column.

SCORING STANDARDS FOR PART 2	VISUAL SUPPORT FORM SELECTED ❶
1. If Part 2 was not evaluated because of stop standards, check OBJ-U. 2. Check the visual support form located **closest to the bottom** with a score of 7/9 or higher in Table 5. 3. Check the visual support form located **closest to the bottom** with a score of 5/6 or higher in Table 4. 4. Check OBJ-U in all other cases.	☐ OBJ-U (objects used in activities) ↳ ✎ "Scoring Part 3: Table 12" ▶ 4C ☑ OBJ (objects representing the activities) ☐ PHO (photos) ☐ PIC (colour pictograms) ☐ BWP (black-and-white pictograms) ☐ WTC (words typed on the computer) ☐ WWH (words written by hand)

Part 3

Goal

The goal of Part 3 is to identify the recommended schedule characteristics for the user. As the visual support form for the user's schedule was decided in Part 2, the evaluation will now determine the following schedule features: presentation mode, initiation, manipulation, identification, length, location, and layout.

Duration

10 to 20 minutes.

Administration

As in Part 2 of the evaluation, Part 3 takes place in the environment where the schedule will be implemented. It is divided into two sections: 3A and 3B. Section 3A is divided into three subsections: 3A.1, 3A.2, and 3A.3. Section 3B is divided into two subsections: 3B.1 and 3B.2.

The procedures to follow differ from one section to the next, and sometimes even within subsections. They are therefore presented separately. The following information, however, applies to both sections.

The subsections must be evaluated in the same order as they appear in the Evaluation Protocol for every user. As in Parts 1 and 2, using reinforcers (e.g., saying, "well done!" or giving the user food or objects they like) is not only recommended but strongly encouraged; this will help the user better understand the task at hand, pay attention, and stay motivated throughout the evaluation.

Moreover, as in Part 2, the user must successfully complete each match throughout all of Part 3. It is thus necessary to assist them so they can complete the match successfully. This can be done through physical, gestural, or verbal prompts if needed, both during demonstrations and evaluations.

During demonstrations (not scored), any help should be proactive so that the user understands the task and what is expected of them. Therefore, as in previous parts, the examiner should show the user every action to perform.

It is important, however, to remember that the evaluation's objective is to assess the user's skills and not teach them new ones. If the user makes a mistake, start over and provide the help required for them to succeed. As a rule, once the demonstrations are complete, wait until the user finishes the action before intervening, as they may correct themselves in the meantime. But, depending on the examiner's judgment, and if it is obvious that the user will make a mistake, assistance may be provided. The score will be impacted if any help is given.

Sequence for Section 3A

The steps presented here apply to all of Section 3A, regardless of the form of visual support selected. However, the materials required for the OBJ form are different than for other visual support forms. As such, material preparation will also differ. The demonstrations, evaluation, and scoring will be explained in more detail for each subsection (3A.1, 3A.2, and 3A.3).

Generally, the evaluation should proceed as follows: the examiner hands the user a schedule cue telling them to go consult their schedule (presented here in strip format mounted on the wall); the user drops the schedule cue into the schedule cue box; the user then takes a visual support from the Velcro strip and brings it to the corresponding matching box location, dropping it into that box.

1. Prepare the Material for Evaluating Section 3A

To know what materials are required for Section 3A, refer to the 🛠 symbol located directly under "Section 3A: Schedule Displayed on the Wall" on p. B24 of the Evaluation Protocol. The materials needed for the OBJ form are different than those required for other forms. Therefore, material preparation will also differ.

1.1. For a Visual Support in OBJ Form

(If this is the visual support form selected.)

a) Prepare the materials listed beside the 🛠 symbol where it says, "If the form of visual support selected (❶ Table 6) is OBJ," in the Evaluation Protocol. Part of the material is the same as that used during the evaluation of Part 2: the object bag from the same category, the three matching boxes, the examiner's tray (optional), and the blue mounting putty. In addition, the examiner will also need the piggy bank and coins[1] as well as the strip-format schedule.

b) While the examiner's tray is optional, its use is recommended. Using the tray ensures that the evaluation runs smoothly, as the examiner will have to carry around a certain amount of material and score the performance at the same time. Place the Evaluation Protocol and a pencil in the bottom of the large basket (i.e., the examiner's tray). As mentioned in Appendix 1, on p. B111 of the Supplementary Material section, put the smaller basket inside the large one and insert the small square basket. If using reinforcers, place those into the small square basket. Put the coins (which will go into the piggy bank) in the small basket, on either side of the small square basket (see Figure 3.1).

c) If removed, put the matching boxes back in the designated locations. The matching boxes should go back in the same locations as in Part 2, which were written down in Table 3 on p. B19 of the Evaluation Protocol.

---

[1] As indicated in Appendix 1, on p. B89 of the Supplementary Material section, a small plastic container and poker chips can be used instead of a piggy bank and coins. To simplify the text, only the words "piggy bank" and "coins" will be used in Part 3 to refer to this material.

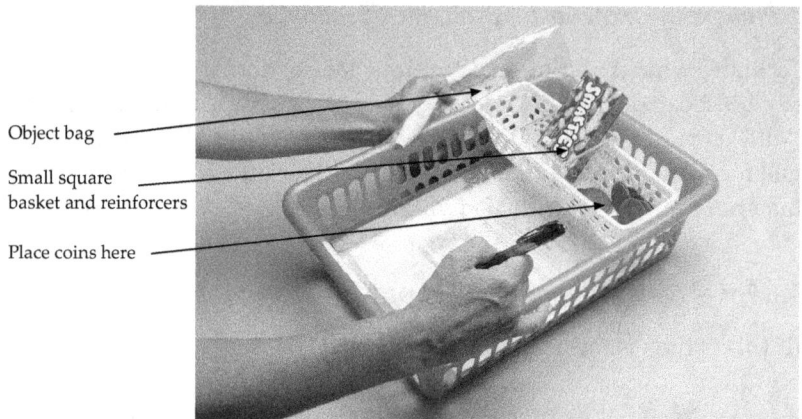

Figure 3.1. Examiner's tray arranged for the evaluation of Section 3A, OBJ form.

Source: Artimage 2015.

> d) Place an example of each of the three visual supports (from the same category as that used in Part 2) on the top of the matching boxes (once again, refer to Table 3 on p. B19 of the Evaluation Protocol to know which visual support to put where).
>
> e) With the blue mounting putty, mount the schedule strip to the wall in an individualized location and write down its location in the box provided for that purpose, on p. B24 of the Evaluation Protocol.
>
> The goal of this part of the evaluation is to see whether the user can take a visual support from the schedule strip and bring it to the corresponding location. Consequently, the schedule strip should be placed at a reasonable distance from the location of each matching box.
>
> For this part of the evaluation, the schedule strip should be placed in an individualized location. Therefore, if the evaluation is conducted in an area where other schedules are displayed, do not use this location to evaluate Part 3. However, once the evaluation is complete, it may be recommended to display the user's schedule in this location.
>
> The following criteria are generally used to identify where to display the schedule:

- The most central location based on the user's daily activities.
- A location that prevents others from moving or touching the visual supports on the schedule (e.g., the schedule may be displayed in the user's bedroom in their home).

It is possible that based on the user's daily activities, a schedule location that meets these criteria is not ideal for the evaluation. This may be due to various reasons (e.g., schedule not visible as user moves around between the different matching boxes, the schedule is located further than stipulated in evaluation criteria, etc.). If this is the case, pick a different location for the duration of the evaluation.

f) Mount the piggy bank to the top left of the schedule strip.

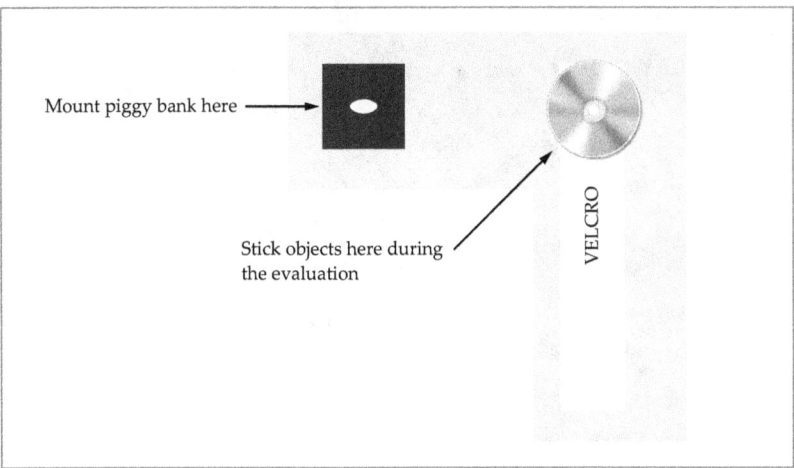

Figure 3.2. Piggy bank mounted on schedule strip.

1.2. For Other Visual Support Forms

a) Prepare the materials listed beside the ✂ symbol where it says "If the form of visual support selected (❶ Table 6) is not OBJ," on p. B24 in the Evaluation Protocol. Part of the material is the same as that used during the evaluation of Part 2: filing box 2–3 + 3H from the same category, the three matching boxes, the examiner's tray (optional), and the blue mounting putty. In addition, the examiner will need the schedule cue box and the schedule strip.

b) While the examiner's tray is optional, its use is recommended. It ensures that the evaluation runs smoothly, as the examiner will have to carry around a certain amount of material and score the performance at the same time. Place the Evaluation Protocol and a pencil in the bottom of the large basket (i.e., the examiner's tray). As mentioned in Appendix 1, on p. B111 of the Supplementary Material section, place the smaller basket inside the large one and insert the small square basket. If using reinforcers, place those into the small square basket (see Figure 3.3).

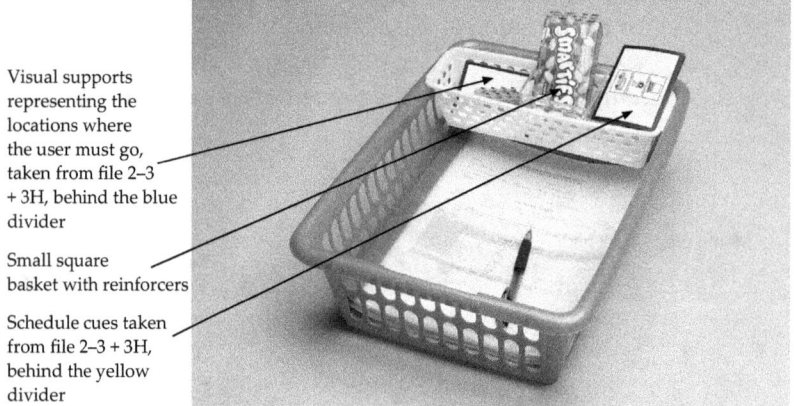

Visual supports representing the locations where the user must go, taken from file 2–3 + 3H, behind the blue divider

Small square basket with reinforcers

Schedule cues taken from file 2–3 + 3H, behind the yellow divider

Figure 3.3. Examiner's tray assembled to evaluate Section 3A, visual support forms other than OBJ.

Source: Artimage 2015.

c) Identify which visual supports will be used to evaluate Section 3A and place them on the examiner's tray.

The visual supports representing the locations where the user needs to go can be found in filing box 2–3 + 3H of the category being evaluated, behind the "2–3.XXX" divider. Here, the "XXX" refers to the form of visual support selected (e.g., 2–3.BWP). Put all the visual supports on the examiner's tray (if using) in the same place as in Part 2 of the evaluation (i.e., to the left of the small square basket that contains the reinforcers). Make sure the visual supports are placed in the correct order (see numbers on back).

The schedule cues can be found in the filing box 2–3 + 3H of the category being evaluated, behind the yellow "3H.XXX" divider. Here, the "XXX" refers to the form of visual support selected (e.g., 3H.BWP). Put all visual supports in the examiner's tray (if using) to the right of the small square basket containing the reinforcers (see Figure 3.3). It is important to note that for visual supports in PHO form and PIC form, the schedule cues are the same. They can be found behind the 3H.PHO/3H.PIC divider.

d) If removed, put the matching boxes back in the designated locations. The matching boxes should go back in the same locations as in Part 2, which are written down in Table 3 on p. B19 of the Evaluation Protocol.

e) Place an example of each of the three visual supports (from the same category as that used in Part 2) on the top of the matching boxes (once again, refer to Table 3 on p. B19 of the Evaluation Protocol to know which visual support to put where). It is very important to use the first three visual supports from filing box 2–3 + 3H of the category being evaluated, which can be found behind the blue "2–3.XXX" divider (here, "XXX" refers to the form of visual support selected), always following the numbered order on the back.

f) Use the blue mounting putty to mount the schedule strip to the wall in an individualized location, and write down the chosen location in the box provided for that purpose on p. B24 in the Evaluation Protocol.

The goal of this part of the evaluation is to see whether the user can take a visual support from the schedule strip and bring it to the corresponding location. Consequently, the schedule strip should be placed at a reasonable distance from the location of each matching box.

For this part of the evaluation, the schedule strip should be placed in an individualized location. Therefore, if the evaluation is conducted in an area where other schedules are displayed, do not use this location to evaluate Part 3. However, once the evaluation is complete, it may be recommended to display the user's schedule in this location.

The following criteria are generally used to identify where to display the schedule:

- The most central location based on the user's daily activities.
- A location that prevents others from moving or touching the visual supports on the schedule (e.g., the schedule may be displayed in the user's bedroom in their home).

It is possible that based on the user's daily activities, a schedule location that meets these criteria is not ideal for the evaluation. This may be due to various reasons (e.g., schedule not visible as user moves around between the different matching boxes, the schedule is located further than stipulated in evaluation criteria, etc.). If this is the case, pick a different location for the duration of the evaluation.

g) Mount the schedule cue box to the top left of the schedule strip.
h) Stick the first schedule cue to the top of the schedule cue box to identify it (the same way as on the matching boxes).

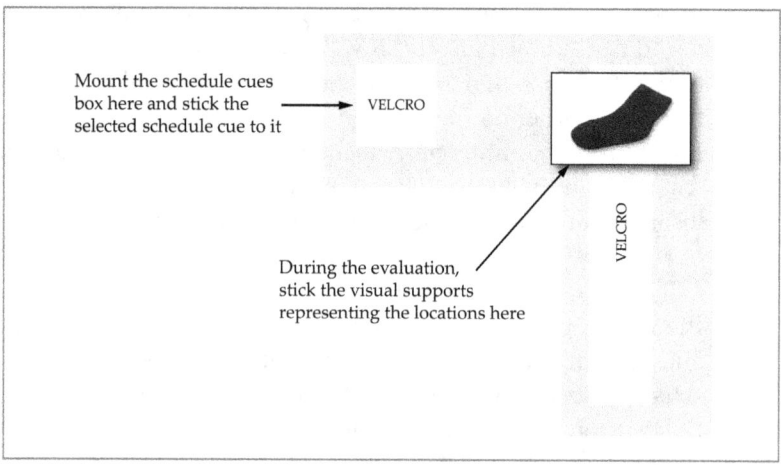

Figure 3.4. Schedule cues box mounted on the schedule strip.

2. Demonstrations, Evaluation, and Scoring

The following detailed procedure applies for all visual support forms, even OBJ, with a few exceptions. In fact, to evaluate the OBJ form, the visual supports representing the locations where the user must go are objects, and the schedule cues are coins that the user must put into the piggy bank. As such, in the text that follows, simply replace "schedule cue" with "coin" and "schedule cue box" with "piggy bank." Furthermore, the examiner does not need to put the objects back in order (as is the case for the other visual support forms), since they are not numbered. However, during both demonstrations and the evaluation, the examiner must make sure to give the user the three objects from the category evaluated (one example of each object from the category) and to vary the order in which they are handed to the user to ensure that the user never goes to the same location twice in a row.

Demonstrations

As in Part 2, demonstrations for Section 3A are not all optional. The Evaluation Protocol will specify whether a demonstration is mandatory ("mand.") or optional ("opt.").

Moreover, as in Parts 1 and 2, demonstrations are not scored. But they must be done all at once for the three visual supports (one demonstration for each visual support). Do not give a demonstration for the first visual support, immediately hand the visual support to the user to match on their own, and then give a demonstration for the second visual support.

For visual supports in OBJ form, the examiner must make sure to give the user the three objects from the category evaluated (one example of each object from the category) and to vary the order in which they are handed to the user to ensure that the user never goes to the same location twice in a row.

For demonstrations of visual support forms other than OBJ, take one visual support at a time for the category evaluated following the numbered order (see numbers on back); as such, demonstrations will automatically be given all at once.

Evaluation and Scoring

Use the same materials as for the demonstrations.

If the visual support form evaluated is OBJ, hand the first visual support to the user, making sure to change the order from the demonstrations. Give the user the three objects from the category evaluated (one example of each object from the category) and vary the order in which they are handed to the user to ensure that the user never goes to the same location twice in a row.

If the visual support is in a form other than OBJ, hand the user the next visual support, following the numbered order.

For Section 3A, the user will need to perform three actions for each location:

- The user takes the schedule cue, goes to the schedule strip, and drops the cue in the schedule cue box.
- The user takes the visual support (the first from the top) from the schedule strip.
- The user walks and drops the visual support into the correct matching box.

In addition, the first action in the Evaluation Protocol is marked "not scored," since the user's performance is not evaluated for this action. The last two actions are also scored separately: assign one point if the user did the actions entirely on their own, and no points if help was provided, even if minimal.

If, for example, the user did not take the visual support from the schedule strip on their own and help was provided for that action, but they walked over to the right location and dropped the visual support in the correct box entirely on their own, assign a score of 0 for the "The user takes the visual support from the schedule strip" (or "The user takes the top visual support from the schedule strip," when there is more than one on the strip) action, and a score of 1 for the "The user walks and drops the visual support into the correct box" action.

However, if the user took the proper visual support from the schedule strip, walked to the right location on their own, but needed help to drop the visual support into the correct matching box, assign a score of 1 for the "The user takes the [top] visual support from the schedule strip" action and 0 for the "The user walks and drops the visual support into the correct box" action.

2.1. Detailed Procedure for Subsection 3A.1

Before starting, make certain the visual supports representing the locations where the user needs to go are placed in the correct order (see numbering on back of visual supports) if evaluating a form other than OBJ. For the OBJ form, make sure to stick an example of each object from the category to the schedule strip one at a time and vary the order in which they are presented.

For this subsection, place the visual supports on the schedule strip one at a time.

Demonstrations

a) **E (Examiner):** Take the first visual support representing a location where the user needs to go and stick it on the schedule strip.
b) **E:** Hand the user the schedule cue, guide them to their schedule, and show[2] them that they have to drop the schedule cue into the schedule cue box.
   U (User): Take the schedule cue, go to the schedule strip, and drop the cue into the schedule cue box.
c) **E:** Show the user that they need to take a visual support from the schedule strip.
   U: Take the visual support from the schedule strip.
d) **E:** Walk with the user to show them where to go and where to drop the visual support (i.e., in the correct matching box). Demonstrating this action is optional depending on the examiner's judgment; as the locations represented by the visual supports are the same as in Part 2, it is possible that the user can already do this action on their own.
   U: Walk and drop the visual support into the correct box.
e) **E:** Stick the second visual support representing one of the locations on the schedule strip.
f) **E and U:** Repeat steps b through d for this visual support.
g) **E:** Stick the third visual support representing one of the locations on the schedule strip.
h) **E and U:** Repeat steps b through d for this visual support.

Evaluation and Scoring

Attempts 1 to 3

a) **E (Examiner):** Take the next visual support representing one of the locations and stick it on the schedule strip.
b) **E:** Hand the schedule cue to the user.

---

2   Here and in the following steps, the verb "show" is purposefully vague and refers to any means required, whether verbal, gestural, or physical, to help the user understand the task at hand. It is, however, important to choose carefully how you show the user what to do so that they are more likely to be able to do it on their own after the demonstrations.

U (User): Take the schedule cue, go to the schedule strip, and drop the schedule cue into the schedule cue box.

c) **U:** Take the visual support from the schedule strip.
E: Score the user's performance.
Reminder: Score the user's performance for each attempt as follows: if the user took the visual support from the schedule strip completely on their own, without any help, assign one point. If they required even minimal help, assign a score of 0 for that attempt.

d) **U:** Walk and drop the visual support into the correct box.
E: Score the user's performance.
Reminder: Score the user's performance for each attempt as follows: if the user walked to the correct location entirely on their own, without any help (do not walk in front of them and lead the way), and dropped the visual support into the correct matching box on their own, assign one point. If they required even minimal help, assign a score of 0 for that attempt.

e) **E and U:** Repeat steps a through d for the next two visual supports (attempts 2 and 3).

f) **E:** Record the results for the first three attempts in the "Subtotal 3A.1: Attempts 1 to 3" column.

If the user scored 3/3 for the two scored actions, evaluating attempts 4 to 6 for 3A.1 is optional. If the decision is made not to evaluate attempts 4 to 6, check "Not evaluated (0/3 or 3/3)" in the "Subtotal 3A.1: Attempts 4 to 6" column and assign a score of 3/3 for both actions. Then add up the two subtotals for 3A.1 in the "Total 3A.1" column, which will inevitably be 6/6. In this case, continue the evaluation at 3A.2.

g) **E:** Determine whether the stop standard for 3A.1 (see the stop standard in this guide) is reached during the first three attempts or if the evaluation of 3A.1 continues for attempts 4 to 6.

Attempts 4 to 6

a) **E (Examiner):** Take the next visual support representing one of the locations and stick it on the schedule strip.

b) **E:** Hand the schedule cue to the user.
U (User): Take the schedule cue, go to the schedule strip, and drop the schedule cue into the schedule cue box.

c) **U:** Take the visual support from the schedule strip.

E: Score the user's performance and determine whether the stop standard for 3A.1 (see below for the stop standard) is reached or whether the evaluation of 3A.1 continues.

If the stop standard is reached, the examiner can choose to let the user finish the match to give the user the opportunity to end this part of the evaluation on a positive note. The user's performance, however, will no longer be scored, and even though any type of help can now be provided, it is no longer necessary to correct them if they make a mistake.

d) **U**: Walk and drop the visual support into the correct box.

E: Score the user's performance and identify whether the stop standard for 3A.1 (see below for the stop standard) is reached or whether the evaluation of 3A.1 continues.

e) **E and U**: Repeat steps a through d for the next two visual supports (attempts 5 and 6), making sure to determine whether the stop standard for 3A.1 (see below for the stop standard) is reached during these attempts or if the evaluation of 3A.1 continues.

f) **E**: Record the results for attempts 4 to 6 in the "Subtotal 3A.1: Attempts 4 to 6" column.

g) **E**: Add up the two subtotals for 3A.1 in the "Total 3A.1" column.

h) **E**: Determine whether the stop standard for 3A.1 is reached after the six attempts or if the evaluation of Part 3 continues.

STOP STANDARD FOR SUBSECTION 3A.1	
STOP STANDARD FOR SUBSECTION 3A.1	PROCEDURE TO FOLLOW IF THE STOP STANDARD IS REACHED
✋ 3 scores of 0 on the same action in 3A.1	✏ "Subtotal 3A.1 Attempts 4 to 6" + "Total 3A.1" + "Scoring Part 3: Tables 10, 11, and 12" ▶ 4C If the user scores 0 three times for the same action in 3A.1: • Stop the evaluation of Part 3. • If the stop standard is reached before evaluating attempts 4 to 6, check "Not evaluated (0/3 or 3/3)" in the "Subtotal 3A.1 Attempts 4 to 6" column and assign a score of 0/3 for both actions.

(Continued)

- If the stop standard is reached while evaluating attempts 4 to 6, assign a score of 0 for the actions not evaluated and write the results down in the "Subtotal 3A.1 Attempts 4 to 6" column.
- Add up the two subtotals in the "Total 3A.1" column.
- Proceed to score Part 3 by filling in Tables 10, 11, and 12 in the Evaluation Protocol:

  In the "3A.1" column in Table 10, write down the results from that subsection. In the "3A.2" column, write down the results from that subsection, checking "Not evaluated (0/6)" for the two actions and assign a score of 0/6 to each. Do the same for column "3A.3."

  In the "Total 3B (3B.1 + 3B.2)" column of Table 11, check "3B not evaluated (0/9)" for the four actions and assign a score of 0/9 to each.

  In Table 12, see the scoring instructions for Part 3 (on p. A104).

- Then jump to Part 4, Section 4C to finish the evaluation.

2.2. Detailed Procedure for Subsection 3A.2

Collect the visual supports representing locations and schedule cues; it may be better to send the user on a break now. If using a form other than OBJ, put the visual supports back in order (see numbers on the back). For visual supports in OBJ form, make sure to stick three visual supports from the category being evaluated to the schedule strip (one example of each object in the category) and to vary the order.

For this subsection, the three visual supports representing locations must be placed on the schedule strip *right from the start*.

Demonstrations

a) **E (Examiner):** Take the first three visual supports representing the locations and stick them on the schedule strip.

b) **E:** Hand the user the schedule cue, guide them to their schedule, and show[3] them that they need to drop the schedule cue into the schedule cue box.
U (User): Take the schedule cue, go to the schedule strip, and drop the cue into the schedule cue box.

c) **E:** Show the user that they need to take the visual support at the top of the schedule strip.
U: Take the top visual support from the schedule strip.

d) **E:** Walk with the user to show them where to go and where to drop the visual support (i.e., in the correct matching box). Demonstrating this action is optional depending on the examiner's judgment; it is possible that the user can already do this action on their own.
U: Walk and drop the visual support into the correct box.

e) **E and U:** Repeat steps b through d for the next two visual supports.

Evaluation and Scoring

Attempts 1 to 3

a) **E (Examiner):** Take the next three visual supports representing the locations and stick them on the schedule strip.

b) **E:** Hand the schedule cue to the user.
U (User): Take the schedule cue, go to the schedule strip, and drop the schedule cue into the schedule cue box.

c) **U:** Take the top visual support from the schedule strip.
E: Score the user's performance.

d) **U:** Walk and drop the visual support into the correct box.
E: Score the user's performance.

e) **E and U:** Repeat steps b through d for the next two visual supports (attempts 2 and 3).

f) **E:** Record the results for the first three attempts in the "Subtotal 3A.2: Attempts 1 to 3" column.

If the user scored 3/3 for the two scored actions, evaluating attempts 4 to 6 for 3A.2 is optional. If the decision is made not to evaluate attempts 4 to 6, check "Not evaluated (0/3 or 3/3)"

---

3   Here and in the following steps, the verb "show" is purposefully vague and refers to any means required, whether verbal, gestural, or physical, to help the user understand the task at hand. It is, however, important to choose carefully how you show the user what to do so that they are more likely to be able to do it on their own after the demonstrations.

in the "Subtotal 3A.2: Attempts 4 to 6" column and assign a score of 3/3 for both actions. Then add up the two subtotals for 3A.2 in the "Total 3A.2" column, which will inevitably be 6/6. In this case, continue the evaluation at 3A.3.

g) **E:** Determine whether the stop standard for 3A.2 (see the stop standard in this guide) is reached during the first three attempts or if the evaluation of 3A.2 continues for attempts 4 to 6.

Attempts 4 to 6

a) **E (Examiner):** Take the next three visual supports representing the locations and stick them on the schedule strip.
b) **E:** Hand the schedule cue to the user.
U (User): Take the schedule cue, go to the schedule strip, and drop the schedule cue into the schedule cue box.
c) **U:** Take the top visual support from the schedule strip.
E: Score the user's performance and determine whether the stop standard for 3A.2 (see the stop standard in this guide) is reached or whether the evaluation of 3A.2 continues.

If the stop standard is reached, the examiner can choose to let the user finish the match to give the user the opportunity to end this part of the evaluation on a positive note. The user's performance, however, will no longer be scored, and even though any type of help can now be provided, it is no longer necessary to correct them if they make a mistake.
d) **U:** Walk and drop the visual support into the correct box.
E: Score the user's performance and determine whether the stop standard for 3A.2 is reached or whether the evaluation of 3A.2 continues.
e) **E and U:** Repeat steps b through d for the next two visual supports (attempts 5 and 6), making sure to determine whether the stop standard for 3A.2 is reached during these attempts or if the evaluation of 3A.2 continues.
f) **E:** Record the results for attempts 4 to 6 in the "Subtotal 3A.2: Attempts 4 to 6" column.
g) **E:** Add up the two subtotals for 3A.2 in the "Total 3A.2" column.
h) **E:** Identify whether the stop standard for 3A.2 is reached after the six attempts or if the evaluation of Part 3 continues.

STOP STANDARD FOR SUBSECTION 3A.2	
STOP STANDARD FOR SUBSECTION 3A.2	PROCEDURE TO FOLLOW IF THE STOP STANDARD IS REACHED
✋ 3 scores of 0 on the same action in 3A.2	✏ "Subtotal 3A.2 Attempts 4 to 6" + "Total 3A.2" + "Scoring Part 3: Tables 10, 11, and 12" ▶ If the user scores 0 three times for the same action in 3A.2: • Stop the evaluation of Part 3. • If the stop standard is reached before evaluating attempts 4 to 6, check "Not evaluated (0/3 or 3/3)" in the "Subtotal 3A.2 Attempts 4 to 6" column and assign a score of 0/3 for both actions. • If the stop standard is reached while evaluating attempts 4 to 6, assign a score of 0 for the actions not evaluated and write the results down in the "Subtotal 3A.2 Attempts 4 to 6" column. • Add up the two subtotals in the "Total 3A.2" column. • Proceed to score Part 3 by filling in Tables 10, 11, and 12 in the Evaluation Protocol: In Table 10, write down the results for Subsection 3A.1 and Subsection 3A.2 in their respective columns. In the "3A.3" column, check "Not evaluated (0/6)" for the two actions and assign a score of 0/6 to each. In the "Total 3B (3B.1 + 3B.2)" column of Table 11, check "3B not evaluated (0/9)" for the four actions and assign a score of 0/9 to each. For Table 12, see the scoring instructions for Part 3 (on p. A104). • Then jump to Part 4 to finish the evaluation.

2.3. Detailed Procedure for Subsection 3A.3

Collect the visual supports representing locations and schedule cues; it may be better to send the user on a break now. If using a form other than OBJ, put the visual supports back in order (see numbers on the back). For visual supports in OBJ form, make sure to stick the visual supports from the category being evaluated as two blocks of three locations (one block of examples for each location, then one block of examples for each location, for a total of six visual supports) on the schedule strip and to vary the order between both blocks.

In this subsection, demonstrations are not permitted. However, the procedure to follow is very similar to that for 3A.1 and 3A.2.

For this subsection, the six visual supports representing locations must be placed on the schedule strip *from the start*.

Evaluation and Scoring

a) **E (Examiner):** Take the first six visual supports representing the locations and stick them on the schedule strip.

b) **E:** Hand the schedule cue to the user.
U (User): Take the schedule cue, go to the schedule strip, and drop the schedule cue into the schedule cue box.

c) **U:** Take the top visual support from the schedule strip.
E: Score the user's performance.

d) **U:** Walk and drop the visual support into the correct box.
E: Score the user's performance.

e) **E and U:** Repeat steps b through d for the next five visual supports (attempts 2 to 6). As of the third attempt, determine for each action whether the first stop standard for 3A.3 is reached or if the evaluation for 3A.3 continues for all six attempts.

If the first stop standard is reached, the examiner can choose to let the user finish part or all the actions for attempts 2 to 6 to give them the opportunity to end this part of the evaluation on a positive note. The user's performance, however, will no longer be scored, and even though any type of help can now be provided, it is no longer necessary to correct them if they make a mistake.

FIRST STOP STANDARD FOR SUBSECTION 3A.3	
FIRST STOP STANDARD FOR SUBSECTION 3A.3	PROCEDURE TO FOLLOW IF THE STOP STANDARD IS REACHED
✋ 2 scores of 0 on the same action in **3A.3**	✏️ "Total 3A.3" + "Scoring Part 3: Tables 10, 11, and 12" ▶ If the user scores 0 twice for the same action in 3A.3: • Stop the evaluation of Part 3. • If the stop standard is reached while evaluating 3A.3, assign a score of 0 for the actions not evaluated and write the results down in the "Total 3A.3" column. • Proceed to score Part 3 by filling in Tables 10, 11, and 12 in the Evaluation Protocol: In Table 10, write down the results for 3A.1, 3A.2, and 3A.3 in their respective columns. In the "Total 3B (3B.1 + 3B.2)" column in Table 11, check "3B not evaluated (0/9)" for the four actions and assign a score of 0/9 to each. For Table 12, see the scoring instructions for Part 3 (on p. A104). • Then jump to Part 4 to finish the evaluation.

f) **E:** If the six attempts are evaluated (because the first stop standard for 3A.3 was not reached), record the results for 3A.3 in the "Total 3A.3" column.

g) **E:** Determine whether the second stop standard for 3A.3 is reached or if the evaluation of Part 3 continues.

SECOND STOP STANDARD FOR SUBSECTION 3A.3	
SECOND STOP STANDARD FOR SUBSECTION 3A.3	PROCEDURE TO FOLLOW IF THE STOP STANDARD IS REACHED
✋ Form of visual support selected (❶ in Table 6) is not WTC or WWH or 3A.3 ≤ 4/6 for one of the two evaluated actions.	✏️ "Scoring Part 3: Tables 10, 11, and 12" ▶ If the form of visual support selected (the one used during the evaluation of Part 3) is not WTC or WWH or if the user obtains a result less than or equal to 4/6 for one of the two actions evaluated in 3A.3: • Stop the evaluation of Part 3. • Proceed to score Part 3 by filling in Tables 10, 11, and 12 in the Evaluation Protocol: In Table 10, write down the results for 3A.1, 3A.2, and 3A.3 in their respective columns. In the "Total 3B (3B.1 + 3B.2)" column in Table 11, check "3B not evaluated (0/9)" for the four actions and assign a score of 0/9 to each. In Table 12, see the scoring instructions for Part 3 (on p. A104). • Then jump to Part 4 to finish the evaluation.

If the second stop standard for 3A.3 is not reached, record the result of Section 3A in Table 7 on p. B28 of the Evaluation Protocol. Then continue the evaluation with Section 3B.

Sequence for Section 3B

Important Reminder: Only evaluate Section 3B if the form of visual support selected (❶) when scoring Part 2 (see Table 6 on p. B23 of the Evaluation Protocol) is WTC or WWH, Subsection 3A.3 was evaluated, and the user scored 5/6 or higher on two actions in that subsection (see Table 7 on p. B28 of the Evaluation Protocol).

The user will need to perform a simple match in this section. This task is merely a pretext to evaluate the schedule on which the user will place a token, write an X, or check off activities as they complete them.

Generally, the evaluation will proceed as follows: the user gets an object from the location indicated in their schedule (presented here in sheet form) to perform the match, then returns to their schedule, where they can see the next object to get and match, and so on.

Figure 3.5 presents an example of the detailed actions the user needs to perform and the number of times to repeat them (three or six based on their schedule). This is an example of a token schedule for the "Work/School" category and the WWH visual support form.

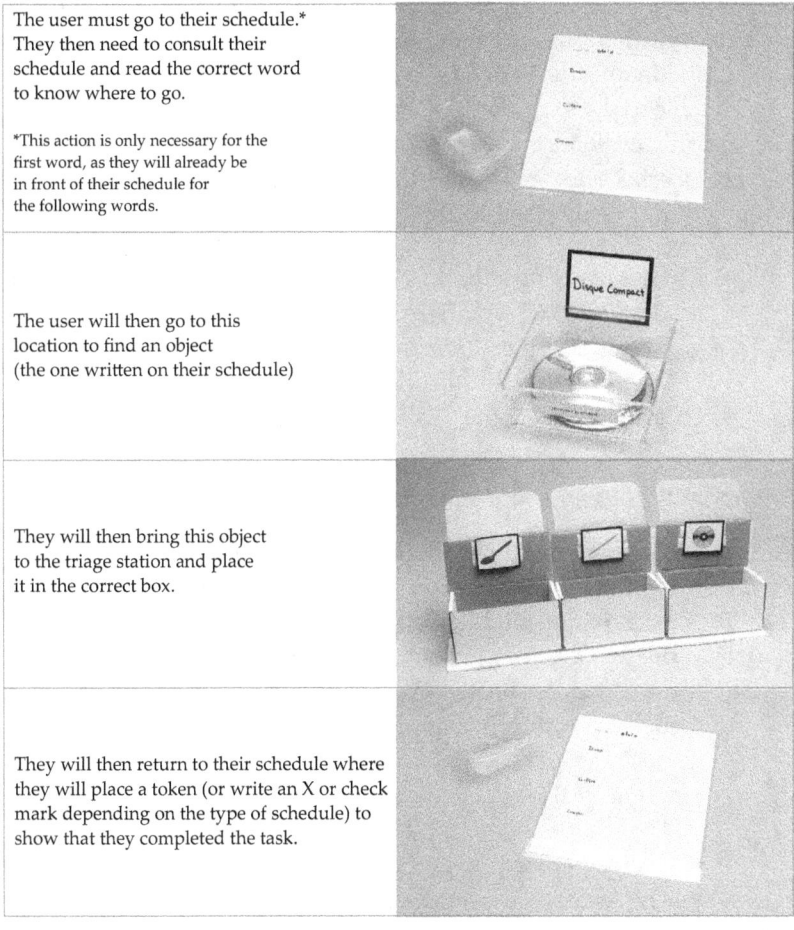

Figure 3.5. Detailed actions for a token schedule, "Work/School" category, and the WWH visual support form.

Source: Artimage 2015.

1. Identify the Visual Support Form, the Category, and the Type of Schedule Being Evaluated

First, check which visual support form, WTC or WWH, will be evaluated in the box provided for that purpose on p. B29 in the Evaluation Protocol. This visual support form corresponds to the visual support form chosen (❶) when scoring Part 2 (see Table 6 on p. B23 of the Evaluation Protocol).

Then select the category to evaluate. It is important to pick a different category from the one evaluated in Section 3A (which was the same one used in Part 2). Check the category evaluated in the box provided for that purpose on p. B29 in the Evaluation Protocol.

Last, identify the type of schedule being evaluated. Two choices are available to the examiner (a token schedule or a checkmark schedule), but only evaluate one. The following guidelines will help identify the type of schedule to evaluate. Check which type of schedule is being evaluated in the box provided on p. B29 in the Evaluation Protocol.

- Choose the "Checkmark Schedule" if the user can write simple letters (to know whether they can, ask them to copy a word you write down on a piece of paper, for example on the verso of the Evaluation Protocol).
- Otherwise, select the "Token Schedule."

2. Prepare the Material for Evaluating Section 3B

a) Prepare the required materials for Section 3B listed next to the ✂ symbol on p. B29 of the Evaluation Protocol under "Checkmark Schedule" or "Token Schedule."

b) Write the user's name with the non-permanent marker on the three schedule sheets for the type of schedule, category, and visual support form evaluated.

c) Choose the schedule's location and write it in the space provided on p. B30 in the Evaluation Protocol.

The location where the schedule will be displayed should be decided according to the following criteria:
- The location where the schedule sheet is displayed must be different from the one where the schedule strip was mounted during the evaluation of Section 3A.
- The schedule sheet should be placed at a reasonable distance from the triage station (about 7 to 8 feet), and from

each of the object baskets (fifteen to thirty feet). For this reason, while the triage station and object baskets have not yet been put into place, it is important to consider their locations here, as one is dependent on the other.

If the evaluation is taking place in an area where other users' schedules are displayed and that meets previous criteria, the schedule sheet for Section 3B can be placed here. If this area does not exist or does not satisfy previous criteria, choose another location simply for the duration of the evaluation. For example, in a residential setting, the user's bedroom or bedroom door may be used for this purpose.

d) In the selected location, place the first schedule sheet (i.e., the one that says "3B.1: Demos" for the type of schedule, category, and visual support form being evaluated), as well as the uncapped marker if using the checkmark schedule, or the token box (without lid) if using the token schedule. There are different options to display the schedule, as illustrated in Figures 3.6 and 3.7. Use the blue mounting putty if required.

e) Assemble and install the triage station and write down its location on the line provided on p. B30 in the Evaluation Protocol.

The triage station is made up of two corrugated plastic sheet panels (bottom and back). Three matching boxes are mounted to the panels (see Figure 1.1 for assembly). Stick a version of the three photos of the category evaluated to the top of the boxes. These photos can be found behind the blue 2–3. PHO

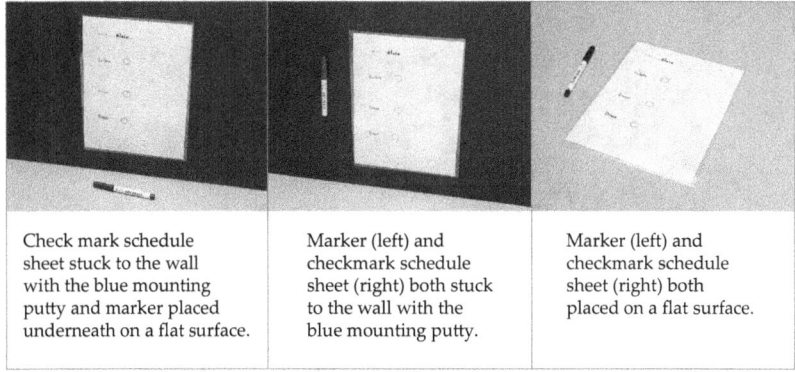

| Check mark schedule sheet stuck to the wall with the blue mounting putty and marker placed underneath on a flat surface. | Marker (left) and checkmark schedule sheet (right) both stuck to the wall with the blue mounting putty. | Marker (left) and checkmark schedule sheet (right) both placed on a flat surface. |

Figure 3.6. Examples for displaying the checkmark schedule.

Source: Artimage 2015.

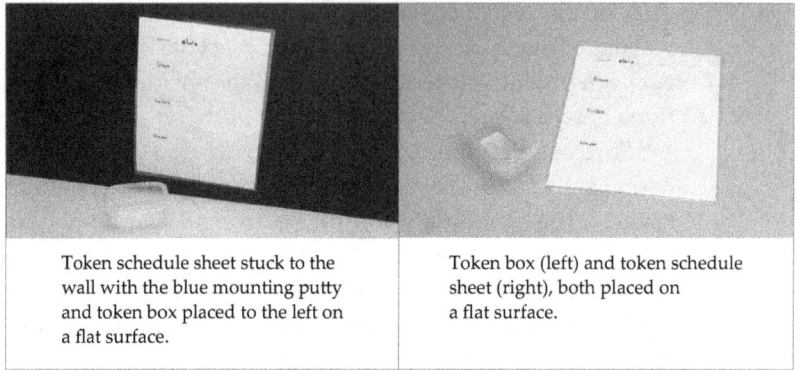

| Token schedule sheet stuck to the wall with the blue mounting putty and token box placed to the left on a flat surface. | Token box (left) and token schedule sheet (right), both placed on a flat surface. |

Figure 3.7. Example for displaying the token schedule.

Source: Artimage 2015.

divider in filing box 2–3 + 3H of the category being evaluated (see Figure 3.8). Make sure that the visual supports are in order (see numbers on back) and mount the first three visual supports in the correct sequence. Please note that the photograph (PHO) is used for the triage station, regardless of the form of visual support being evaluated.

The triage station must be installed about seven to eight feet away from where the schedule sheet is mounted, on a flat surface such as a table or dresser (which is usually moved to the desired location for the evaluation). The examiner can also use one or two chairs placed together.

Figure 3.8. Triage station for the "Work/School" category.

Source: Artimage 2015.

f) Install the object baskets identified as "3B: Basket for Objects" and write down their locations in Table 8 on p. B30 of the Evaluation Protocol by also checking the category being evaluated.

First, put six identical objects from the object bag of the category being evaluated into a basket; do the same with the two other baskets.

Then place the three object baskets in three different locations from the ones used in Section 3A. The locations do not need to have a link with the objects for this part of the evaluation. They should be about 15 to 30 feet from the schedule sheet. It is important to choose a flat surface close to a wall, as shown in Figure 3.9.

Identify locations using words to indicate the objects the user must get. To do this, use the visual supports from filing box 2–3 + 3H of the category being evaluated, behind the blue divider corresponding to the visual support form evaluated (WTC or WWH). Use the blue mounting putty to mount the visual supports to the wall, making sure not to put any on the Velcro.

Last, write down the locations chosen in Table 8 on p. B30 of the Evaluation Protocol by also checking the category evaluated. Excerpt 7 shows an example of Table 8 filled out for an evaluation of the "Other" category.

Figure 3.9. Location identification using visual supports with names, WWH visual support form.

Source: Artimage 2015.

Excerpt 7. Schedule Evaluation Protocol, Table 8. Location of 3B Baskets: Object Baskets (Different than in Section 3A)

TABLE 8. LOCATION OF 3B BASKETS: OBJECT BASKETS (DIFFERENT THAN IN SECTION 3A)		
CHECK THE CATEGORY BEING EVALUATED	VISUAL SUPPORTS	WRITE DOWN THE VISUAL SUPPORT LOCATIONS (only for the category being evaluated)
☐ Home	Toothbrush	L1:
	Sock	L2:
	Lego	L3:
☐ Work/School	Spoon	L1:
	Pencil	L2:
	Disc	L3:
☑ Other	Ball	L1: On the kitchen counter.
	Marker	L2: On the small table in the living room.
	Sponge	L3: On the dresser near the entrance.

g) While the examiner's tray is optional, its use is recommended to ensure that the evaluation goes smoothly. In this instance, it can be used to carry the Evaluation Protocol, pencil (to score), the two schedule sheets (with the third placed in the selected location), and the reinforcers, if applicable (see Figure 3.10).

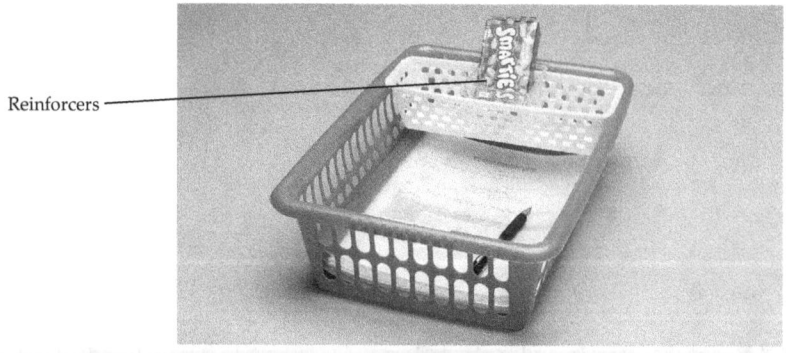

Figure 3.10. Examiner's tray assembled for Subsection 3B.

Source: Artimage 2015.

3. Demonstrations, Evaluation, and Scoring

For Subsection 3B, the user will need to complete several actions, four of which will be scored:

- "The user consults their schedule" (not scored).
- "The user reads the correct word on the schedule sheet to know where to go and walks to the location where the object indicated is located" (scored).
- "The user takes the object from this location, brings it to the triage station, and drops it in the corresponding box" (scored).
- "The user writes an X or checkmark in the circle to the right of the word corresponding to the object they just matched *or* places a token to the right of the word (showing that they have completed the task)" (scored).

The user will repeat all these actions, starting with reading the correct word, as many times as there are words on their schedule (three to six). Demonstrations and the evaluations of the two subsections in 3B are performed using three different schedule sheets. Which schedule to use can be found in the top of the table (see ① and ② in Excerpt 8) in the Evaluation Protocol. The sheet for 3B.1 demonstrations is titled "3B.1: Demos," while the schedule sheets for the evaluations of Subsections 3B.1 and 3B.2 are titled "3B.1: 3 Attempts" and "3B.2: 6 Attempts," respectively. As their name suggests, the difference between the two subsections rests in the number of attempts (corresponding to the number of times the user needs to go to get objects).

As the user does not know the procedure to follow for Section 3B, demonstrations (not scored) are mandatory for the four scored actions in Subsection 3B.1 for every location. As such, a note indicating "1 mand. demo/location" is found opposite each action in the "3B.1: Demos" column in the Evaluation Protocol. In this section, the demonstrations will be performed with the help of the "3B.1: Demos" schedule sheet for the category and the visual support form being evaluated.

Moreover, every time a new schedule sheet is used ("3B.1: Demos," "3B.1: 3 Attempts," or "3B.2: 6 Attempts"), the examiner must tell the user that they need to consult their schedule for the first word only. This action is not scored and is not written down in the tables in Subsections 3B.1 and 3B.2 of the Evaluation Protocol (a note at the bottom of the tables, however, reminds the examiner when this action should be performed; see Excerpt 8).

As in Section 3A, score the four actions performed by the user separately, assigning one point if the user performs the action entirely on their own or no points if help was provided, even if minimal. For the action "The user reads the correct word on the schedule sheet," the examiner will assume the user read the word properly, unless they remain motionless in front of the schedule or go to a different location from the one indicated on the schedule. The examiner will then provide the required help so that they read the correct word or go to the correct location. A score of 0 will then be assigned for that action.

Excerpt 8. Schedule Evaluation Protocol, Subsection 3B.1

SUBSECTION 3B.1					
✋ Subtotal **3B.1** ≤ 1/3 on one of the evaluated actions		✏️ "Table 9" + "Scoring Part 3: Tables 10, 11, and 12" ▶			
ACTIONS DONE BY USER (3 attempts, 1 trip per location)	**SCHEDULE SHEET**				**SUBTOTAL 3B.1**
	3B.1: ① **DEMOS**	**3B.1: 3 ATTEMPTS** ②			
		1	2	3	
The user reads the correct word on the schedule sheet and walks to the location where the object indicated is located. *Note: For the action "The user reads the correct word on the schedule sheet," the examiner will assume that the user has read the correct word, unless they remain motionless in front of the schedule or go to a different location than the one indicated on the schedule.*	1 mand. demo/ location	/1	/1	/1	/3
The user takes the object from this location, brings it to the triage station, and drops it into the corresponding box.	1 mand. demo/ location	/1	/1	/1	/3
The user heads back to their schedule.	1 mand. demo/ location	/1	/1	/1	/3
The user writes an X or checkmark in the circle to the right of the word corresponding to the object they just matched *or* places a token to the right of the word (showing that they have completed the task).	1 mand. demo/ location	/1	/1	/1	/3

(!) *Note:* When a new schedule sheet is used (3B.1: Demos and 3B.1: 3 Attempts), the examiner must communicate to the user that they need to go consult their schedule (not scored) only for the first word.

① Demonstrations for all actions using the "3B.1: Demos" schedule sheet.

② Evaluation using the "3B.1: 3 Attempts" schedule sheet.

3.1. Detailed Procedure for Subsection 3B.1

Demonstrations

a) **E (Examiner):** Show[4] the user that they need to consult their schedule.
U (User): Go to the schedule (as this first action is not scored in 3B.1 and 3B.2, it does not figure in the table in the Evaluation Protocol).

b) **E:** Show the user that they need to read the correct word (name of object) on the "3B.1: Demos" schedule sheet and guide them to the location where the object indicated on their schedule is located.
U: Read the right word on the schedule sheet and walk to the correct location where the object is located.

c) **E:** Show the user that they need to bring this object to the triage station where they will place it in the corresponding matching box.
U: Take the object from that location, bring it to the triage station, and place it in the corresponding matching box.

d) **E:** Guide the user back to their schedule.
U: Go back to their schedule.

e) **E:** Show the user that once the action is completed, they need to write an X or checkmark (for the checkmark schedule) in the circle to the right of the word that corresponds to the object they just matched. For the token schedule, they need to place a token to the right of that word.
U: Using the pencil found beside the schedule, write an X or checkmark in the circle to the right of the word corresponding to the matched object (checkmark schedule), or take a token from the token box and place it to the right of the word corresponding to the matched object (token schedule).

f) **E and U:** Repeat steps b through e for the other two words on the schedule sheet.

g) **E:** Remove the "3B.1: Demos" schedule sheet.

---

[4] Here and in the following steps, the verb "show" is purposefully vague and refers to any means required, whether verbal, gestural, or physical, to help the user understand the task at hand. It is, however, important to choose carefully how you show the user what to do so that they are more likely to be able to do it on their own after the demonstrations.

Evaluation and Scoring

Replace the previous schedule sheet with the "3B.1: 3 Attempts" sheet for the schedule type, category, and form of visual support to evaluate.

   a) **E (Examiner):** Show the user that they need to consult their schedule.
   U (User): Go consult their schedule (as this first action is not scored in 3B.1, it does not figure in the table in the Evaluation Protocol).
   b) **U:** Read the correct word on the schedule sheet and walk to the location where the object indicated is located.
   For the action "The user reads the correct word on the schedule sheet," the examiner will assume that the user has read the correct word, unless they stand motionless in front of their schedule or walk to a different location than the one indicated on the schedule. The examiner will help the user read the correct word and go to the correct location as required, and will then assign a score of o for this action.
   E: Score the user's performance.
   c) **U:** Take the object from this location, bring it to the triage station, and place it in the corresponding matching box.
   E: Score the user's performance.
   d) **U:** Go back to their schedule.
   E: Score the user's performance.
   e) **U:** Using the pencil found beside the schedule (checkmark schedule), write an X or checkmark in the circle to the right of the word corresponding to the matched object. Or for the token schedule, place a token to the right of the word corresponding to the matched object.
   E: Score the user's performance.
   f) **E and U:** Repeat steps b through e for the other two words on the schedule sheet.
   g) **E:** Remove the "3B.1: 3 Attempts" schedule sheet.
   h) **E:** Write down the results for 3B.1 in the column provided for this purpose ("Subtotal 3B.1").
   i) **E:** Determine whether the stop standard for 3B.1 has been reached or if the evaluation of Part 3 continues.

STOP STANDARD FOR SUBSECTION 3B.1	
STOP STANDARD FOR SUBSECTION 3B.1	PROCEDURE TO FOLLOW IF THE STOP STANDARD IS REACHED
✋ Subtotal **3B.1** ≤ 1/3 for one of the actions evaluated	✏️ "Table 9" + "Scoring Part 3: Tables 10, 11, and 12" ▶ If the user's subtotal is less than or equal to 1/3 for one of the actions evaluated in 3B.1: • Stop the evaluation of Part 3. • Write the results for Section 3B into Table 9. Write down the results for Subsection 3B.1 in the "Subtotal 3B.1" column. In the "Subtotal 3B.2" column, check "3B.2 not evaluated (0/6)" for all four actions and assign a score of 0/6 for each. Last, write down the total in the "Total 3B (3B.1 + 3B.2)" column, which will inevitably match the 3B.1 subtotal. • Proceed to score Part 3 by filling in Tables 10, 11, and 12 in the Evaluation Protocol (see scoring instructions for Part 3 on p. A104). • Then jump to Part 4 to finish the evaluation.

If the stop standard for 3B.1 is not reached, then continue with the evaluation.

3.2. Detailed Procedure for Subsection 3B.2

Replace the previous schedule sheet with the "3B.2: 6 Attempts" sheet for the type of schedule, category, and form of visual support to evaluate.

    a) **E (Examiner):** Show the user that they need to consult their schedule.
    U (User): Go to consult their schedule (as this first action is not scored in 3B.2, it does not figure in the table in the Evaluation Protocol).
    b) **U:** Read the correct word on the schedule sheet and walk to the location where the object indicated is located.

For the action "The user reads the correct word on the schedule sheet," the examiner will assume that the user has read the right word, unless they stand motionless in front of their schedule or walk to a different location than the one indicated on the schedule. The examiner will help the user read the correct word and go to the correct location as required, and will then assign a score of 0 for this action.

   E: Score the user's performance.
c) U: Take the object from this location, bring it to the triage station, and place it in the corresponding matching box.
   E: Score the user's performance.
d) U: Go back to their schedule.
   E: Score the user's performance.
e) U: Using the pencil placed beside the schedule (checkmark schedule), write an X or checkmark in the circle to the right of the word corresponding to the object that was just matched. For the token schedule, take a token from the token box and place it to the right of the word corresponding to the matched object.
   E: Score the user's performance.
f) **E and U:** Repeat steps b through e for the other five words on the schedule sheet. Starting at the third attempt, determine whether the stop standard for 3B.2 is reached during each action or if the evaluation of 3B.2 continues until the sixth attempt. If a stop standard is reached, the examiner can choose to let the user finish part or all actions for attempts 3 to 6 to allow them to complete the evaluation on a positive note. However, as the user's performance is no longer scored, the examiner can provide help, but it is no longer necessary to correct them if they make a mistake.

CREATING VISUAL SCHEDULES

STOP STANDARD FOR SUBSECTION 3B.2	
STOP STANDARD FOR SUBSECTION 3B.2	PROCEDURE TO FOLLOW IF THE STOP STANDARD IS REACHED
✋ 2 scores of 0 for the same action in 3B.2	✏️ "Table 9" + "Scoring Part 3: Tables 10, 11, and 12" ▶ If the user scores 0 twice on the same action in 3B.2: • Stop the evaluation of Part 3. • If the stop standard is reached while evaluating 3B.2, assign a score of 0 to any non-evaluated actions and write the results down in the "Subtotal 3B.2" column. • Write the results for Section 3B into Table 9. Write down the subtotals for 3B.1 and 3B.2 in their respective columns. Then add up the subtotals and write the total down in the "Total 3B (3B.1 + 3B.2)" column. • Proceed to score Part 3 by filling in Tables 10, 11, and 12 in the Evaluation Protocol (see scoring instructions for Part 3 on p. A104). • Then jump to Part 4 to finish the evaluation.

g) **E:** If the six attempts were evaluated (because the stop standard for 3B.2 was not reached), write the results for 3B.2 down in the "Subtotal 3B.2" column.

h) **E:** Proceed with the scoring of Section 3B in Table 9 on p. B33 of the Evaluation Protocol. In the "Subtotal 3B.1" and "Subtotal 3B.2" columns, write down the results for these subsections. Then add up the total in the "Total 3B (3B.1 + 3B.2)" column.

i) **E:** Proceed with the scoring of Part 3.

4. Scoring Part 3 in the Evaluation Protocol

If Part 3 was not evaluated because a stop standard in Part 1 or Part 2 was reached, only fill in Table 12. In this case, jump directly to step c.

If Part 3 was evaluated, whether in part or in full, fill in Tables 10, 11, and 12 according to the following guidelines.

a) **Table 10**

If Table 7 was completed on p. B28 in the Evaluation Protocol, (results of Section 3A), copy those results into Table 10. This only applies if Section 3B was evaluated (in part or in full). Otherwise, write down the results of the subsections evaluated for Section 3A, referring to each subsection, and check "not evaluated" when applicable.

b) **Table 11**

If Table 9 was completed on p. B33 in the Evaluation Protocol, (results for Section 3B), copy those results into Table 11. This only applies if Section 3B was evaluated (in part or in full). Otherwise (i.e., if Section 3B was not evaluated), in the "Total 3B (3B.1 + 3B.2)" column, check "3B not evaluated (0/9)" for the four actions and assign a score of 0/9 for each.

c) **Table 12**

Part 3 enables the examiner to determine the following schedule features: presentation mode, manipulation, identification, initiation, length, location, and layout.

To properly determine these characteristics, follow the scoring standards **from top to bottom** (also provided in the Evaluation Protocol), as in Part 2. Just like in Part 2, the guidelines for Table 12 are very important: "Follow the scoring standards for Part 3 **from top to bottom**. The highest standard on the list corresponding to the user's results is the proper score for them." This will be checked off in the "Characteristics" column. It is important to follow this guideline to ensure that schedule characteristics are properly identified for the user, as their results may correspond to more than one scoring standard. As such, start with the first standard, and if it applies, check the corresponding recommendation. Otherwise, move on to the next standard and so on until a standard corresponds to the user's results. Please note that scoring standards are written in shortened form using the symbols explained throughout this guide and in the Evaluation Protocol.

Part 4

Goal

The goal of Part 4 is to identify the activities that will be on the schedule and provide details on the schedule's location and identification.

Duration

About 20 minutes.

Administration

Interview the person who knows the user best in the setting where the schedule will be implemented and fill out the questionnaire in the Evaluation Protocol.

Part 4 of the evaluation is divided into three sections: 4A, 4B, and 4C. These must be administered in order. The first two sections should only be evaluated if the user obtained specific scores in the previous parts of the evaluation. Instructions at the beginning of the section will specify whether the evaluation should be performed or not. However, Section 4C must be evaluated in all instances, regardless of the user's performance throughout the previous sections and subsections (even if the user cannot match two objects in Part 1 of the evaluation, for example).

Sequence

1. Detailed Procedure for Section 4A: Identifying the Schedule with a Cue That Relates to the User's Interests

First, determine whether this section needs to be filled out. It should only be filled out if the recommendation associated with the schedule identification (❺) is "C) Visual cue related to the user's interests" when scoring Part 3 (Table 12 on p. B35 of the Evaluation Protocol).

If that's the case, fill in this part of the questionnaire. Then, based on the examiner's clinical judgment, make a recommendation for a meaningful cue to identify the user's schedule.

Excerpt 9 (below) provides an example of a user's results for Part 3, followed by information gathered by the examiner during the interview and a recommendation for schedule identification.

Excerpt 9. Schedule Evaluation Protocol. Table 12. Scoring of Part 3. "Identification" Characteristic + Section 4A

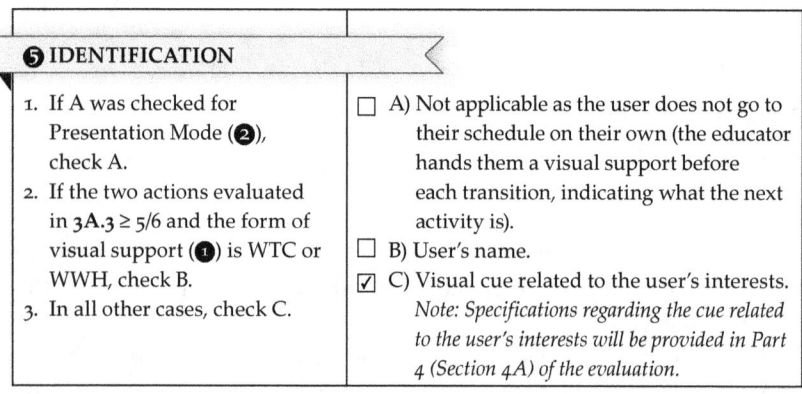

❺ IDENTIFICATION	
1. If A was checked for Presentation Mode (❷), check A. 2. If the two actions evaluated in 3A.3 ≥ 5/6 and the form of visual support (❶) is WTC or WWH, check B. 3. In all other cases, check C.	☐ A) Not applicable as the user does not go to their schedule on their own (the educator hands them a visual support before each transition, indicating what the next activity is). ☐ B) User's name. ☑ C) Visual cue related to the user's interests. *Note: Specifications regarding the cue related to the user's interests will be provided in Part 4 (Section 4A) of the evaluation.*

Here, the Identification score in Table 12 indicates that Section 4A must be filled out.

During the interview, the examiner gathers the following information for Section 4A.

(Continued)

IDENTIFY THE USER'S INTERESTS OR FIELDS OF INTEREST		
Star Trek, music, appliance brand names.		
SPECIFY OBJECTS, PHOTOS, OR IMAGES THE USER PARTICULARLY LIKES (THEY MAY OR MAY NOT BE A PART OF THE INTERESTS DESCRIBED ABOVE)		
OBJECTS	PHOTOS	IMAGES
Music CDs	Magazine photos of appliances	Star Trek movie images
Star Trek DVDs	Photos of home appliances	
Star Trek costume parties	Photos of Star Trek movies	
	Photo of user and their entourage (home or school)	

The information gathered by the examiner will allow them to specify a cue to identify the user's schedule:

❺ IDENTIFICATION

Scoring Standard:
Based on the previous information, specify the visual cue that relates to the user's interests and that is recommended to identify their schedule.

C) Visual cue related to the user's interests:

Image representing their favourite movie: Star Trek

(!) *Note: If C-2 was checked for "Initiation" (❻) when scoring Part 3 (Table 12 in the Evaluation Protocol), it is important that the visual cue chosen is suitable as it will need to be transportable and available in several copies.*

2. Detailed Procedure for Section 4B: Finding an Individualized Location

First, determine whether this section needs to be filled out. It should only be filled out if the recommendation associated with the schedule's location (❸) is "C) Individualized location (e.g., user's bedroom, workplace, etc.)" when scoring Part 3 (Table 12 on p. B35 of the Evaluation Protocol).

If this is the case, fill in this part of the questionnaire. Then, based on the examiner's clinical judgment, make a recommendation for an individualized location for the schedule.

Several factors should be considered when deciding where to place the schedule, in particular: where does the user spend most of their time; what location would be central to their activities; and last, is there a possibility that another user may behave in a way that would influence these recommendations?

Determine where the schedule will be implemented (at home, school, or work) by checking the appropriate box in questions 1 and 2, and answer the two questions for that setting only. Then answer questions 3 and 4.

Let us consider the following situation as an example: the schedule is implemented in the home setting. The user spends most of their time in the living room, and the most central location based on their daily activities is the hallway that leads to the living room. Either of these locations can then be chosen depending on how heavily trafficked they are. Additionally, if another person who lives there tends to remove things from the walls and put them in their mouth, it may be better to place the schedule on the wall in the user's bedroom.

Several factors should be considered: based on their current level of competence, will the user be able to go consult their schedule on their own if it is not in their field of vision on a regular basis? How often does the other person behave in this manner when there are things on the wall? What interventions have been done to date regarding this behaviour? Were several interventions tried, and for how long? What were the results? All these factors, combined with the examiner's clinical judgment, will influence the recommendation on where to place the schedule.

Excerpt 10 (below) provides an example of Section 4B completed.

3. Detailed Procedure for Section 4C: Schedule Content (Activities and Representative Visual Supports)

The elements that will make up the user's schedule should now be chosen. To do this, identify the activities in which the user will take part in the target setting, their level of interest in each one, and what would best represent this activity on their schedule.

Please note that the representative visual support will be included on the schedule in the recommended form (❶), determined after completing the evaluation, unless otherwise specified. For example, if the fork has been selected to represent supper, then depending on the visual support form recommended in this evaluation, the schedule should include a fork (OBJ), a photo of a fork (PHO), or a pictogram of a fork (PIC or BWP). If the visual support form recommended is a written word, write the representative word for the activity in the right-hand column of the table for the setting in the Evaluation Protocol. For example, for the "supper" activity, this could include the words "supper," "meal," or "eat."

Excerpt 10. Schedule Evaluation Protocol, Section 4B

For questions 1 and 2, check the setting where the schedule will be implemented in the two tables below. Then only answer the questions for that setting.

1. WHERE DOES THE USER SPEND MOST OF THEIR TIME?		
☑ At home	☐ At school	☐ At work
☐ Their bedroom ☑ The living room ☐ The kitchen ☐ Other: _____	☐ At their desk ☐ In the play/leisure area ☐ Moves from one room to another ☐ Other: _____	☐ At their desk ☐ In the common room ☐ Moves from one room to another ☐ Other: _____

2. WHAT IS THE MOST CENTRAL LOCATION?		
☑ At home	☐ At school	☐ At work
☑ The hallway ☐ The living room ☐ The kitchen ☐ Other: _____	☐ At their desk ☐ In the play/leisure area ☐ Group transition area ☐ Other: _____	☐ The hallway ☐ The workshop ☐ The common room ☐ Other: _____

(!) *Note: Generally, choose a schedule location based on its functional qualities as they relate to the user's movements throughout the day. It can be the location where the user spends most of their time, a central location they pass frequently, etc. However, the examiner may recommend a different location than the one that meets these criteria because of certain considerations. Answer questions 3 and 4 to find the most suitable location.*

3. DOES ANOTHER PERSON IN THAT LOCATION behave in a way that limits the possible schedule locations or requires specific adaptations, as the schedule would be accessible to them (e.g., a person who tends to remove anything stuck on the walls and for whom current interventions do not seem to be effective)? If yes, specify the behaviour, restrictions, and required adaptations as they relate to the schedule and its location.

Another user removes anything stuck on the walls and puts it in their mouth. However, this person doesn't go into other users' bedrooms. As such, the user's bedroom would probably be the best place to stick the schedule on the wall.

(Continued)

> 4. ARE THERE ANY OTHER FACTORS that need to be considered regarding the individualized location of the user's schedule? If yes, please specify what they are and include any required adaptations in relation to the schedule and its location.
>
> No.

❸ LOCATION	
Scoring standard: According to the previous information, specify the recommendation for the individualized location.	C) Individualized location (e.g., user's bedroom, workplace, etc.) *Stuck on the wall in the user's bedroom*

Follow the instructions below (also available in the Evaluation Protocol) to fill out the table with the help of the person interviewed:

1. Fill in the table for the setting (home, work, or school) by checking the box for the setting where the schedule will be implemented.
2. Then check all the user's daily activities in the table for that setting. Write down any other activity done by the user in the empty rows at the bottom of the table.
3. On a scale of 1 to 3, rate the user's interest in each activity, with 1 = not interested, 2 = somewhat interested, and 3 = very interested.
4. In the right-hand column of the table, indicate the representative visual support[1] that will allow the user to identify the activity. To do this, circle the visual support in the "Suggestions for Visual Supports Representative of Activities" column if relevant for the user. Otherwise, write the recommendation down in the "Other Representative Visual Supports" column.

Excerpt 11 (on the following page) provides an example of Section 4C completed for the home setting.

---

[1] Representative visual supports will be found in the schedule in the form recommended following the completion of this evaluation (see scoring of Part 3, Table 12, ❶, of the Evaluation Protocol). If a different form is recommended for a given visual support, it should be noted in the right-hand column.

Excerpt 11. Schedule Evaluation Protocol, Section 4C, Home Setting

☐ HOME SETTING			
ACTIVITIES	LEVEL OF INTEREST	SUGGESTIONS FOR VISUAL SUPPORTS REPRESENTATIVE OF ACTIVITIES	OTHER REPRESENTATIVE VISUAL SUPPORTS
☑ Bath	1	Soap, ~~washcloth~~, bubble bath container, etc.	
☑ Breakfast	3	Utensil (specify): <u>fork</u> napkin, peanut butter jar, etc.	
☑ Walk	2	Coat, purse, ~~cap~~, etc.	
☑ Lunch	3	Utensil (specify): <u>fork</u> napkin, plate, lunchbox, etc.	
☑ Dinner	3	Utensil (specify): <u>fork</u> napkin, plate, etc.	
☑ Bedtime	1	Pyjamas, pillow, etc.	Night cream jar
☑ Brushing teeth	1	Toothbrush, ~~toothpaste~~ etc.	
☐ Massage		Jar of cream, bottle of oil, etc.	
☑ Music	3	Radio, music instrument, compact disk, etc.	MP3 player
☑ Restaurant outing: <u>McDonald's</u>	3	Empty French fry container, brand logo, etc.	McDonald's cup
☐ Transportation		Small car, taxi logo, etc.	
☑ Workshop	2	Picture of workshop, miniature table, etc.	Wood block
☐ Break		Empty pop can, empty juice box, compact disc, photo of place where user spends their break, mug, glass, etc.	
☑ Activities in the community		Park, sports, etc.	
☑ Other: <u>Leaving to go bowling</u>	3		Towel to clean bowling balls
☑ Other: <u>Family visit</u>	3		Photo of family
☐ Other:			

Here, transportation has not been checked, while "Leaving to go bowling" has been added. In this particular case, the visual support on the schedule represents the activity the person is going to, rather than the means of transportation. In other cases, a visual support representing a school bus to indicate "Leaving for school" can be chosen. Knowing the user's level of understanding and what means the most to them, another visual support was suggested for the outing to McDonald's, and the "Family visit" activity was added.

RECOMMENDATIONS REPORT

Recommendations Report

The form to fill out can be found in the Recommendations Report, which is included in the Supplementary Material.
First, fill in the nominative data section, the user description, the evaluation goal, and the observations made throughout the evaluation.

Schedule Characteristics

Then go to the section on the schedule's different characteristics in the Recommendations Report (Supplementary Material, p. B50). To know what to check and specify, refer to the symbols for the different schedule characteristics (see example below) in the "Scoring Part 3" section (Table 12) and "Scoring Part 4" section of the Evaluation Protocol. Corresponding symbols can be found in the Recommendations Report.

In the Recommendations Report, check the corresponding characteristics that were checked in Table 12 ("Scoring Part 3" section on p. B35 of the Evaluation Protocol). The following example illustrates the procedure to follow for one of the characteristics (Table 12). The information found here must be copied in the Recommendations Report in the corresponding box using the number ("❷" in this example) and schedule characteristic ("Presentation Mode") as references.

> **② PRESENTATION MODE**
>
> 1. If Part 3 was not evaluated because of a stop standard, check A.
> 2. If one of the two evaluated actions in **3A.1** is ≤ 3/6, check A.
> 3. If the four actions evaluated at **3B** ≥ 8/9, check B-2.
> 4. In all other cases, check B-1.
>
> ☐ A) The educator hands the user the visual support before each activity.
> ☑ B) Stationary schedule displayed on:
>   ☑ 1) The wall
>   ☐ 2) A table

Check the corresponding statement(s) in the Recommendations Report.

> **② PRESENTATION MODE**
>
> ☐ The educator hands the user the visual support before each activity.
> ☑ Stationary schedule displayed on:
>   ☑ The wall
>   ☐ A table
>   ☐ Other: _____
> ☐ Portable schedule
> ☐ Other: _____

Further details for schedule identification are required in the Recommendations Report if a visual support related to the user's interest is recommended. In this case, find the symbol for the schedule identification in Part 4, Section 4A, on p. B38 of the Evaluation Protocol and copy the recommendation in the corresponding place in the Recommendations Report.

Similarly, additional details for the schedule's location are required. If an individualized location is recommended, find the schedule location symbol in Part 4, Section 4B, on p. B40 of the Evaluation Protocol and copy the recommendation in the corresponding place in the Recommendations Report.

The Recommendations Report offers a greater choice of schedule characteristics than the Evaluation Protocol. These additional choices are useful specifically if the schedule's characteristics will be modified in the future using the Adjustment Protocol. There are, in fact, many more possibilities than those offered in the Recommendations Report. The choices offered were limited to those deemed beneficial for the evaluation using the Evaluation Protocol or Adjustment Protocol. When the SET was first created, the decision was made to first only evaluate certain schedule characteristics to limit the evaluation time. If a larger number of possibilities were to be evaluated, the evaluation would have taken much longer without eliminating the need to subsequently re-evaluate and readjust. It was thus deemed more efficient to evaluate basic characteristics from the start, try them out, re-evaluate them, and then introduce more possibilities according to the results obtained in the re-evaluation. This is why the Adjustment Protocol was created.

Moreover, it is important to know that if the examiner chooses to fill in the Recommendations Report after adjusting a schedule characteristic using the Adjustment Protocol, they will then need to select which schedule characteristics to check on their own and provide the details required, as this information is not included in the Adjustment Protocol.

It is strongly recommended that examiners opt for the characteristics presented in the Evaluation Protocol. However, experienced examiners can choose to adapt the characteristics for a user (e.g., a combination of visual supports or a different way of manipulating the schedule, etc.). That is why the "Other" option is included for most characteristics, allowing the examiner to write their recommendations in the Recommendations Report.

Schedule Content

Now, go to the next section in the Recommendations Report. First, write down the activities included in the user's schedule and the recommended representative visual supports for each activity based on the information obtained in Section 4C. Remember that these visual supports will be included in the form recommended (❶) unless otherwise indicated. Also, if using boxes or envelopes, write down their recommended locations.

Typically, a schedule will be implemented according to a sequence of back-to-back activities. However, if the recommended mode of presentation is "The examiner hands the user a visual support before each activity," then the examiner may consider recommending non-sequential activities when implementing the schedule. If the schedule can be displayed on a wall in the short term, choosing back-to-back activities is recommended right from the start.

Several elements can influence the examiner's choice regarding which activities or the number of visual supports to include in the schedule. The user's interest in the activities, what time of day is conducive to teaching or learning, how often these activities are repeated throughout the day, and many other factors will influence their recommendations. As such, the examiner will need to choose which activities to keep from the list in the table in Section 4C. If needed, more activities can be added.

The example below shows the content of a user's schedule, with a recommended preliminary implementation for a half-day of school. In this specific case, the afternoon activities listed in Section 4C are not included in the Recommendations Report. The form of visual support recommended for this user is the black-and-white pictogram (BWP), and hence the visual supports representing activities on the schedule are in BWP form.

As in the previous section, if the examiner chooses to fill in the Recommendations Report after adjusting a schedule characteristic using the Adjustment Protocol, they will need to identify the information to fill in for this section themselves, as this information is not provided in the Adjustment Protocol.

ACTIVITIES ON THE SCHEDULE	REPRESENTATIVE VISUAL SUPPORTS	BOX/ENVELOPE LOCATIONS
Undress	Image of a locker	To the left of the lockers
Bring the notebook to the teacher	Image of a book	In the box provided for this purpose by the teacher
Play area	Image of a radio	At the entrance of the play area, on the wall to the left
Independent work	Image of a person sitting alone at their desk	On the divider at the entrance of their individual study area
Individual learning with teacher	Image of two people sitting around a desk	On the wall to the right of the user's desk in their individual study area
Recess	Image of a ball	On the wall to the left of the door leading to the schoolyard
Music	Image of a flute	On the wall at the entrance of the music classroom
Computer	Image of a computer	On the back wall to the left of the computer desk
Lunch	Image of a lunchbox	On the back of the lunch table chair identified with the user's name

Procedures to Follow

Then detail the procedures to follow by writing down the steps to perform, both for the user and the educator, as illustrated in the following example.

STEPS TO DO BY EDUCATOR	STEPS TO DO BY USER
The educator hands the user the schedule cue.	The user takes the cue.
	They walk over to their schedule.
	They drop the schedule cue into the corresponding envelope.
	They take the first visual support from the schedule.
	They go to the corresponding location.
	They drop the visual support into the corresponding envelope.
	They start the activity.

Comments and Signature

In this section, write down any relevant comments regarding the schedule implementation. For example, if the user reacts a certain way to being touched or if they present behaviours that may require adapting the procedure, it is important to share this information with the educators who will be managing the schedule.

The following note is included in the Recommendations Report: "Make sure to regularly introduce variations in the daily sequence of activities." However, choosing to limit these variations for a short period is acceptable in the first phase of schedule implementation. But it is crucial that as soon as the user seems to be mastering their schedule, variations are integrated. Otherwise it will be difficult to know whether the user understands their schedule or if they learned the routine by heart. If the sequence of activities is the same, day in and day out, the user will have a harder time adapting to change and the unexpected. It is therefore important to remember that one of the main goals of the schedule is to encourage flexibility in people with ASD.

As with all evaluations, it is important to sign and date the Recommendations Report.

SCHEDULE ADJUSTMENT PROTOCOL

Schedule Adjustment Protocol

When the SET was created, the goal was to provide educators working with individuals who have autism spectrum disorder with a tool that would help them implement a schedule for a given user. As such, this was the purpose behind the Evaluation Protocol and all the materials in the SET kit. Following the evaluation's results, the schedule characteristics recommended are those that would require the least intervention from the educator but that the user will be able to integrate quickly and autonomously. This first step therefore focuses on the user's independence (i.e., performing the required steps on their own without outside help).

After a while, the user may be ready to integrate a different type of schedule, adapted to the skills and abilities they have developed. It is important to note, however, that increasing a schedule's level of difficulty simply because the user is at ease using their schedule may not necessarily be beneficial. As such, if a user can use their schedule on their own and it meets their needs, modifying it without a valid reason is not recommended.

There are a few valid reasons to modify the characteristics of a user's schedule (e.g., a change in their environment such as transitioning to high school or a workplace). One major consideration is reducing the time the educator devotes to managing the schedule daily. As such, the Adjustment Protocol does not present an exhaustive list of possible adjustments but rather focuses on the most common ones and the ones that will help reduce the time the educator spends managing the schedule.

The Adjustment Protocol, which is included in the Supplementary Material section, should therefore be employed if the user has already been using a schedule independently for a while (one created with the Evaluation Protocol or by some other process) and it is evident that there would be significant advantages to adjusting one or more of the characteristics of the schedule, including reducing the amount of time the educator has to spend managing it.

The Adjustment Protocol will help adjust different characteristics in the schedule to encourage a greater level of independence. Thus, it provides the opportunity for the user to be more independent in managing their schedule and facilitates schedule management for educators by reducing the support they need to provide to the user.

Use the Adjustment Protocol to Modify These Seven Characteristics

1. **Layout:** Mount the schedule on a wall from top to bottom or from left to right.
2. **Location:** Place the schedule in a group transition area.
3. **Presentation:** Make the schedule transportable.
4. **Length:** Increase the number of visual supports on the schedule.
5. **Visual support form:**
   - Switch to the OBJ form of visual support (objects representing activities) instead of the OBJ-U form (objects used in activities).
   - Switch to a visual support form with a simpler graphic representation or a smaller visual support (higher level of difficulty).
6. **Initiation:** At the end of the activity, the user:
   - Takes the schedule cue on their own and brings it over to their schedule.
   - Consults their schedule without bringing the schedule cue but by using visual cues letting them know it is time to go consult their schedule.
   - Consults their schedule on their own using natural cues at the end of the activity.
7. **Manipulation:** At the end of the activity, the user:

- Removes the visual support representing the completed activity from their schedule and drops it into a container labelled "Finished" placed next to the schedule (the visual supports thus disappear as the activities are completed).
- Flips over the visual support representing the completed activity.
- Checks off or writes an X on their schedule, or places a token next to the visual support representing the completed activity.

Schedule Adjustment Sequence

The schedule adjustment process is divided into two parts. The first aims to determine whether an adjustment should be made and what characteristic should be adjusted. The second allows the examiner to proceed with the adjustment and its evaluation.

Materials Required for the Adjustment

Adjusting the schedule is done using this guide, the materials in the SET kit, and any additional materials prepared by the person making the adjustment, as well as the Adjustment Protocol, Evaluation Protocol, Independence Evaluation Grid, and Recommendations Report (these documents are included in the Supplementary Material section and must be photocopied and enlarged for the evaluation).

The Adjustment Protocol contains all the information for the schedule adjustment. At times, it refers to the Evaluation Protocol as well as the corresponding materials from the SET kit to proceed with certain evaluations. The Independence Evaluation Grid helps evaluate whether the user meets prerequisites for schedule adjustments and whether an adjustment should be kept after its introduction. The Recommendations Report, which can be filled out after adjusting the schedule, contains all the relevant information describing the user's adjusted schedule.

Administration

Part 1

Part 1 identifies whether a schedule adjustment should be tried depending on the user's level of independence in using their current schedule and which characteristic to adjust.

A) Identify If the Adjustment's Prerequisites Are Met

The schedule should only be adjusted if one of the following criteria is met:

- ☐ Following the schedule evaluation using the Evaluation Protocol, the schedule was implemented according to the recommendations. After a week, the user was fully independent in using their schedule and has maintained this independence for at least a week.
- ☐ Following the adjustment of a schedule characteristic using the Adjustment Protocol, the user's level of independence was evaluated (as recommended in the "Independence Evaluation" step in the introduction and evaluation phases for each adjustment) and meets the different criteria for this step, regarding both their independence and the time to wait before introducing another adjustment.
- ☐ The user has been using their schedule independently for at least three months.

B) Evaluate the Level of Independence for the Current Schedule

To establish whether the user meets the independence prerequisites for a schedule adjustment, the examiner must fill in the Independence Evaluation Grid (see Excerpt 12). Follow the instructions in the grid as well as the instructions below:

- Fill in the Independence Evaluation Grid four times per day for three days, making sure to randomly evaluate different activities.
  a) If the user needed help to execute a step in their schedule, they are not considered fully independent.
  b) If the user executes all the steps on their own in the evaluation, they are considered fully independent. Identify which characteristic to adjust.

C) Identify the Characteristics to Adjust

If the user meets the schedule adjustment prerequisites, consult Table 1 in the Adjustment Protocol to identify which characteristics to adjust based on the current characteristics and the intended goal.

In Table 1, adjustments follow a certain chronological logic. However, following this order is not required for all adjustments, only for the first three (if applicable):

1. "Use OBJ visual support form (objects representing activities) and drop the visual supports into containers where the activities take place."
2. "Display the schedule on the wall (from top to bottom)."
3. "Increase the number of visual supports on the schedule."

These three adjustments must be done first and in chronological order. However, if only adjustments 2 and 3 are required, do them in that order and skip adjustment 1. Likewise, if only adjustment 3 is required, skip adjustments 1 and 2.

As such, if the form used is OBJ-U (objects used in activities), start the adjustment by modifying that characteristic and guide the user in using the OBJ form (objects representing activities).

If the presentation mode is "The educator hands the user a visual support before each activity," adjust that characteristic and guide the user in using a wall-mounted schedule.

If the schedule is mounted on the wall, increase the number of visual supports to a number deemed appropriate by the educator (typically corresponds to a half or full day of activities).

In other cases (e.g., if the user uses a form other than OBJ-U, the schedule is mounted on the wall, and the number of visual supports is deemed appropriate by the educator), the examiner can choose to make the adjustment they find most relevant for the user based on the intended goal and benefits. In Table 1, the "Current Schedule Characteristic" column corresponds to the prerequisites that allow the examiner to select which criteria to adjust. Once the characteristic is identified, ensure that the user meets the prerequisites specific to each adjustment in the "Prerequisites for This Adjustment" section (Part 2 of the Adjustment Protocol), as it provides more detailed information and, at times, additions (not specified in Table 1).

Adjusting more than one characteristic at a time is not recommended (except for certain proposed adjustments that will modify two schedule characteristics at the same time if they are linked).

Excerpt 12. Completed Independence Evaluation Grid (One Day Out of Three Required)

Independence Evaluation Grid

Instructions
- Fill in the user's name and evaluation date and check the day of the evaluation (first, second, or third).
- List the steps the user must currently perform to use their schedule.
- During the evaluation, specify the time and, using the legend at the bottom of the grid, specify the type of help provided during the different steps.
- Evaluate the user's independence in using their schedule over three days, four times per day. It is important to ensure you randomly evaluate the schedule's use during different activities.
- If help was required to perform one of the steps, the user is not considered fully independent.

User's name: Alexis Bérubé				
Date: 02/06/2009 (DD/MM/YY)	Day: ☑ 1 ☐ 2 ☐ 3			
STEPS	**TIME**			
	9:15 a.m.	10:30 a.m.	12:00 p.m.	1:45 p.m.
The user takes the schedule cue.	I	I	I	I
They walk over to their schedule strip and drop the cue into the schedule cue box.	I	I	I	I
They take the top visual support from the schedule.	I	G	I	G
They walk to the matching box and drop the visual support into the correct box.	I	I	I	I
They start the activity.	I	I	I	I

Legend: I = Independent, P = Physical prompt, G = Gestural prompt, V = Verbal prompt.

In this situation, we can conclude that the user is not fully independent in using their schedule as they received gestural help twice during a specific step. It is therefore not possible to adjust a schedule characteristic with the Adjustment Protocol for now. Rather, they should be taught how to use their schedule before evaluating their independence once again.

Part 2

Part 2 presents each adjustment and the information needed to make the adjustment.

After choosing the characteristic to adjust, the examiner must go to the corresponding section in the Adjustment Protocol where they will find the prerequisites and the procedure to follow. Table 1 in the Adjustment Protocol indicates the page containing the procedure to adjust for the chosen characteristic.

Generally, the examiner should first introduce the adjusted characteristic and evaluate the user's level of independence. Depending on the user's performance, three options are offered:

- Revert to the schedule's initial characteristics.
- Keep the adjusted schedule and wait for a certain period of time before trying new adjustments.
- Keep the adjusted schedule and, if desired, proceed with a new adjustment.

For certain adjustments, a pre-evaluation step will determine whether the examiner should or should not proceed with the implementation. In other cases, this procedure is not required.

For each characteristic to adjust, the intended goal is clearly indicated, and the different introduction and evaluation steps are explained.

The guidelines provided in the Adjustment Protocol leave more room for the examiner's own initiative than those in the Evaluation Protocol. They are thus easier to adapt to a variety of situations but require greater experience in schedule implementation. Furthermore, and contrary to the Evaluation Protocol, the materials required for adjustments are not included in the SET kit, as they are unique to the user and entirely customized. However, the materials to use in the pre-evaluation are the same as those used in the Evaluation Protocol.

Adjustment Prerequisites

Prerequisites indicate the schedule's current characteristics and the intended goal of the adjustment, which can be found in Table 1. However, in addition to reiterating the information in Table 1, they also provide specifications and, at times, additions specifying the required prerequisites for that adjustment.

The intended adjustment should only be made if the user's situation meets all these prerequisites.

Adjustment Benefits

These are the benefits the user and/or educator will reap from the adjustment.

Pre-Evaluation

For certain adjustments, a pre-evaluation step will determine whether the examiner should or should not proceed with the implementation and what exactly the modification should be. The required materials and success criteria (when applicable) are then specified to determine whether the adjustment should be implemented. The materials correspond to a given part, section, or subsection in the Evaluation Protocol and the guide, as well as the corresponding materials in the SET kit.

Introduction and Evaluation Phases

These phases include the schedule modifications required to introduce the new adjusted schedule, the support to provide to the user when teaching them the new characteristics during the introduction phase, and the success criteria for the evaluation of the user's independence.

Schedule Modifications

The schedule modifications may require preparing, moving, or adding materials. Modification principles are outlined for each adjustment. However, considering that the initial schedule characteristics are quite varied (except for those outlined as prerequisites for a specific adjustment), this list is not exhaustive.

Introduction and Teaching

The modified schedule is introduced, and the user is taught how to use it. Any support the user requires to adapt to the new characteristic(s) must be provided.

Independence Evaluation

This section outlines the timeline to use the new schedule before evaluating the user's autonomy with the Independence Evaluation Grid, and the evaluation methods and criteria that will determine whether to keep the modification or revert to the previous schedule. It also indicates how long to wait before making another adjustment if desired.

Excerpt 13. Schedule Adjustment Protocol, Adjustment 9, Characteristic to Adjust: Schedule Manipulation

---

ADJUSTMENT 9

Characteristics to adjust: Manipulation.
Goal: At the end of the activity, to have the user flip over the visual support representing the completed activity on their schedule.

PREREQUISITES FOR THIS ADJUSTMENT

- ☐ At the end of the activity, the user removes the visual support representing the activity from their schedule and drops it into a container labelled "Finished" placed beside their schedule.
AND
- ☐ At the end of the activity, the aim is for the user to flip over the visual support representing the completed activity on their schedule.

ADJUSTMENT BENEFITS

- Facilitates the schedule's management by the educator, as certain daily routines are recurring and the educator will simply need to flip the visual supports back over.
- Allows the educator to check if the user is in fact at the activity indicated on the schedule.
- Allows the user to view the number of activities they have completed.
- Familiarizes the user with the fact that the visual supports can stay on the schedule.

INTRODUCTION AND EVALUATION PHASES

Schedule Modifications

Make the required modifications, specifically:

- Remove the box or envelope labelled "Finished" that was placed beside the schedule.
- Stick a strip of Velcro on both sides of the visual supports.

Introduction and Teaching

Provide the user with the support they need to learn their new schedule. Specifically, teach them how to take the visual supports on the schedule, flip them over, and stick them back on the schedule when an activity is finished, instead of dropping them into a box or envelope labelled "Finished."

Independence Evaluation

After two days of using this new schedule, evaluate the user's independence:

- Fill in the Independence Evaluation Grid four times per day for one day, making sure to evaluate different activities randomly.
  - If the user needed help in executing a step of the schedule, revert to the previous schedule and wait at least two months before attempting this adjustment again.
  - If the user is fully independent with their schedule, wait until they maintain this level of independence for at least two weeks before attempting another adjustment, and only if it will make using and managing the schedule easier.

If desired, you can fill in the Recommendations Report with the new schedule characteristics.

Recommendations Report

Following the schedule adjustment, the examiner can fill out the Recommendations Report again. This report provides all the relevant information to describe the adjusted schedule. Additionally, it is important to remember that more than one characteristic can be modified. For example, if a schedule will now be mounted on the wall, when it was not previously, the educator will also need to change its identification in addition to its presentation mode.

Moreover, when the examiner fills out the Recommendations Report after the initial evaluation, very precise information regarding what to check and include in the "Schedule Characteristics" and "Schedule Content" sections is provided in the Evaluation Protocol. Similarly, the instructions provided in the guide explaining how to fill in these sections also refer to the Evaluation Protocol. However, the situation is quite different when the examiner decides to fill in the Recommendations Report after adjusting a schedule characteristic. In this case, the examiner will need to identify the different characteristics of the adjusted schedule on their own, check corresponding statements, and add any specifications as needed.

Pre-Experimental Results

While designing and refining the SET, the authors conducted a short trial to essentially examine the content validity and ease of use. This step guided them in improving the tool's content and form.

To do this, they used various content validity and construct validity indices. For content validity, they asked experts' opinions on the tool's ease of use and the results obtained using the tool. For construct validity, they compared the results on the visual support forms prescribed by the SET with direct experiments of three schedule types, including the one prescribed by the tool.

First, the authors devised a satisfaction questionnaire made up of 16 questions on various important aspects in the tool's development (materials, protocols, result compilation methodology, the evaluation's different parts, the SET Guide, and the evaluation duration).

Then the authors asked for the collaboration of experts working with an ASD clientele. These experts were all specialized educators who have been applying individualized schedules inspired by the TEACCH® approach with an ASD clientele for several years. They are all recognized trainers and specialists in the field. The four experts each evaluated three people with ASD (two of these experts, however, evaluated the same three users). The nine individuals evaluated by these experts all had an autism spectrum disorder with or without an intellectual disability and were all elementary-aged schoolchildren.

The four experts filled out the satisfaction questionnaire after using the tool with the three users. They rated their satisfaction on a scale of 0 to 4 (with 0 = strongly disagree, 1 = disagree, 2 = I don't know [no opinion], 3 = agree, and 4 = strongly agree). The satisfaction percentage was calculated by considering scores of 3 or 4 as satisfactory (a score of 3 to 4 meant agreement, while a score of 0, 1, or 2 meant disagreement). As such, the satisfaction percentage was calculated by dividing the number of total agreements by the number of questions and multiplying by 100. The average satisfaction for the 16 questions was 90%. Eleven of the 16 questions received an absolute score of 100%. For the five other questions, the level of satisfaction varied between 50% and 75%. The interview with the person who knows the user best (Part 4 of the evaluation) and the evaluation duration received the lowest scores (50%). The guide's ease of understanding and the exhaustiveness of the information in the Schedule Evaluation Protocol scored 75%. Modifications to make to the Schedule Evaluation Protocol, Evaluation Guide, and the tool itself were thus defined in part by the dissatisfaction indices revealed in the questionnaire.

Then, for information purposes, the authors used two measurement indices for the predictive validity of the tool's results. To do this, the first index recorded was the visual support form result compared to the expert's clinical judgment on the most appropriate choice of visual support. The second predictive validity index was obtained by comparing the evaluation's results for the most relevant type of schedule for the user with the efficiency of use of three different schedule types, one of which was the one prescribed by the tool. These two indices were only obtained from two experts who used the SET with six users, as they were the only ones to have filled in all the documents required for these two measurements.

After evaluating each user, the authors asked the experts for their professional recommendations on the form of visual support (objects, photos, black-and-white pictograms, colour pictograms, words typed on the computer, and words written by hand) for every user. Five recommendations of six were the same as those obtained with the tool. However, one recommendation of the six combined two forms of visual supports (colour pictograms and words typed on the computer), which included the form recommended in the evaluation. Considering this last result as a partial agreement (0.5) rather than a full agreement (1), it is possible to calculate a partial agreement percentage of 92%.

However, the authors wanted to obtain a more formal predictive index (i.e., the efficacy of the schedule type prescribed by the SET in real-life situations). To obtain this predictive validity index, they asked the same two experts to try three different schedule types with the six users, including the one prescribed by the SET, and to measure their efficacy in reaching a success criterion.

The experts tried the three schedule types with each user: one with a lower level of difficulty than the one prescribed by the SET, and one with a higher level of difficulty, and last, the one prescribed by the SET. The individuals with ASD had to alternately go to three different locations using one or the other of the preselected schedules, and successfully complete two consecutive attempts for each location within a maximum of seven trips to the same location, or fifteen in total.

They were also allowed two sets of attempts to meet these criteria; however, after nine consecutive failed attempts, the test was ended regardless of the location. The results for the six individuals with ASD revealed a 100% prediction level calculated as a percentage of absolute agreement (the type of schedule prescribed by the tool compared to the most effective type of schedule).

These results were promising but were too few to satisfactorily draw conclusions on the SET's psychometric qualities. This pre-experimentation did, however, allow the authors to substantially improve Part 4 of the evaluation, the evaluation's duration using stop standards based on users' results, the quantity of information provided in the Evaluation Protocol, and the overall presentation of the SET Guide.

The authors decided to publish the SET to allow the greatest number of educators to use it and, eventually, conduct studies on its psychometric value. However, it is important to remember that the authors' first intention in developing the SET was to create a clinical tool that would help educators who work directly with individuals with ASD, and who are not specialized in evaluation, to identify an individualized, effective schedule for these users. Hence, for the authors, the most important criterion resides in the tool's usefulness for professionals working in the field to help people with ASD, particularly to build autonomy and improve communication.

Bibliography

Artuso, Danièle. 1995. *L'aide au très jeune enfant atteint d'autisme*. Cannes: Éditions AFD.

Aussilloux, Charles, Amaria Baghdadli, and René Pry. 1998. "Prise en charge des adolescents autistes." *Revue psychologie française* 43 (3): 225–230.

Bambera, Linda M., and Christina Ager. 1992. "Using Self-Scheduling to Promote Self-Directed Leisure Activity in Home and Community Settings." *Journal of the Association for Persons with Severe Handicaps* 17: 67–76.

Banda, Devender R., Eric Grimmet, and Stephanie L. Hart. 2009. "Activity Schedules: Helping Students with Autism Spectrum Disorders in General Education Classrooms Manage Transition Issues." *Teaching Exceptional Children* 41, no. 4 (March–April): 16–21.

Bryan, Linley C., and David L. Gast. 2000. "Teaching On-Task and On-Schedule Behaviors to High-Functioning Children with Autism via Picture Activity Schedules." *Journal of Autism and Developmental Disorders* 30 (6): 553–567.

Carbonneau, France, Russell Clark, Karine Gagnon, Myriam Hurtubise, and Joanne Larose. 2009. *Programme-cadre des services spécialisés de réadaptation en Montérégie pour les personnes présentant un trouble envahissant du développement*. Longueuil: Centre de réadaptation en déficience intellectuelle Montérégie-Est, Centre montérégien de réadaptation et Services de réadaptation du Sud-Ouest et du Renfort.

Davis, Daniel K., Steven E. Stock, and Michael L. Wehmeyer. 2002. "Enhancing Independent Task Performance for Individuals with Mental Retardation through Use of a Handheld Self-Directed Visual and Audio Prompting

System." *Education and Training in Mental Retardation and Developmental Disabilities* 37: 209–218.

———. 2002. "Enhancing Independent Time Management Skills of Individuals with Mental Retardation Using a Palmtop Personal Computer." *Mental Retardation* 40 (5): 358–365.

Dettmer, Sarah, Richard L. Simpson, Brenda Smith Myles, and Jennifer B. Ganz. 2000. "The Use of Visual Supports to Facilitate Transitions of Students with Autism." *Focus on Autism and Other Developmental Disabilities* 15 (3): 163–169.

Dougherty, J. 1995. "L'intervention structurée selon le modèle TEACCH." Training notes. Chapel Hill, N.C.: TEACCH.

———. 1999. *TEACCH Approach: Advanced Content*. Chapel Hill, N.C.: TEACCH.

Duttlinger, Cari, Kevin Michael Ayres, Alicia Bevill-Davis, and Karen H. Douglas. 2012. "The Effects of a Picture Activity Schedule for Students with Intellectual Disability to Complete a Sequence of Tasks Following Verbal Directions." *Focus on Autism and Other Developmental Disabilities* 28 (1): 32–43.

Eckenrode, Laurie, Pat Fennell, and Kathy Hearsey. 2004. *Tasks Galore for the Real World*. Raleigh, N.C.: Tasks Galore.

Faherty, Catherine. 1998. *TEACCH Structured Teaching Assessment*. Chapel Hill, N.C.: TEACCH.

Foubert, Martine, and Bernadette Rogé. 1998. "Les prises en charge d'adultes autistes." *Revue psychologie française* 43 (3): 231–238.

Fouse, Beth, and Maria Wheeler. 1997. *A Treasure Chest of Behavioral Strategies for Individuals with Autism*. Arlington, Tex.: Future Horizons.

Goupil, Georgette. 1997. *Élèves en difficulté d'adaptation et d'apprentissage*. 2nd ed. Boucherville, Que.: Gaëtan Morin.

Hall, Laura J., Lynn E. McClannahan, and Patricia J. Krantz. 1995. "Promoting Independence in Integrated Classrooms by Teaching Aides to Use Activity Schedules and Decreased Prompts." *Education and Training in Mental Retardation and Developmental Disabilities* 30 (3): 208–217.

Hodgdon, Linda A. 1995. *Visual Strategies for Improving Communication: Practical Supports for School and Home*. Troy, Mich.: QuirkRoberts Publishing.

Hoff, Ulla, and Paule Mercier. 2002. *L'accompagnement de l'élève TED intégré au primaire : s'outiller pour relever le défi*. Québec: Commission scolaire des Découvreurs.

Hume, Kara. 2009. *Implementation Checklist for Visual Schedules*. Chapel Hill, N.C.: The National Professional Development Center on Autism Spectrum Disorders, Frank Porter Graham Child Development Institute, University of North Carolina. https://csesa.fpg.unc.edu/sites/csesa.fpg.unc.edu/files/ebpbriefs/VisualSchedules_Checklist_0.pdf.

Hume, Kara. 2011. *Structured Teaching Strategies: A Series Article 2: Visual Schedules in the School Setting*. Bloomington, Ind.: Indiana Resource

Center for Autism. https://www.iidc.indiana.edu/doc/resources/structured-teaching-strategies-visual-schedules.pdf.

Hungelmann, Angela M. 2001. "An Analysis of TEACCH-Based Home Programming for Young Children with Autism." *Dissertation Abstracts International: The Sciences & Engineering* 61 (10B): 55–67.

Juhel, Jean-Charles. 2003. *La personne autiste et le syndrome d'Asperger*. Québec: Les Presses de l'Université Laval.

Koyama, Takanori, and Hui-Ting Wang. 2011. "Use of Activity Schedule to Promote Independent Performance of Individuals with Autism and Other Intellectual Disabilities." *Research in Developmental Disabilities* 32: 2235–2242.

Krantz, Patricia J., Michael T. MacDuff, and Lynn E. McClannahan. 1993. "Programming Participation in Family Activities for Children with Autism: Parents' Use of Photographic Activity Schedules." *Journal of Applied Behavior Analysis* 26: 137–139.

Leroux, Gilbert. 1993. "Notes de rencontres pour l'implantation des classes d'inspiration TEACCH." Unpublished document. Montréal: Commission scolaire de Montréal, École Saint-Pierre-Apôtre.

Lopata, Christopher, Marcus L. Thomeer, Martin Andrew Volkner, Robert E. Nida, and Gloria K. Lee. 2008. "Effectiveness of a Manualized Summer Social Treatment Program for High-Functioning Children with Autism Spectrum Disorders." *Journal on Autism and Developmental Disorder* 38 (5): 980–904. https://doi.org/10.1007/s10803-007-0460-7.

MacDuff, Gregory S., Patricia J. Krantz, and Lynn E. McClannahan. 1993. "Teaching Children with Autism to Use Photographic Activity Schedules: Maintenance and Generalization of Complex Response Chains." *Journal of Applied Behavior Analysis* 26: 89–95.

Massey, Noelle, and John J. Wheeler. 2000. "Acquisition and Generalization of Activity Schedules and Their Effects on Task Engagement in a Young Child with Autism in an Inclusive Pre-School Classroom." *Education and Training in Mental Retardation and Developmental Disabilities* 35 (3): 326–335.

Marcus, Lee, and John D. Overton. 2008. "Workshop on High Functioning Autism." Fédération québecoise de l'autisme, Montréal, QC, 2008.

Matson, Johnny L., Jonathan Wilkins, and Jennifer Macken. 2009. "The Relationship of Challenging Behaviors to Severity and Symptoms of Autism Spectrum Disorders." *Journal of Mental Health Research in Intellectual Disabilities* 2: 29–44.

Maurice, Catherine. 2005. *Intervention béhaviorale auprès des jeunes enfants autistes*. Montréal: Chenelière Éducation.

McClannahan, Lynn E., and Patricia J. Krantz. 1997. "In Search of Solutions to Prompt Dependence: Teaching Children with Autism to Use Photographic Activity Schedules." In *Environment and Behaviour*, edited by E. M. Pinkston and D. M. Baer, 271–278. Boulder, Colo.: Westview Press.

———. 1999. *Activity Schedules for Children with Autism: Teaching Independent Behaviour.* Bethesda, Md.: Woodbine House.

Mesibov, Gary B. 1997. "Formal and Informal Measures on the Effectiveness of the TEACCH Programme." *Autism* 1: 25–35.

Mesibov, Gary B., Marie Howley, and Signe Naftel. 2003. *Accessing the Curriculum for Pupils with Autistic Spectrum Disorders: Using the TEACCH Program to Help Inclusion.* London: David Fulton Publishers.

Mesibov, Gary B., Eric Schopler, Bruce Schaffer, and Rhoda Landrus. 1994. *Profil psycho-éducatif pour adolescents et adultes (AAPEP).* Bruxelles: De Boeck Université.

Mesibov, Gary B., Victoria A. Shea, Eric Schopler, Lynn W. Adams, Elif Merkler, Sloane Burgess, Matthew W. Mosconi, Suzannah M. Chapman, Christine Tanner, and Mary E. Van Bourgondien. 2005. *The TEACCH Approach to Autism Spectrum Disorders.* New York: Kluwer Academic/Plenum Publishers.

Missouri Autism Guidelines Initiative. 2012. *Autism Spectrum Disorders: Guide to Evidence-Based Interventions.* Consensus Publication.

Montreuil, Nicole, and Ghislain Magerotte. 1994. *Pratique de l'intervention individualisée.* Bruxelles: De Boeck/Wesmael.

Morrison, Rebecca S., Diane M. Sainato, Delia Benchaaban, and Sayaka Endo. 2002. "Increasing Play Skills of Children with Autism Using Activity Schedules and Correspondence Training." *Journal of Early Intervention* 25 (1): 58–72.

National Autism Center. 2015. *Evidence-Based Practice and Autism in the Schools: A Guide to Providing Appropriate Interventions to Students with Autism Spectrum Disorder.* 2nd ed. Randolph, Mass.: Center of May Institute.

Office of Special Education and Student Services. 2011. *Models of Best Practice in the Education of Students with Autism Spectrum Disorders.* Richmond, Va.: Department of Education.

O'Reilly, Mark F., Jeff Sigafoos, Giulio E. Lancioni, Chaturi D. Edrisinha, and Alonzo A. Andrews. 2005. "An Examination of the Effects of a Classroom Activity Schedule on Levels of Self-Injury and Engagement for a Child with Severe Autism." *Journal of Autism and Developmental Disorders* 35 (3): 305–311.

Panerai, Simonetta, Letizia Ferrante, Valeria Caputo, and Carmela Impellizzeri. 1998. "Use of Structured Teaching for Treatment of Children with Autism and Severe and Profound Mental Retardation." *Education and Training in Mental Retardation and Developmental Disabilities* 33 (4): 367–374.

Peeters, Théo. 1996. *L'autisme : de la compréhension à l'intervention.* Paris: Dunod.

Rogé, Bernadette. 2003. *Autisme, comprendre et agir.* Paris: Dunod.

———. 2003. "L'autisme et la déficience intellectuelle." In *La déficience intellectuelle,* edited by M. J. Tassé and D. Morin, 69–89. Boucherville, Que.: Gaëtan Morin.

Sattler, Jerome M. 2002. "Autistic Disorder." In *Assessment of Children: Behavioral and Clinical Applications*, 390–400. San Diego, Calif.: Jerome M. Sattler.

Schopler, Eric, Robert-Jay Reichler, and Margaret Lansing. 1988. *Stratégies éducatives de l'autisme*. Paris: Masson.

Schopler, Eric, and Robert-Jay Reichler. 1994. *Profil psycho-éducatif (PEP-R) : évaluation et intervention individualisée pour enfants autistes ou présentant des troubles du développement*. Bruxelles: De Boeck/Wesmael.

Schopler, Eric, and Bernadette Rogé. 1998. "Approche éducative de l'autisme : le programme TEACCH. Sa transposition en France." *Revue psychologie française* 43 (3): 199–212.

Schopler, Eric, Nurit Yirmiya, Cory Shulman, and Lee M. Marcus, eds. 2001. *The Research Basis for Autism Intervention*. New York: Kluwer Academic/Plenum Publishers.

Schopler, Eric, Margaret D. Lansing, Robert J. Reichler, and Lee M. Marcus. 2005. *Psychoeducational Profile (PEP-3): TEACCH Individualized Psychoeducational Assessment*. 3rd ed. Austin, Tex.: PROED.

Siegel, Bryna. 2003. *Helping Children with Autism Learn: Treatment Approaches for Parents and Professionals*. Oxford: Oxford University Press.

Stromer, Robert, Jonathan W. Kimball, Elisabeth M. Kinney, and Bridget A. Taylor. 2006. "Activity Schedules, Computer Technology, and Teaching Children with Autism Spectrum Disorders." *Focus on Autism and Other Developmental Disabilities* 21 (1): 14–24.

Tissot, Catherine, and Roy Evans. 2003. "Visual Teaching Strategies for Children with Autism." *Early Child Development and Care* 173 (4): 425–433.

University of North Carolina. n.d. "Structured TEACCHIng: Individualized Schedules." Online course, University of North Carolina, TEACCH Autism Program, Services Across a Lifespan, Chapel Hill, NC. https://www.piedmontahec.org/courses-and-events/68401/structured-teacching-individualized-schedules.

University of North Carolina at Chapel Hill, Department of Psychiatry, TEACCH Division. 1996. *Visually Structured Tasks: Independent Activities for Students with Autism and Other Visual Learners*. Chapel Hill, N.C.: TEACCH.

———. 2010. *TEACCH Structured Teaching Assessment: A Guide to Individualizing Schedules and Work Systems*. Chapel Hill, N.C.: TEACCH.

Virginia Department of Education, Office of Special Education and Student Services. 2010. *Guidelines for Educating Students with Autism Spectrum Disorders*. Virginia. https://www.doe.virginia.gov/home/showpublisheddocument/7942/638010930376470000.

Wheeler, John J., and Stacy L. Carter. 1998. "Using Visual Cues in the Classroom for Learners with Autism as a Method for Promoting Positive Behavior." *B.C. Journal of Special Education* 21 (3): 64–73.

Zimbelman, Merilee, Angelia M. Paschal, Suzanne R. Hawley, Craig A. Molgaard, and Theresa St. Romain. 2006. "Addressing Physical Inactivity among Developmentally Disabled Students through Visual Schedules and Social Stories." *Research in Developmental Disabilities* 28 (4): 386–396.

SUPPLEMENTARY MATERIAL*
Schedule Evaluation Tool

*It is essential that the following documents are photocopied on 8.5" × 11" sheets of paper: Schedule Evaluation Protocol, Recommendations Report, Schedule Adjustment Protocol, Independence Evaluation Grid, and all Schedule Sheets in Appendix 2. They will need to be enlarged.

SCHEDULE EVALUATION TOOL

Johanne Mainville, Sonia Di Lillo,
Nathalie Poirier, and Nathalie Plante

SCHEDULE EVALUATION PROTOCOL

INFORMATION ON THE EVALUATED USER		
First name		
Last name		
Sex assigned at birth	☐ M ☐ F	
Date of birth (DD/MM/YYYY)	/ /	
Visual problems (colour blindness, squinting, etc.)	☐ Yes	Specify:
	☐ No	
Place of residence		
Examiner		
Date of evaluation (DD/MM/YYYY)	/ /	

Table of Contents

List of Tables B4
Legend of Symbols B5
Example of a Subsection From Part 1 .... B6

PART 1 .... B8

    Section 1A B8
        Subsection 1A.OBJ (Object–Object) B8

    Section 1B B9
        Subsection 1B.PHO (Photo–Photo) B9
        Subsection 1B.PIC (Colour Pictogram–Colour Pictogram) B10
        Subsection 1B.BWP (Black-And-White Pictogram–Black-And-White Pictogram) B11
        Subsection 1B.WTC (Words Typed on the Computer–Words Typed on the Computer) B11
        Subsection 1B.WWH (Words Written by Hand–Words Written by Hand) B12

    Section 1C B13
        Subsection 1C.PHO (Photo–Object) B13
        Subsection 1C.PIC (Colour Pictogram–Object) B13
        Subsection 1C.BWP (Black-And-White Pictogram–Object) B14
        Subsection 1C.WTC (Words Typed on the Computer–Object) B15
        Subsection 1C.WWH (Words Written by Hand–Object) B16

    Scoring Part 1 .... B17

PART 2 .... B19

    Visual Support Form 1 .... B20
    Visual Support Form 2 .... B21
    Visual Support Form 3 .... B22

    Scoring Part 2 .... B23

PART 3 .... B24

   Section 3A: Schedule Displayed on the Wall B24
      Section 3A.1 One Visual Support on the
      Schedule Strip B25
      Section 3A.2 Three Visual Supports on the
      Schedule Strip B27
      Section 3A.3 Six Visual Supports on the
      Schedule Strip B28

   Section 3B: Token or Checkmark Schedule B29
      Subsection 3B.1 .... B31
      Subsection 3B.2 .... B32

   Scoring Part 3 .... B34

PART 4 .... B38

   Section 4A: Identifying the Schedule With a
   Cue Related to the User's Interests B38

   Section 4B: Identifying an Individualized
   Location B39

   Section 4C: Schedule Content (Activities on the
   Schedule and Representative Visual Supports) B41
      Home Setting B42
      Work Setting B43
      School Setting B44

List of Tables

PART 1
Table 1. Results for Part 1 .... B17
Table 2. Scoring Part 1 .... B17

PART 2
Table 3. Location of Visual Supports B19
Table 4. Results for Part 1 (Totals Only) B23
Table 5. Results for Part 2 .... B23
Table 6. Scoring Part 2 .... B23

PART 3
Table 7. Results for Section 3A B28
Table 8. Location of 3B Baskets: Object Baskets B30
Table 9. Results for Section 3B B33
Table 10. Results for Section 3A B34
Table 11. Results for Section 3B B34
Table 12. Scoring Part 3 .... B35

Legend of Symbols

SYMBOL	MEANING
🚩	Section or subsection where evaluation may directly begin (found in three locations).
🛠	Materials needed to evaluate a part, section, or subsection.
✋	Stop the evaluation here (stop standard) and follow the outlined procedure.
✏️	Score the section or subsection indicated after this symbol.
▶	Continue the evaluation at the part, section, or subsection that directly follows the scoring indicated before the symbol.
▶▶	Skip ahead several sections or subsections and continue the evaluation at the location indicated after this symbol.
↻	Return to the section or subsection indicated to the right of this symbol and proceed with the evaluation based on the results obtained by the user.
1 opt. demo	Number of optional demonstrations allowed.
1 mand. demo	Number of mandatory demonstrations.
$\leq$	Less than or equal to…
$\geq$	Greater than or equal to…
❷ PRESENTATION MODE	
	Relevant information for the Schedule Recommendations Report. The corresponding number and title can be found in the report.

Example of a Subsection From Part 1

① SECTION 1B

③
- Filing box 1B + 1C
- Bottom panel and back panel
- 3 matching boxes

② **SUBSECTION 1B.PHO (PHOTO–PHOTO)** ⑤ ⑥

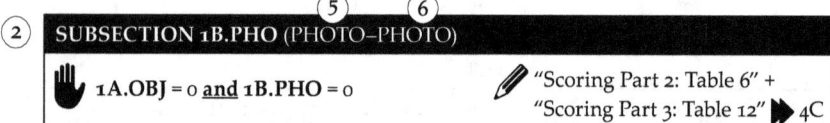

1A.OBJ = 0 **and** 1B.PHO = 0   "Scoring Part 2: Table 6" + "Scoring Part 3: Table 12" ▶ 4C

⑦ CATEGORY	④ DEMOS	ORDER OF VISUAL SUPPORTS ON MATCHING BOXES	SCORING	COMMENTS AND OBSERVATIONS
Home	1 opt. demo/ support	Toothbrush Sock Lego	/3	
Work/School	1 opt. demo/ support	Spoon Pencil Disc	/3	
Other	1 opt. demo/ support	Ball Marker Sponge	/3	☐ Other not ⑧ evaluated (3/3)
		TOTAL **1B.PHO**	⑨ /9	☐ 1B.PHO not ⑩ evaluated (9/9)

- ① Section name
- ② Subsection name
- ③ Material to use for Section 1B (including Subsection 1B.PHO)
- ④ Indications for demonstrations (not scored)
- ⑤ The first word, "PHOTO," indicates which form of visual support to hand to the user. In this example, the photos can be found in filing box 1B + 1C (as specified in the list of materials) behind the 1B.PHO divider.
- ⑥ The second word, "PHOTO," indicates what form of visual support to mount to the top of the matching boxes. In this example, the photos come from the same place as in ⑤.

⑦ Start the evaluation with the first category in the column and continue the evaluation following the order in the column.
⑧ Check this box if this category was not evaluated because the user matched all the visual supports in the first two categories correctly (perfect score).
⑨ User's total score for this subsection.
⑩ If the evaluation started in a later subsection and the user scored 9/9 on that subsection, 1B.PHO does not need to be evaluated, so check this box and assign the highest score.

PART 1

- 3 object bags: Home bag, Work/School bag, and Other bag
- Filing box 1B + 1C
- Bottom panel and back panel
- 3 matching boxes

(!) **Note:** *During Part 1 of the evaluation, it is very important to collect the objects after the user has matched them.*

SECTION 1A

 START THE EVALUATION HERE
Only if the user's skill level is unknown or they are unable to match two identical pictograms.

- 3 object bags: Home bag, Work/School bag, and Other bag
- Bottom panel and back panel
- 3 matching boxes

SUBSECTION 1A.OBJ (OBJECT–OBJECT)				
CATEGORY	DEMOS	ORDER OF VISUAL SUPPORTS ON MATCHING BOXES	SCORING	COMMENTS AND OBSERVATIONS
Home	2 opt. demos/ support	Toothbrush Sock Lego	/3	
Work/ School	2 opt. demos/ support	Spoon Pencil Disc	/3	
Other	2 opt. demos/ support	Ball Marker Sponge	/3	
		SUBTOTAL	/9	
		TOTAL **1A.OBJ** (SUBTOTAL X 2)	/18	☐ **1A.OBJ** not evaluated (18/18)

SECTION 1B

- Filing box 1B + 1C
- Bottom panel and back panel
- 3 matching boxes

SUBSECTION 1B.PHO (PHOTO–PHOTO)

✋ 1A.OBJ = 0 **and** 1B.PHO = 0   ✏️ "Scoring Part 2: Table 6" + "Scoring Part 3: Table 12" ▶ 4C

CATEGORY	DEMOS	ORDER OF VISUAL SUPPORTS ON MATCHING BOXES	SCORING	COMMENTS AND OBSERVATIONS
Home	1 opt. demo/ support	Toothbrush Sock Lego	/3	
Work/School	1 opt. demo/ support	Spoon Pencil Disc	/3	
Other	1 opt. demo/ support	Ball Marker Sponge	/3	☐ Other not evaluated (3/3)
		TOTAL **1B.PHO**	/9	☐ **1B.PHO** not evaluated (9/9)

▶ START THE EVALUATION HERE

Only if the user can match two identical pictograms and does not have functional reading skills.

- Filing box 1B + 1C
- Bottom panel and back panel
- 3 matching boxes

SUBSECTION 1B.PIC (COLOUR PICTOGRAM–COLOUR PICTOGRAM)

✋ If the evaluation starts here **and** during the first evaluation of this subsection, or if **1C.WTC** was evaluated previously	↩ 1A.OBJ if 1B.PIC ≤ 8/9
✋ 1B.PHO = 0 **and** 1B.PIC = 0 **and** 1A.OBJ ≤ 8/18	✏ "Scoring Part 2: Table 6" + "Scoring Part 3: Table 12" ▶ 4C
✋ 1B.PHO = 0 **and** 1B.PIC = 0 **and** 1A.OBJ ≥ 10/18	✏ "Scoring Part 1: Tables 1 and 2" ▶

CATEGORY	ORDER OF VISUAL SUPPORTS ON MATCHING BOXES	DEMOS AND SCORING—IF EVALUATION STARTS HERE (or if 1C.WTC was evaluated previously)	SCORING— IF IB.PHO WAS EVALUATED PREVIOUSLY	COMMENTS AND OBSERVATIONS
Home	Toothbrush Sock Lego	1 opt. demo/ support /3	/3	
Work/School	Spoon Pencil Disc	1 opt. demo/ support /3	/3	
Other	Ball Marker Sponge	1 opt. demo/ support /3	/3 ☐ Other not evaluated (3/3)	
	TOTAL	/9	/9	
	TOTAL 1B.PIC (highest score if subsection evaluated twice)	/9	☐ 1B.PIC not evaluated (0/9 or 9/9)	

Schedule Evaluation Protocol B11

SUBSECTION 1B.BWP (BLACK-AND-WHITE PICTOGRAM–BLACK-AND-WHITE PICTOGRAM)

✋ 1B.PIC = 0 **and** 1B.BWP = 0   ➡ 1C

CATEGORY	ORDER OF VISUAL SUPPORTS ON MATCHING BOXES	SCORING	COMMENTS AND OBSERVATIONS
Home	Toothbrush Sock Lego	/3	
Work/School	Spoon Pencil Disc	/3	
Other	Ball Marker Sponge	/3	☐ Other not evaluated (3/3)
	TOTAL 1B.BWP	/9	☐ 1B.BWP not evaluated (0/9 or 9/9)

SUBSECTION 1B.WTC (WORDS TYPED ON THE COMPUTER–WORDS TYPED ON THE COMPUTER)

✋ 1B.WTC = 0   ➡ 1C

CATEGORY	ORDER OF VISUAL SUPPORTS ON MATCHING BOXES	SCORING	COMMENTS AND OBSERVATIONS
Home	Toothbrush Sock Lego	/3	
Work/School	Spoon Pencil Disc	/3	
Other	Ball Marker Sponge	/3	☐ Other not evaluated (3/3)
	TOTAL 1B.WTC	/9	☐ 1B.WTC not evaluated (0/9 or 9/9)

SUBSECTION 1B.WWH (WORDS WRITTEN BY HAND–WORDS WRITTEN BY HAND)			
CATEGORY	ORDER OF VISUAL SUPPORTS ON MATCHING BOXES	SCORING	COMMENTS AND OBSERVATIONS
Home	Toothbrush Sock Lego	/3	
Work/School	Spoon Pencil Disc	/3	
Other	Ball Marker Sponge	/3	☐ Other not evaluated (3/3)
	TOTAL 1B.WWH	/9	☐ 1B.WWH not evaluated (0/9 or 9/9)

SECTION 1C

- Bag 1C (visual supports mounted on matching boxes)
- Filing box 1B + 1C (visual supports handed to user)
- Bottom panel and back panel
- 3 matching boxes

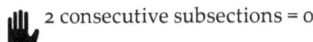 2 consecutive subsections = 0

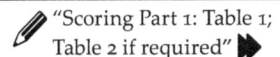 "Scoring Part 1: Table 1; Table 2 if required"

SUBSECTION 1C.PHO (PHOTO–OBJECT)

CATEGORY	DEMOS	ORDER OF VISUAL SUPPORTS ON MATCHING BOXES	SCORING	COMMENTS AND OBSERVATIONS
Home	1 opt. demo/support	Toothbrush Sock Lego	/3	
Work/School	1 opt. demo/support	Spoon Pencil Disc	/3	
Other	1 opt. demo/support	Ball Marker Sponge	/3	☐ Other not evaluated (3/3)
		TOTAL 1C.PHO	/9	☐ 1C.PHO not evaluated (0/9 or 9/9)

SUBSECTION 1C.PIC (COLOUR PICTOGRAM–OBJECT)

CATEGORY	ORDER OF VISUAL SUPPORTS ON MATCHING BOXES	SCORING	COMMENTS AND OBSERVATIONS
Home	Toothbrush Sock Lego	/3	
Work/School	Spoon Pencil Disc	/3	
Other	Ball Marker Sponge	/3	☐ Other not evaluated (3/3)
	TOTAL 1C.PIC	/9	☐ 1C.PIC not evaluated (0/9 or 9/9)

SUBSECTION 1C.BWP (BLACK-AND-WHITE PICTOGRAM–OBJECT)			
CATEGORY	ORDER OF VISUAL SUPPORTS ON MATCHING BOXES	SCORING	COMMENTS AND OBSERVATIONS
Home	Toothbrush Sock Lego	/3	
Work/School	Spoon Pencil Disc	/3	
Other	Ball Marker Sponge	/3	☐ Other not evaluated (3/3)
TOTAL 1C.BWP		/9	☐ 1C.BWP not evaluated (0/9 or 9/9)

▶ START THE EVALUATION HERE

Only if the user has functional reading skills.

- Bag 1C (visual supports mounted on matching boxes)
- Filing box 1B + 1C (visual supports handed to the user)
- Bottom panel and back panel
- 3 matching boxes

SUBSECTION 1C.WTC (WORDS TYPED ON THE COMPUTER–OBJECT)	
✋ If the evaluation starts here and during the first evaluation only	↻ 1B.PIC if 1C.WTC ≤ 8/9
✋ 1B.WTC = 0 **and** 1B.WWH = 0	✏ "Scoring Part 1: Table 1; Table 2 if required" ▶
✋ 1C.BWP = 0 **and** 1C.WTC = 0	✏ "Scoring Part 1: Table 1; Table 2 if required" ▶

CATEGORY	ORDER OF VISUAL SUPPORTS ON MATCHING BOXES	DEMOS AND SCORING—IF EVALUATION STARTS HERE	SCORING— IF 1C.BWP WAS EVALUATED PREVIOUSLY	COMMENTS AND OBSERVATIONS
Home	Toothbrush Sock Lego	1 opt. demo/ support /3	/3	
Work/School	Spoon Pencil Disc	1 opt. demo/ support /3	/3	
Other	Ball Marker Sponge	1 opt. demo/ support /3	/3 ☐ Other not evaluated (3/3)	
	TOTAL	/9	/9	
	TOTAL 1C.WTC (highest score if subsection evaluated twice)	/9	☐ 1C.WTC not evaluated (0/9)	

SUBSECTION 1C.WWH (WORDS WRITTEN BY HAND–OBJECT)			
CATEGORY	ORDER OF VISUAL SUPPORTS ON MATCHING BOXES	SCORING	COMMENTS AND OBSERVATIONS
Home	Toothbrush Sock Lego	/3	
Work/School	Spoon Pencil Disc	/3	
Other	Ball Marker Sponge	/3	☐ Other not evaluated (3/3)
	TOTAL 1C.WWH	/9	☐ 1C.WWH not evaluated (0/9)

SCORING PART 1

TABLE 1. RESULTS FOR PART 1

Record the results obtained for each visual support form in the different subsections of Part 1, then fill in the "Subtotal" and "Total" columns.

	Visual Support Form	Section 1A	Section 1B	Section 1C	Subtotal	Divide by	Total (round off to the nearest whole number)
Top ↑	OBJ	/18			/18	÷ 3	/6
	PHO		/9	/9	/18	÷ 3	/6
	PIC		/9	/9	/18	÷ 3	/6
	BWP		/9	/9	/18	÷ 3	/6
	WTC		/9	/9	/18	÷ 3	/6
Bottom	WWH		/9	/9	/18	÷ 3	/6

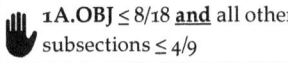 1A.OBJ ≤ 8/18 **and** all other subsections ≤ 4/9

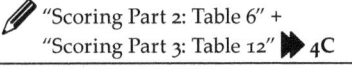 "Scoring Part 2: Table 6" + "Scoring Part 3: Table 12" ▶ 4C

In all other cases, follow the scoring standards for Part 1 (Table 2)

TABLE 2. SCORING PART 1

Follow the scoring standards for Part 1 **from top to bottom** and fill in the "Visual Supports Selected for the Evaluation of Part 2" column

SCORING STANDARDS FOR PART 1	VISUAL SUPPORTS SELECTED FOR THE EVALUATION OF PART 2
1. In Table 1, going **from bottom to top**, circle the first two highest scores in the "Total" column. Exception: If five scores out of six are 0, circle the one score greater than 0 as well as the visual support form located the **closest to the top** that received a score of 0.	Visual Support Form 1 (the **closest to the top** in the "Visual Support Form" column in Table 1):
2. From these two circled visual support forms, take the one closest to the top in the "Visual Support Form" column in Table 1 and enter it into the "Visual Support Form 1" box in the right hand column of this table.	Visual Support Form 2 (the **closest to the bottom** in the "Visual Support Form" column of Table 1):

*See remaining instructions (3 and 4) on the next page.

3. From these two circled visual support forms, take the one closest to the bottom in the "Visual Support Form" column in Table 1 and enter it into the "Visual Support Form 2" box in the right hand column of this table. 4. If Visual Support Forms 1 and 2 are not located directly one above the other in the "Visual Support Form" column in Table 1, enter one of the following in the "Visual Support Form 3" box in the right hand column of this table: 　a) The visual support form located **between** the two if there is only one 　b) The visual support form with the highest score if there is more than one 　c) If the scores are the same, the visual support form located closest to Visual Support Form 1 in the "Visual Support Form" column of Table 1	Visual Support Form 3 (**between** Support Form 1 and Support Form 2 in the "Visual Support Form" column of Table 1):

PART 2

Referring to Table 2 on p. B17, write down the visual support forms selected in the "VISUAL SUPPORT FORM 1," "VISUAL SUPPORT FORM 2," and, if applicable, "VISUAL SUPPORT FORM 3" boxes.

Choose the category to evaluate and fill in Table 3.

TABLE 3. LOCATION OF VISUAL SUPPORTS		
CHECK THE CATEGORY BEING EVALUATED	VISUAL SUPPORTS	WRITE DOWN THE VISUAL SUPPORT LOCATIONS (only for the category being evaluated)
☐ Home	Toothbrush	L1:
	Sock	L2:
	Lego	L3:
☐ Work/School	Spoon	L1:
	Pencil	L2:
	Disc	L3:
☐ Other	Ball	L1:
	Marker	L2:
	Sponge	L3:

- Filing box 2–3 + 3H (for the category evaluated)
- If one of the forms of visual supports being evaluated is OBJ: 1 object bag (for the category evaluated)
- 3 matching boxes
- Examiner's tray (optional)
- Blue mounting putty (optional)

VISUAL SUPPORT FORM 1

✋ Subtotal for attempts 1 to 6 for Visual Support Form 1 = 0/6	✏️ "Subtotal attempts 7 to 9" + "Total Visual Support Form 1" + "Scoring Part 2: Tables 4, 5, and 6" + "Scoring Part 3: Table 12" ▶ 4C
✋ Total for Visual Support Form 1 ≤ 3/9	✏️ "Scoring Part 2: Tables 4, 5, and 6" + "Scoring Part 3: Table 12" ▶ 4C

ACTIONS DONE BY USER (6 attempts, 2 trips per location)	DEMOS	1	2	3	4	5	6	SUBTOTAL ATTEMPTS 1 TO 6
The user takes the visual support.	2 demos/ location 1 mand. + 1 opt.							Not scored
The user walks and drops the visual support in the correct box.	2 demos/ location 1 mand. + 1 opt.	/1	/1	/1	/1	/1	/1	/6

⚠️ *Note: Visual Support Form 1 is the only one for which a second demonstration is allowed.*

⚠️ *Note: Collect the visual supports from the matching boxes and put them back in order before continuing with attempts 7 to 9 (if required).*

ACTIONS DONE BY USER (3 attempts, 1 trip per location)	7	8	9	SUBTOTAL ATTEMPTS 7 TO 9	TOTAL VISUAL SUPPORT FORM 1
The user takes the visual support.				Not scored	Not scored
The user walks and drops the visual support in the correct box.	/1	/1	/1	/3 ☐ Not evaluated (0/3 or 3/3)	/9

VISUAL SUPPORT FORM 2

🖐 Subtotal for attempts 1 to 6 for Visual Support Form 2 = 0/6	✏️ "Subtotal attempts 7 to 9" + "Total Visual Support Form 2" ▶ If no Visual Support Form 3 was selected, "Scoring Part 2: Tables 4, 5, and 6" ▶
🖐 Total for Visual Support Form 2 ≥ 7/9	✏️ "Scoring Part 2: Tables 4, 5, and 6" ▶

ACTIONS DONE BY USER (6 attempts, 2 trips per location)	DEMOS	1	2	3	4	5	6	SUBTOTAL ATTEMPTS 1 TO 6
The user takes the visual support.	1 mand. demo/ location							Not scored
The user walks and drops the visual support in the correct box.	1 mand. demo/ location	/1	/1	/1	/1	/1	/1	/6

ACTIONS DONE BY USER (3 attempts, 1 trip per location)	7	8	9	SUBTOTAL ATTEMPTS 7 TO 9	TOTAL VISUAL SUPPORT FORM 2
The user takes the visual support.				Not scored	Not scored
The user walks and drops the visual support in the correct box.	/1	/1	/1	/3 ☐ Not evaluated (0/3 or 3/3)	/9

VISUAL SUPPORT FORM 3

✋ Subtotal for attempts 1 to 6 for Visual Support Form 3 = 0/6

✏️ "Subtotal attempts 7 to 9" + "Total Visual Support Form 3" + "Scoring Part 2: Tables 4, 5, and 6" ▶

ACTIONS DONE BY USER (6 attempts, 2 trips per location)	DEMOS	1	2	3	4	5	6	SUBTOTAL ATTEMPTS 1 TO 6
The user takes the visual support.	1 mand. demo/location							Not scored
The user walks and drops the visual support in the correct box.	1 mand. demo/location	/1	/1	/1	/1	/1	/1	/6

ACTIONS DONE BY USER (3 attempts, 1 trip per location)	7	8	9	SUBTOTAL ATTEMPTS 7 TO 9	TOTAL VISUAL SUPPORT FORM 3
The user takes the visual support.				Not scored	Not scored
The user walks and drops the visual support in the correct box.	/1	/1	/1	/3 ☐ Not evaluated (0/3 or 3/3)	/9

Schedule Evaluation Protocol B23

SCORING PART 2

TABLE 4. RESULTS FOR PART 1 (TOTALS ONLY)

Copy results from Part 1, Table 1 on p. B17 ("Total" column only)

	VISUAL SUPPORT FORM	TOTAL (round off to the nearest whole number)
Top ↑ Bottom	OBJ	/6
	PHO	/6
	PIC	/6
	BWP	/6
	WTC	/6
	WWH	/6

TABLE 5. RESULTS FOR PART 2

Copy the visual support forms selected for the evaluation of Part 2 (Table 2, p. B17) in the "Visual Support Forms" column. Then, write down the results of Part 2 referring to each form of visual support evaluated and check "not evaluated" if applicable.

	VISUAL SUPPORT FORMS	TOTAL
VISUAL SUPPORT FORM 1		/9
VISUAL SUPPORT FORM 2		/9 or ☐ not evaluated
VISUAL SUPPORT FORM 3 (IF APPLICABLE)		/9 or ☐ not evaluated

TABLE 6. SCORING PART 2

Follow the scoring standards for Part 2 **from top to bottom**. The highest standard in the list corresponding to the user's results is the right one for the user; check it in the "Visual Support Form Selected ❶" column.

SCORING STANDARDS FOR PART 2	VISUAL SUPPORT FORM SELECTED ❶
1. If Part 2 was not evaluated because of stop standards, check OBJ-U. 2. Check the visual support form located **closest to the bottom** with a score of 7/9 or higher in Table 5. 3. Check the visual support form located **closest to the bottom** with a score of 5/6 or higher in Table 4. 4. Check OBJ-U in all other cases.	☐ OBJ-U (objects used in activities) ✋✏ "Scoring Part 3: Table 12" ▶ 4C ☐ OBJ (objects representing the activities) ☐ PHO (photos) ☐ PIC (colour pictograms) ☐ BWP (black-and-white pictograms) ☐ WTC (words typed on the computer) ☐ WWH (words written by hand)

✋ Total (Table 5) Visual Support Forms 1, 2, <u>and</u> 3 (only visual support forms evaluated) ≤ 5/9   ✏ "Scoring Part 3: Table 12" ▶ 4C

PART 3

SECTION 3A
SCHEDULE DISPLAYED ON THE WALL

| If the form of visual support selected (❶ in Table 6, p. B23) is OBJ:
☐ 3 matching boxes
☐ 1 object bag (same category as in Part 2)
☐ Piggy bank and coins[1]
☐ Schedule strip
☐ Blue mounting putty
☐ Examiner's tray (optional) | **OR** | If the form of visual support selected (❶ in Table 6, p. B23) is not OBJ:
☐ 3 matching boxes
☐ Schedule cue box
☐ Filing box 2–3 + 3H (same category as in Part 2)
☐ Schedule strip
☐ Blue mounting putty
☐ Examiner's tray (optional) |

Location of schedule strip on a wall (individualized location):

---

1. As specified in Appendix 1 (p. B89), you can use a small plastic container and poker chips here instead of a piggy bank and coins. To simplify the text, the terms "piggy bank" and "coins" will be used in Part 3.

3A.1 ONE VISUAL SUPPORT ON THE SCHEDULE STRIP

✋ 3 scores of 0 on the same action in 3A.1

✏️ "Subtotal **3A.1** attempts 4 to 6" + "Total **3A.1**" + "Scoring Part 3: Tables 10, 11, and 12" ▶ 4C

ACTIONS DONE BY USER	DEMOS	ATTEMPT 1
* The user takes the schedule cue, goes to the schedule strip, and drops the cue in the schedule cue box.	1 mand. demo	Not scored
The user takes the visual support from the schedule strip.	1 mand. demo	/1
The user walks and drops the visual support into the correct box.	1 opt. demo	/1

(!) **Note:** *For the OBJ visual support form, the text preceded by an asterisk in all tables should read as follows: "The user takes the coin, goes to the schedule strip, and drops the coin in the piggy bank."*

ACTIONS DONE BY USER	DEMOS	ATTEMPT 2
* The user takes the schedule cue, goes to the schedule strip, and drops the cue in the schedule cue box.	1 mand. demo	Not scored
The user takes the visual support from the schedule strip.	1 mand. demo	/1
The user walks and drops the visual support into the correct box.	1 opt. demo	/1

ACTIONS DONE BY USER	DEMOS	ATTEMPT 3	SUBTOTAL 3A.1 ATTEMPTS 1 to 3
* The user takes the schedule cue, goes to the schedule strip, and drops the cue in the schedule cue box.	1 mand. demo	Not scored	Not scored
The user takes the visual support from the schedule strip.	1 mand. demo	/1	/3
The user walks and drops the visual support into the correct box.	1 opt. demo	/1	/3

ACTIONS DONE BY USER	ATTEMPT 4
* The user takes the schedule cue, goes to the schedule strip, and drops the cue in the schedule cue box.	Not scored
The user takes the visual support from the schedule strip.	/1
The user walks and drops the visual support into the correct box.	/1

ACTIONS DONE BY USER	ATTEMPT 5
* The user takes the schedule cue, goes to the schedule strip, and drops the cue in the schedule cue box.	Not scored
The user takes the visual support from the schedule strip.	/1
The user walks and drops the visual support into the correct box.	/1

ACTIONS DONE BY USER	ATTEMPT 6	SUBTOTAL 3A.1 ATTEMPTS 4 to 6
* The user takes the schedule cue, goes to the schedule strip, and drops the cue in the schedule cue box.	Not scored	Not scored
The user takes the visual support from the schedule strip.	/1	/3 ☐ Not evaluated (0/3 or 3/3)
The user walks and drops the visual support into the correct box.	/1	/3 ☐ Not evaluated (0/3 or 3/3)

ACTIONS DONE BY USER–TOTAL	TOTAL 3A.1
* The user takes the schedule cue, goes to the schedule strip, and drops the cue in the schedule cue box.	Not scored
The user takes the visual support from the schedule strip.	/6
The user walks and drops the visual support into the correct box.	/6

3A.2 THREE VISUAL SUPPORTS ON THE SCHEDULE STRIP

(!) *Note: Collect the visual supports representing locations and put them back in order, and collect the schedule cues before evaluating Subsection 3A.2.*

✋ 3 scores of 0 on the same action in 3A.2	✏️ "**Subtotal 3A.2** attempts 4 to 6" + "Total **3A.2**" + "Scoring Part 3: Tables 10, 11, and 12" ▶

ACTIONS DONE BY USER (3 attempts, 1 trip per location)	DEMOS	1	2	3	SUBTOTAL 3A.2 ATTEMPTS 1 TO 3
* The user takes the schedule cue, goes to the schedule strip, and drops the cue in the schedule cue box.	1 mand. demo/ location				Not scored
The user takes the top visual support from the schedule strip.	1 mand. demo/ location	/1	/1	/1	/3
The user walks and drops the visual support into the correct box.	1 opt. demo/ location	/1	/1	/1	/3

ACTIONS DONE BY USER (3 attempts, 1 trip per location)	4	5	6	SUBTOTAL 3A.2 ATTEMPTS 4 TO 6	TOTAL 3A.2
* The user takes the schedule cue, goes to the schedule strip, and drops the cue in the schedule cue box.				Not scored	Not scored
The user takes the top visual support from the schedule strip.	/1	/1	/1	/3 ☐ Not evaluated (0/3 or 3/3)	/6
The user walks and drops the visual support into the correct box.	/1	/1	/1	/3 ☐ Not evaluated (0/3 or 3/3)	/6

3A.3 SIX VISUAL SUPPORTS ON THE SCHEDULE STRIP

(!) *Note: Collect the visual supports representing locations and put them back in order, and collect the schedule cues before evaluating Subsection 3A.3.*

2 scores of 0 on the same action in 3A.3			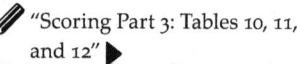 "Total **3A.3**" + "Scoring Part 3: Tables 10, 11, and 12" ▶				
ACTIONS DONE BY USER (6 attempts, 2 trips per location)	1	2	3	4	5	6	**TOTAL 3A.3**
* The user takes the schedule cue, goes to the schedule strip, and drops the cue in the schedule cue box.							Not scored
The user takes the top visual support from the schedule strip.	/1	/1	/1	/1	/1	/1	/6
The user walks and drops the visual support into the correct box.	/1	/1	/1	/1	/1	/1	/6

✋ Form of visual support selected (❶ in Table 6) is not **WTC** or **WWH** or 3A.3 ≤ 4/6 for one of the two evaluated actions.	✏ "Scoring Part 3: Tables 10, 11, and 12" ▶

TABLE 7. RESULTS FOR SECTION 3A

Record results for Section 3A by referring to each subsection.

ACTIONS DONE BY USER	3A.1	3A.2	3A.3
The user takes the [top] visual support from the schedule strip.	/6	/6	/6
The user walks and drops the visual support into the correct box.	/6	/6	/6

SECTION 3B
TOKEN OR CHECKMARK SCHEDULE

(!) **Note:** Only evaluate Section **3B** if the form of visual support selected (●) when scoring Part 2 (see Table 6, p. B23) is **WTC** or **WWH**, Subsection **3A.3** was evaluated, and the user scored 5/6 or higher on two actions in that subsection (see Table 7, p. B28).

Indicate the visual support form, category, and type of schedule being evaluated. Indicate the locations of the schedule and triage station and fill in Table 8 on p. B30.

Form of visual support selected (● in Table 6, p. B23)		
☐ WTC	☐ WWH	
Category chosen for Section 3B (different than the one used when evaluating Section 3A)		
☐ Home	☐ Work/School	☐ Other
Type of schedule evaluated		
☐ Choose the checkmark schedule if the user can write simple letters (to know whether they can, ask them to copy a word you write down on a piece of paper, for example on the verso of the Evaluation Protocol). ☐ Otherwise, choose the token schedule.		

	CHECKMARK SCHEDULE			**TOKEN SCHEDULE**
🛠️	☐ Three "Checkmark Schedule" sheets for the category and visual support form evaluated from the envelope labelled "Token and Checkmark Schedule Sheets" ☐ Filing box 2–3 + 3H (corresponding to the category chosen for 3B) ☐ One object bag (corresponding to the category chosen for 3B) ☐ Bottom and back panels ☐ Three matching boxes ☐ Three 3B baskets: baskets for objects ☐ Non-permanent marker ☐ Examiner's tray (optional) ☐ Blue mounting putty	OR	🛠️	☐ Three "Token Schedule" sheets for the category and visual support form evaluated from the envelope labelled "Token and Checkmark Schedule Sheets" ☐ Token box ☐ Filing box 2–3 + 3H (corresponding to the category chosen for 3B) ☐ One object bag (corresponding to the category chosen for 3B) ☐ Bottom and back panels ☐ Three matching boxes ☐ Three 3B baskets: baskets for objects ☐ Non-permanent marker ☐ Examiner's tray (optional) ☐ Blue mounting putty

Schedule location (different than the location of the schedule sheet used during the evaluation of 3A):

___

Location of triage station:

___

TABLE 8. LOCATION OF 3B BASKETS: OBJECT BASKETS (DIFFERENT THAN IN SECTION 3A)		
CHECK THE CATEGORY BEING EVALUATED	**VISUAL SUPPORTS**	**WRITE DOWN THE VISUAL SUPPORT LOCATIONS** (only for the category being evaluated)
☐ Home	Toothbrush	L1:
	Sock	L2:
	Lego	L3:
☐ Work/School	Spoon	L1:
	Pencil	L2:
	Disc	L3:
☐ Other	Ball	L1:
	Marker	L2:
	Sponge	L3:

Schedule Evaluation Protocol   B31

SUBSECTION 3B.1

✋ Subtotal **3B.1** ≤ 1/3 on one of the evaluated actions   ✏️ "Table 9" + "Scoring Part 3: Tables 10, 11, and 12" ▶

ACTIONS DONE BY USER (3 attempts, 1 trip per location)	SCHEDULE SHEET				SUBTOTAL 3B.1
	3B.1: DEMOS	3B.1: 3 ATTEMPTS			
		1	2	3	
The user reads the correct word on the schedule sheet and walks to the location where the object indicated is located. *Note: For the action "The user reads the correct word on the schedule sheet," the examiner will assume that the user has read the correct word, unless they remain motionless in front of the schedule or go to a different location than the one indicated on the schedule.*	1 mand. demo/ location	/1	/1	/1	/3
The user takes the object from this location, brings it to the triage station, and drops it into the corresponding box.	1 mand. demo/ location	/1	/1	/1	/3
The user heads back to their schedule.	1 mand. demo/ location	/1	/1	/1	/3
The user writes an X or checkmark in the circle to the right of the word corresponding to the object they just matched *or* places a token to the right of the word (showing that they have completed the task).	1 mand. demo/ location	/1	/1	/1	/3

⓵ **Note:** *When a new schedule sheet is used (3B.1: Demos and 3B.1: 3 Attempts), the examiner must communicate to the user that they need to go consult their schedule (not scored) only for the first word.*

SUBSECTION 3B.2

✋ 2 scores of 0 for the same action in **3B.2** ✏️ "Table 9" + "Scoring Part 3: Tables 10, 11, and 12" ▶

ACTIONS DONE BY USER (6 attempts, 2 trips per location)	SCHEDULE SHEETS 3B.2: 6 ATTEMPTS						SUBTOTAL 3B.2
	1	2	3	4	5	6	
The user reads the correct word on the schedule sheet and heads to the location where the object indicated is located. *Note: For the action "The user reads the correct word on the schedule sheet," the examiner will assume that the user has read the correct word, unless they remain motionless in front of the schedule or go to a different location than the one indicated on the schedule.*	/1	/1	/1	/1	/1	/1	/6
The user takes the object from this location, brings it to the triage station, and drops it into the corresponding box.	/1	/1	/1	/1	/1	/1	/6
The user heads back to their schedule.	/1	/1	/1	/1	/1	/1	/6
The user writes an X or checkmark in the circle to the right of the word corresponding to the object they just matched *or* places a token to the right of the word (showing that they have completed the task).	/1	/1	/1	/1	/1	/1	/6

❗ *Note: When a new schedule sheet is used (3B.2: 6 Attempts) the examiner must communicate to the user that they need to go consult their schedule (not scored) only for the first word.*

TABLE 9. RESULTS FOR SECTION 3B

Record the results for Section 3B by referring to each subsection and checking "not evaluated" if applicable.

ACTIONS DONE BY THE USER	SUBTOTAL 3B.1	SUBTOTAL 3B.2	TOTAL 3B (3B.1 + 3B.2)
The user reads the correct word on the schedule sheet and heads to the location where the object indicated is located.	/3	/6 or ☐ 3B.2 not evaluated (0/6)	/9
The user takes the object from this location, brings it to the triage station, and drops it into the corresponding box.	/3	/6 or ☐ 3B.2 not evaluated (0/6)	/9
The user heads back to their schedule.	/3	/6 or ☐ 3B.2 not evaluated (0/6)	/9
The user writes an X or checkmark in the circle to the right of the word corresponding to the object they just matched *or* places a token to the right of the word (showing that they have completed the task).	/3	/6 or ☐ 3B.2 not evaluated (0/6)	/9

SCORING PART 3

TABLE 10. RESULTS FOR SECTION 3A

If Table 7 (p. B28) was already filled in, copy the results for Section 3A. Otherwise, record results for Section 3A by referring to each subsection and checking "not evaluated" if applicable.

ACTIONS DONE BY USER	3A.1	3A.2	3A.3
The user takes the [top] visual support from the schedule strip.	/6	/6 or ☐ not evaluated (0/6)	/6 or ☐ not evaluated (0/6)
The user walks and drops the visual support into the correct box.	/6	/6 or ☐ not evaluated (0/6)	/6 or ☐ not evaluated (0/6)

TABLE 11. RESULTS FOR SECTION 3B

If Table 9 (p. B33) was already filled in, copy the results for Section 3B. Otherwise, record the results for Section 3B by referring to each subsection and checking "not evaluated" if applicable.

ACTIONS DONE BY USER	SUBTOTAL 3B.1	SUBTOTAL 3B.2	TOTAL 3B (3B.1 + 3B.2)
The user reads the correct word on the schedule sheet and heads to the location where the object indicated is located.	/3	/6 or ☐ 3B.2 not evaluated (0/6)	/9 or ☐ 3B not evaluated (0/9)
The user takes the object from this location, brings it to the triage station, and drops it into the corresponding box.	/3	/6 or ☐ 3B.2 not evaluated (0/6)	/9 or ☐ 3B not evaluated (0/9)
The user heads back to their schedule.	/3	/6 or ☐ 3B.2 not evaluated (0/6)	/9 or ☐ 3B not evaluated (0/9)
The user writes an X or a checkmark in the circle to the right of the word corresponding to the object they just matched *or* places a token to the right of the word (showing that they have completed the task).	/3	/6 or ☐ 3B.2 not evaluated (0/6)	/9 or ☐ 3B not evaluated (0/9)

TABLE 12. SCORING PART 3

Follow the scoring standards for Part 3 from **top to bottom.** The highest standard on the list corresponding to the user's results is the proper score for them. Check this off in the "Characteristics" column.

SCORING STANDARDS FOR PART 3	CHARACTERISTICS
❶ FORM OF VISUAL SUPPORT	
1. Check the form of visual support selected (❶) at the end of Part 2 (Table 6, p. B23).	☐ OBJ-U (objects used in activities) ☐ OBJ (objects representing activities) ☐ PHO (photos) ☐ PIC (colour pictograms) ☐ BWP (black-and-white pictograms) ☐ WTC (words typed on the computer) ☐ WWH (words written by hand)
❷ PRESENTATION MODE	
1. If Part 3 was not evaluated because of a stop standard, check A. 2. If one of the two evaluated actions in **3A.1** is ≤ 3/6, check A. 3. If the four actions evaluated in 3B ≥ 8/9, check B-2. 4. In all other cases, check B-1.	☐ A) The educator hands the user a visual support before each activity. ☐ B) Stationary schedule displayed on: 　☐ 1) The wall; 　☐ 2) A table.
❸ MANIPULATION	
1. If the form of visual support (❶) is OBJ-U, check A-1. 2. If the four actions evaluated in 3B ≥ 8/9 **and** the token schedule was evaluated (because the user cannot write checkmarks), check B. 3. If the four actions evaluated in 3B ≥ 8/9 **and** the checkmark schedule was evaluated, check C. 4. In all other cases, including if Part 3 was not evaluated because of a stop standard, check A-2.	☐ A) Moves around with the visual support: 　☐ 1) Uses the object in the activity. 　☐ 2) Drops the visual support into a container where the activity takes place (box, envelope, etc.). ☐ B) Adds a token at the end of the activity. ☐ C) Writes an X or a checkmark at the end of the activity.

TABLE 12. SCORING PART 3 (*continued*)

❺ IDENTIFICATION

1. If A was checked for Presentation Mode (❷), check A.
2. If the two actions evaluated in **3A.3** ≥ 5/6 and the form of visual support (❶) is WTC or WWH, check B.
3. In all other cases, check C.

☐ A) Not applicable as the user does not go to their schedule on their own (the educator hands them a visual support before each transition, indicating what the next activity is).
☐ B) User's name.
☐ C) Visual cue related to the user's interests.
Note: Specifications regarding the cue related to the user's interests will be provided in Part 4 (Section 4A) of the evaluation.

❻ INITIATION

1. If A was checked for Presentation Mode (❷), check A.
2. If the form of visual support (❶) is OBJ, check B-1.
3. If B or C was checked for Manipulation (❽), check D-1.
4. If the two actions evaluated at **3A.3** ≥ 5/6 **and** the form of visual support (❶) is WTC or WWH, check C-1.
5. In all other cases, check C-2.

☐ A) The user does not go to their schedule on their own; the educator hands them a visual support before each transition, indicating what the next activity is.
☐ B) The user is handed a visual cue in object form indicating they need to go consult their schedule.
　☐ 1. This object should be integratable or the user should be able to insert it into a container (e.g., a piggy bank, stackable baskets, interlocking Mega Bloks, etc.).
☐ C) The user is handed a 2D visual cue (other than object form) indicating they need to go consult their schedule.
　☐ 1. The word "schedule" written in the recommended form (❶).
　☐ 2. The same cue used to identify the schedule, which is related to the user's interests.
　Note: Specifications regarding the cue related to the user's interests will be provided in Part 4 (Section 4A) of the evaluation.
☐ D) The user goes to consult their schedule on their own without a cue.
　☐ 1. They have access to tools that help them recognize when an activity is finished (e.g., a timer, a visual cue at the end of the activity, a sequence or list with a cue indicating to return to their schedule at the end of the activity, etc.).

TABLE 12. SCORING PART 3 (continued)

❼ LENGTH

1. If the four actions evaluated in 3B ≥ 8/9, check D.
2. If the two actions evaluated in 3A.3 ≥ 5/6, check C.
3. If the two actions evaluated in 3A.2 ≥ 4/6, check B.
4. In all other cases, including if Part 3 was not evaluated because of a stop standard, check A.

- ☐ A) 1 visual support at a time
- ☐ B) 3 visual supports at a time
- ☐ C) ½ day
- ☐ D) Full day

❽ LOCATION

1. If A was checked for Presentation Mode (❷), check A.
2. If the two actions evaluated in 3A.3 ≥ 5/6 **and** other users have visual schedules displayed in the group transition area, check B and specify the group transition area in the space provided (*except* if this location is deemed irrelevant for the person evaluated).
3. In all other cases, check C.

- ☐ A) Not applicable as the user does not go to their schedule on their own (the educator hands them a visual support before each transition, indicating what the next activity is).
- ☐ B) Group transition area.
- ☐ C) Individualized location (e.g., the user's bedroom, workplace, etc.).
  Note: Specifications on the individualized location will be provided in Part 4 (Section 4B) of the evaluation.

❾ LAYOUT

1. If A was checked for Presentation Mode (❷), check A.
2. In all other cases, check B.

- ☐ A) Not applicable as the user does not go to their schedule on their own (the educator hands them a visual support before each transition, indicating what the next activity is).
- ☐ B) From top to bottom.

PART 4

SECTION 4A
IDENTIFYING THE SCHEDULE WITH A CUE RELATED TO THE USER'S INTERESTS

(!) **Note:** *Only evaluate Section 4A if C was checked for "Identification" (**5**) when scoring Part 3 (Table 12, p. B35).*

IDENTIFY THE USER'S INTERESTS OR FIELDS OF INTEREST

SPECIFY OBJECTS, PHOTOS, OR IMAGES THE USER PARTICULARLY LIKES (THEY MAY OR MAY NOT BE A PART OF THE INTERESTS DESCRIBED ABOVE).

OBJECTS	PHOTOS	IMAGES

5 IDENTIFICATION

Scoring Standard:
Based on the previous information, specify the visual cue that relates to the user's interests and that is recommended to identify their schedule.

C) Visual cue related to the user's interests:

_____

(!) **Note:** *If C-2 was checked for "Initiation" (**6**) when scoring Part 3 (Table 12, p. B35), it is important that the visual cue chosen is suitable, as it will need to be transportable and available in several copies.*

SECTION 4B
IDENTIFYING AN INDIVIDUALIZED LOCATION

(!) *Note: Only evaluate Section 4B if C was checked for "Location" (❸) when scoring Part 3 (Table 12, p. B35).*

For questions 1 and 2, check the setting where the schedule will be implemented in the two tables below. Then only answer the questions for that setting.

1. WHERE DOES THE USER SPEND MOST OF THEIR TIME?		
☐ At home	☐ At school	☐ At work
☐ Their bedroom ☐ The living room ☐ The kitchen ☐ Other: _____	☐ At their desk ☐ In the play/leisure area ☐ Moves from one room to another ☐ Other: _____	☐ At their desk ☐ In the common room ☐ Moves from one room to another ☐ Other: _____

2. WHAT IS THE MOST CENTRAL LOCATION?		
☐ At home	☐ At school	☐ At work
☐ The hallway ☐ The living room ☐ The kitchen ☐ Other: _____	☐ At their desk ☐ In the play/leisure area ☐ Group transition area ☐ Other: _____	☐ The hallway ☐ The workshop ☐ The common room ☐ Other: _____

(!) *Note: Generally, choose a schedule location that is based on its functional qualities as they relate to the user's movements throughout the day. It can be the location where the user spends most of their time, a central location they pass frequently, etc. However, the examiner may recommend a different location than the one that meets these criteria because of certain considerations. Answer questions 3 and 4 to find the most suitable location.*

3. DOES ANOTHER PERSON IN THAT LOCATION behave in a way that limits the possible schedule locations or requires specific adaptations as the schedule would be accessible to them (e.g., a person who tends to remove anything stuck on the walls and for whom current interventions do not seem to be effective)? If yes, specify the behaviour, restrictions, and required adaptations as they relate to the schedule and its location.

4. ARE THERE ANY OTHER FACTORS that need to be considered regarding the individualized location of the user's schedule? If yes, please specify what they are and include any required adaptations in relation to the schedule and its location.

❸ LOCATION

Scoring standard:
According to the previous information, specify the recommendation for the individualized location.

C) Individualized location (e.g., user's bedroom, workplace, etc.):

SECTION 4C
SCHEDULE CONTENT (ACTIVITIES ON THE SCHEDULE AND REPRESENTATIVE VISUAL SUPPORTS)

1. Fill in the table for the setting (home, work, or school) by checking the box for the setting where the schedule will be implemented.
2. Then check all the user's daily activities in the table for that setting. Write down any other activity done by the user in the empty rows at the bottom of the table.
3. On a scale of 1 to 3, rate the user's interest in each activity:

    1 = not interested, 2 = somewhat interested, and 3 = very interested.

4. In the right-hand column of the table, indicate the representative visual support that will allow the user to identify the activity. To do this, circle the visual support in the "Suggestions for Visual Supports Representative of Activities" column if relevant for the user. Otherwise, write the recommendation down in the "Other Representative Visual Supports" column.

(!) *Note: Representative visual supports will be found in the schedule in the form recommended following the completion of this evaluation (see scoring of Part 3, Table 12, p. B35* ❶*). If a different form is recommended for a given visual support, it should be noted in the right-hand column.*

☐ HOME SETTING			
ACTIVITIES	LEVEL OF INTEREST	SUGGESTIONS FOR VISUAL SUPPORTS REPRESENTATIVE OF ACTIVITIES	OTHER REPRESENTATIVE VISUAL SUPPORTS
☐ Bath		Soap, washcloth, bubble bath container, etc.	
☐ Breakfast		Utensil (specify): _____ napkin, peanut butter jar, etc.	
☐ Walk		Coat, handbag, cap, etc.	
☐ Lunch		Utensil (specify): _____ napkin, plate, lunchbox, etc.	
☐ Dinner		Utensil (specify): _____ napkin, plate, etc.	
☐ Bedtime		Pyjamas, pillow, etc.	
☐ Brushing teeth		Toothbrush, toothpaste, etc.	
☐ Massage		Jar of cream, bottle of oil, etc.	
☐ Music		Radio, musical instrument, CD, etc.	
☐ Restaurant outing		Empty French fry container, brand logo, etc.	
☐ Transportation		Small car, taxi logo, etc.	
☐ Workshop		Picture of workshop, miniature table, etc.	
☐ Break		Empty soda can, empty juice box, CD, photo of place where user spends their break, mug, glass, etc.	
☐ Activities in the community		Park, sports, etc.	
☐ Other:			
☐ Other:			
☐ Other:			

☐ WORK SETTING			
ACTIVITIES	LEVEL OF INTEREST	SUGGESTIONS FOR VISUAL SUPPORTS REPRESENTATIVE OF ACTIVITIES	OTHER REPRESENTATIVE VISUAL SUPPORTS
☐ Lunch		Utensil (specify): _____ napkin, plate, lunchbox, etc.	
☐ Coffee		Mug, spoon, etc.	
☐ Snack		Glass, empty juice box, empty pop can, etc.	
☐ Music		Radio, musical instrument, CD, etc.	
☐ Transportation		Small car, taxi logo, etc.	
☐ Independent work		Photo of work desk, miniature desk, etc.	
☐ Break		Empty pop can, CD, photo of place where user spends their break, etc.	
☐ Bathroom		Roll of toilet paper, photo of bathroom, etc.	
☐ Walk		Coat, purse, cap, etc.	
☐ Movie		Photo of TV, DVD, etc.	
☐ Other:			
☐ Other:			
☐ Other:			
☐ Other:			
☐ Other:			
☐ Other:			
☐ Other:			

☐ SCHOOL SETTING			
ACTIVITIES	LEVEL OF INTEREST	SUGGESTIONS FOR VISUAL SUPPORTS REPRESENTATIVE OF ACTIVITIES	OTHER REPRESENTATIVE VISUAL SUPPORTS
☐ Lunch		Utensil (specify): _____ napkin, plate, lunchbox, etc.	
☐ Snack		Glass, empty juice box, empty pop can, etc.	
☐ Music		Radio, musical instrument, CD, etc.	
☐ Arts and crafts		Crayons, construction paper, glue stick, etc.	
☐ Transportation		Small car, taxi logo, etc.	
☐ Independent work		Photo of work desk, miniature desk, etc.	
☐ Break		Empty pop can, CD, photo of place where user spends their break, etc.	
☐ Bathroom		Roll of toilet paper, photo of bathroom, etc.	
☐ Walk		Coat, purse, cap, etc.	
☐ Recess		Ball, photo of schoolyard, etc.	
☐ Movie		Photo of TV, DVD, etc.	
☐ Learning		Photo of educator, pencil, etc.	
☐ Physical education		Sports clothing, sports equipment, etc.	
☐ Art		Photo of art teacher, paintbrush, musical instrument, etc.	
☐ After-school program		Photo of educator, favourite activity, etc.	
☐ Other:			
☐ Other:			
☐ Other:			

☐ Other:			
☐ Other:			
☐ Other:			
☐ Other:			

SCHEDULE EVALUATION TOOL

Johanne Mainville, Sonia Di Lillo,
Nathalie Poirier, and Nathalie Plante

RECOMMENDATIONS REPORT

NOMINATIVE DATA	
First name	
Last name	
Sex assigned at birth	☐ M ☐ F
Date of birth (DD/MM/YYYY)	/ /
Address	
Telephone number	

Table of Contents

Description of Person B49

Goal of Evaluation B49

Observations During Evaluation B49

Schedule Characteristics B50

Schedule Content B52

Procedures to Follow B53

Comments B53

DESCRIPTION OF PERSON

GOAL OF EVALUATION

OBSERVATIONS DURING EVALUATION

SCHEDULE CHARACTERISTICS

❶ VISUAL SUPPORT FORMS

- ☐ OBJ-U (Objects used in activities)
- ☐ OBJ (Objects representing activities)
- ☐ PHO (Photos)
- ☐ PIC (Colour pictograms)
- ☐ BWP (Black-and-white pictograms)
- ☐ WTC (Words typed on the computer)
- ☐ WWH (Words written by hand)
- ☐ Other: _____

❷ PRESENTATION MODE

- ☐ The educator hands the user a visual support before each activity.
- ☐ Stationary schedule displayed on:
  - ☐ The wall
  - ☐ A table
  - ☐ Other _____
- ☐ Portable schedule
- ☐ Other: _____

❸ LOCATION

- ☐ Individualized location: _____
- ☐ Group transition area
- ☐ Not applicable

❹ LAYOUT

- ☐ From top to bottom
- ☐ From left to right
- ☐ Not applicable

❺ IDENTIFICATION

- ☐ User's name
- ☐ Visual cue related to the user's interests: _____
- ☐ Other: _____
- ☐ Not applicable

❻ INITIATION

- ☐ The user does not go to their schedule on their own; the educator hands them a visual support before each transition indicating what the next activity is.
- ☐ The user is handed a visual cue in object form indicating they need to go consult their schedule. Specify the initiation cue:
  - ☐ This object should be integratable or the user should be able to insert it into a container (e.g., a piggy bank, stackable baskets, interlocking Mega Bloks, etc.).
  - ☐ Other: _____
- ☐ The user is handed a 2D visual cue (other than object form) indicating they need to go consult their schedule. Specify the initiation cue:
  - ☐ The word "schedule" written in the recommended form ❶.
  - ☐ The same cue used to identify the schedule, which is related to the user's interests.
  - ☐ Other: _____

	☐ The user takes the schedule cue on their own at the end of the activity and brings it with them as they consult their schedule. Specify the initiation cue: ☐ The word "schedule" written in the recommended form ❶. ☐ The same cue used to identify the schedule, which is related to the user's interests. ☐ Other: _____ ☐ The user goes to consult their schedule on their own without a cue. Specify: ☐ They have access to tools that help them recognize when an activity is finished (e.g., a timer, a visual cue at the end of the activity, a sequence or list with a cue indicating to return to their schedule at the end of the activity, etc.). ☐ They understand the activity is finished without any tools, by relying on natural cues. ☐ Other: _____ ☐ Other: _____
❼ LENGTH	**❽ MANIPULATION**
☐ 1 visual support at a time ☐ A sequence of ____ visual supports at a time ☐ ½ day ☐ Full day ☐ Other _____	☐ Moves around with the visual support: ☐ Uses the object in the activity. ☐ Drops the visual support into a container where the activity takes place (box, envelope, etc.). ☐ Other: _____ ☐ Removes the visual support and, at the end of the activity, drops it into a container labelled "Finished" placed beside the schedule. ☐ Turns the visual support over at the end of the activity. ☐ Adds a token at the end of the activity. ☐ Writes an X or a checkmark at the end of the activity. ☐ Other: _____

SCHEDULE CONTENT

(!) **Note:** *The representative visual support will be included in the schedule in the visual support form recommended above (unless otherwise specified).*

ACTIVITIES ON THE SCHEDULE	REPRESENTATIVE VISUAL SUPPORTS	BOX/ENVELOPE LOCATIONS

PROCEDURES TO FOLLOW

STEPS TO DO BY THE EDUCATOR	STEPS TO DO BY THE USER

COMMENTS:

(!) *Note: Make sure to regularly introduce variations into the daily sequence of activities.*

SIGNATURE	
Name of examiner	
Signature	
Date (DD/MM/YYYY)	/ /

SCHEDULE EVALUATION TOOL

Johanne Mainville, Sonia Di Lillo,
Nathalie Poirier, and Nathalie Plante

SCHEDULE ADJUSTMENT PROTOCOL

INFORMATION ON THE EVALUATED USER[1]	
First name	
Last name	
Sex assigned at birth	☐ M ☐ F
Date of birth (DD/MM/YYYY)	/ /
Visual problems (colour blindness, squinting, etc.)	☐ Yes Specify:
	☐ No
Place of residence	
Examiner	
Date of evaluation (DD/MM/YYYY)	/ /

---

[1] In this document, the term "user" refers to the person with autism spectrum disorder (ASD), and the term "educator" to the person who manages the user's schedule or helps them use it.

Table of Contents

List of Tables B57

PART 1 .... B58

Prerequisites for a Schedule Adjustment B58
Evaluate the Level of Independence for
the Current Schedule B58
Identify the Characteristic(s) to Adjust B59

PART 2 .... B63

Adjustment 1	Characteristics to Adjust: Visual Support Form and Schedule Manipulation B63
Adjustment 2	Characteristics to Adjust: Presentation Mode and Layout B65
Adjustment 3	Characteristics to Adjust: Schedule Length B67
Adjustment 4	Characteristics to Adjust: Schedule Identification and Location B69
Adjustment 5	Characteristics to Adjust: Initiation B71
Adjustment 6	Characteristics to Adjust: Initiation B73
Adjustment 7	Characteristics to Adjust: Initiation B75
Adjustment 8	Characteristics to Adjust: Schedule Manipulation B76
Adjustment 9	Characteristics to Adjust: Schedule Manipulation B78
Adjustment 10	Characteristics to Adjust: Schedule Manipulation B80
Adjustment 11	Characteristics to Adjust: Visual Support Form B81
Adjustment 12	Characteristics to Adjust: Presentation Mode B84

List of Tables

Table 1. Identification of Schedule
Characteristic(s) to Adjust B60

Table 2. Number of Visual Supports
to Add to the Schedule B68

PART 1

Prerequisites for a Schedule Adjustment

The schedule should only be adjusted if one of the following criteria is met:

- ☐ Following the schedule evaluation using the Schedule Evaluation Protocol,[2] the schedule was implemented according to the recommendations. After a week, the user was fully independent in using their schedule and has maintained this independence for at least a week.
  OR
- ☐ Following the adjustment of a schedule characteristic using the Adjustment Protocol, the user's level of independence was evaluated (as recommended in the "Independence Evaluation" step in the introduction and evaluation phases for each adjustment) and meets the different criteria for this step, regarding both their independence and the time to wait before introducing another adjustment.
  OR
- ☐ The user has been using their schedule independently for at least three months.

Evaluate the Level of Independence for the Current Schedule

To establish whether the user meets the independence prerequisites for a schedule adjustment, the examiner must fill in the Independence Evaluation Grid.

---

[2] Henceforth, this document will simply be referred to as the Evaluation Protocol.

Instructions:

- Fill in the Independence Evaluation Grid four times per day for three days, making sure to randomly evaluate different activities.
    a) If the user needed help to execute a step in their schedule, they are not considered fully independent.
    b) If the user executes all the steps on their own in the evaluation, they are considered fully independent. Identify which characteristic to adjust.

Identify the Characteristic(s) to Adjust

If the user meets the schedule adjustment prerequisites, consult Table 1 to identify which characteristic(s) to adjust based on the current characteristics and the intended goal. Once the characteristic has been identified, you must make sure the user meets the specific criteria for each adjustment in the "Prerequisites for This Adjustment" section, as it provides more detailed information and even some additions (which are not specified in Table 1).

Important: Take the notes indicated at the beginning of Table 1 into consideration (you can also consult a more detailed explanation in the SET Guide, on p. A128).

TABLE 1. IDENTIFICATION OF SCHEDULE CHARACTERISTIC(S) TO ADJUST

(!) Notes: Making more than one adjustment at a time is not recommended.
Adjustments follows a certain chronological logic. However, following this order is not required for all adjustments, only for the first three, which must be done before attempting any others.

	CURRENT SCHEDULE CHARACTERISTIC	INTENDED GOAL	CHARACTERISTIC(S) TO ADJUST	PAGE IN THE ADJUSTMENT PROTOCOL
Adjustment 1	☐ Uses OBJ-U visual support form (objects used in activities).	→ To use the OBJ visual support form (objects representing activities) and drop the visual supports into containers where the activities take place.	Visual support form and schedule manipulation	p. B63
Adjustment 2	☐ Before each activity, the educator hands the user a visual support representing the activity.	→ To display the schedule on the wall (from top to bottom).	Presentation mode and layout	p. B65
Adjustment 3	☐ The schedule is displayed on the wall, and you would like to increase the number of visual supports.	→ To increase the number of visual supports on the schedule.	Schedule length	p. B67
Adjustment 4	☐ The schedule is in an individualized location.	→ To move the schedule to a group transition area.	Schedule identification and location	p. B69
Adjustment 5	☐ At the end of an activity, the user does not go to their schedule on their own. The educator must hand the user a cue letting them know it is time to go consult their schedule.	→ At the end of the activity, to have the user take the schedule cue and walk back to consult their schedule on their own, bringing the cue with them.	Initiation	p. B71

(continued)

TABLE 1. IDENTIFICATION OF SCHEDULE CHARACTERISTIC(S) TO ADJUST *(continued)*

	CURRENT SCHEDULE CHARACTERISTIC	INTENDED GOAL	CHARACTERISTIC(S) TO ADJUST	PAGE IN THE ADJUSTMENT PROTOCOL
Adjustment 6	☐ At the end of an activity, the user takes the schedule cue on their own and brings it to their schedule.	→ At the end of an activity, to have the user use a visual cue to let them know to go consult their schedule without bringing the cue with them.	Initiation	p. B73
Adjustment 7	☐ At the end of an activity, the user uses a visual cue to let them know to go consult their schedule without bringing the cue with them.	→ At the end of an activity, to have the user consult their schedule on their own without bringing cues with them. To have them rely on natural cues indicating the activity is finished.	Initiation	p. B75
Adjustment 8	☐ The user moves from one activity to the next with visual cues and drops them into boxes or envelopes where the activities take place. At the end of the activity, the user goes back to consult their schedule on their own and without a schedule cue.	→ At the end of the activity, to have the user remove the visual support representing the activity from their schedule and drop it into a container labelled "Finished" placed beside their schedule.	Schedule manipulation	p. B76
Adjustment 9	☐ At the end of the activity, the user goes back to their schedule on their own without carrying a schedule cue, removes the visual support representing the activity from their schedule, and drops it into a container labelled "Finished" placed beside their schedule.	→ At the end of the activity, to have the user flip over the visual support representing the completed activity on their schedule.	Schedule manipulation	p. B78

(continued)

TABLE 1. IDENTIFICATION OF SCHEDULE CHARACTERISTIC(S) TO ADJUST (*continued*)

	CURRENT SCHEDULE CHARACTERISTIC	INTENDED GOAL	CHARACTERISTIC(S) TO ADJUST	PAGE IN THE ADJUSTMENT PROTOCOL
Adjustment 10	☐ At the end of an activity, the user goes back to their schedule without carrying a schedule cue, removes the visual support representing the completed activity from the schedule, and drops it into a container labelled "Finished" or flips the visual support over. The user must use one of the following visual support forms: words typed on the computer (WTC) or words written by hand (WWH), and their schedule must include at least six visual supports at a time.	→ At the end of the activity, to have the user write an X or a checkmark on their schedule or place a token next to the visual support representing the completed activity.	Schedule manipulation	p. B80
Adjustment 11	☐ The user demonstrates the ability to use a visual support with a simpler graphic representation (or a smaller visual support).	→ To have the user use a visual support with a simpler graphic representation or a smaller visual support (greater level of difficulty).	Visual support form	p. B81
Adjustment 12	☐ At the end of an activity, the user writes an X or checkmark on their schedule, or crosses out the completed activity, or simply consults their schedule displayed on a wall or a table without performing any action to indicate the activity is completed.	→ To have the user move around with their schedule sheet (transportable schedule).	Presentation mode	p. B84

PART 2

ADJUSTMENT 1

Characteristics to adjust: Visual support form and manipulation.
Goal: To have the user use the OBJ visual support form (objects representing activities) and drop the visual supports into containers where the activities take place.

PREREQUISITES FOR THIS ADJUSTMENT

- ☐ The current form of visual support used is OBJ-U (objects used in activities).
  AND
- ☐ The user has been using their schedule independently for at least a month.
  AND
- ☐ The aim is for the user to use the OBJ visual support form (objects representing activities) and drop the visual supports representing activities in a container where the activities take place.

ADJUSTMENT BENEFITS

- Offers greater latitude in choosing the visual supports representing activities.
- This step is required to eventually display the schedule on the wall.

PRE-EVALUATION

Required Materials

Section 1A (Subsection 1A.OBJ) in the Evaluation Protocol and in the SET Guide (i.e. from the beginning of Part 1 until the end of "4.1 Detailed Procedure for Subsection 1A") and the corresponding materials in the SET kit.

Procedure

Evaluate Section 1A (Subsection 1A.OBJ) in the Evaluation Protocol following the instructions for this section in the SET Guide (i.e., from the beginning of Part 1 to the end of Section 4.1 "Detailed Procedure for 1A Subsections"). However, for this adjustment, some of the instructions given in the SET Guide and the indications in the Evaluation Protocol should be disregarded:

- On p. A15 of the SET Guide, disregard the "Identify where to start the evaluation" step.
- On p. B10 of the Evaluation Protocol, disregard the guideline with the flag icon: "Start the evaluation here if the user's skill level is unknown or if they cannot match two identical pictograms."
- On p. A15 of the SET Guide, disregard the "Use the stop standards to identify which section or subsection to evaluate next" steps; in particular, do not continue the evaluation at Subsection 1B.PHO as indicated in the SET Guide.

Success Criteria

If the user obtains a subtotal score that is equal to or greater than 7/9 for Subsection 1A.OBJ (or equal to or greater than 14/18 in the "Total 1A.OBJ" box).

INTRODUCTION AND EVALUATION PHASES

Schedule Modifications

Make the required modifications, specifically:

- Choose new objects to represent the activities (otherwise, the user may continue to use them in the activities instead of dropping them into the containers). These objects must be available in several copies.
- Place containers where the activities take place and mount a copy of the objects representing the activities on each container. The containers must therefore be big enough to fit a visual support.

Introduction and Teaching

Provide the user with the support they need to learn their new schedule. Specifically, teach them how to drop the visual supports representing activities in the containers where the activities take place.

Independence Evaluation

After five days of using this new schedule, evaluate the user's independence:

- Fill in the Independence Evaluation Grid four times per day for one day, making sure to evaluate different activities randomly.
    ◦ If the user needed help in executing a step of the schedule, revert to the previous schedule and wait at least three months before attempting this adjustment again.
    ◦ If the user is fully independent with their schedule, wait at least two months before attempting another adjustment (i.e., adjusting the presentation mode and layout by displaying the schedule on the wall).
    If desired, you can fill in the Recommendations Report with the new schedule characteristics.

ADJUSTMENT 2

Characteristics to adjust: Presentation mode and layout.
Goal: To display the schedule on the wall (from top to bottom).

PREREQUISITES FOR THIS ADJUSTMENT

☐ The visual support form used is not OBJ-U (objects used in activities).
AND
☐ Before each activity, the educator hands the user a visual support representing the next activity.
AND
☐ You want to display the schedule on the wall (from top to bottom) to increase the user's independence.

ADJUSTMENT BENEFITS

This step is required to eventually increase the number of visual supports on the schedule, which would considerably benefit both the user and educator.

INTRODUCTION AND EVALUATION PHASES

Schedule Modifications

Make the required modifications, specifically:

- Make a schedule strip and mount it on the wall in the selected location.
- Mount a schedule cue box or envelope in that same location.
- Make the cue used to identify the schedule.
- Then make the schedule cues (probably the same as the schedule identification cue) and stick one on the schedule cue box or envelope.
- Stick a strip of Velcro on the back of the visual supports representing the activities (these visual supports are the same as in the initial schedule).

Introduction and Teaching

Provide the user with the support they need to learn their new schedule. Specifically, teach them how to go consult their schedule when they are handed the schedule cue, how to drop the schedule cue into the schedule cue box or envelope, and how to take the visual support representing the activity from the schedule strip. Only one visual support is mounted on the schedule strip for this adjustment.

Independence Evaluation

After two weeks of using this new schedule, evaluate the user's independence:

- Fill in the Independence Evaluation Grid four times per day for three days, making sure to evaluate different activities randomly.

- If the user is fully independent using their schedule but they needed help for one week to achieve this level of independence, keep this new schedule and wait at least three months before attempting the next adjustment (i.e., increasing the number of visual supports on the schedule).

If desired, you can fill in the Recommendations Report with the new schedule characteristics.

- If the user is fully independent using their schedule and they only needed help for less than a week to achieve this level of independence, you can attempt the next adjustment (i.e., increasing the number of visual supports on the schedule).

If desired, you can fill in the Recommendations Report with the new schedule characteristics.

ADJUSTMENT 3

Characteristics to adjust: Schedule length.
Goal: To increase the number of visual supports on the schedule.

PREREQUISITES FOR THIS ADJUSTMENT

- [ ] The schedule is displayed on the wall, and only one or a few visual supports representing the activities are mounted on it.
  AND
- [ ] To increase the user's level of independence, you want to increase the number of visual supports on the schedule.

ADJUSTMENT BENEFITS

- Facilitates the schedule's management for the educator:
  - Allows for the planning out of a longer period of time.
  - Reduces the number of times the educator will have to mount a series of visual supports representing activities on the schedule strip. Once the number increases enough, the educator will not need to know the order of the content in the user's schedule and will not need to have all the visual supports handy.
- Will allow the user to:

- Anticipate upcoming activities in the order they should be completed.
- Know they will be able to do certain activities they like, helping them develop greater flexibility (e.g., they will accept doing certain harder or less liked activities knowing the ones they like will follow, or they will accept a change in their schedule's order or content, or both, more easily).

INTRODUCTION AND EVALUATION PHASES

Schedule Modifications

Use Table 2 to determine the number of visual supports to add to the schedule. Generally, this number will be the current number of visual supports displayed on the schedule divided by two. Table 2 provides guidance for up to nine visual supports, but it is possible to increase this number to the desired length, typically a half or full day of activities.

TABLE 2. NUMBER OF VISUAL SUPPORTS TO ADD TO THE SCHEDULE		
INITIAL NUMBER OF VISUAL SUPPORTS ON SCHEDULE	NUMBER OF VISUAL SUPPORTS TO ADD	TOTAL NUMBER OF VISUAL SUPPORTS
1	2	3
2	1	3
3	2	5
4	2	6
5	3	8
6	3	9

Introduction and Teaching

Provide the user with the support they need to learn their new schedule.

Independence Evaluation

After five days of using this new schedule, evaluate the user's independence:

- Fill in the Independence Evaluation Grid four times per day for one day, making sure to evaluate different activities randomly.
  - If the user needed help in executing a step of the schedule, revert to the previous schedule and wait at least two months before attempting this adjustment again.
  - If the user is fully independent with their schedule, it is possible to attempt adjusting the length of the schedule again until you achieve the desired length or until a full day of activities is displayed on the schedule.

If desired, you can fill in the Recommendations Report with the new schedule characteristics.
  - Wait until the user maintains their level of independence for two weeks before attempting a new characteristic adjustment if this will make the schedule easier to use or manage.

ADJUSTMENT 4

Characteristics to adjust: Schedule identification and location.
Goal: To move the schedule to a group transition area.

PREREQUISITES FOR THIS ADJUSTMENT

- ☐ The schedule is in an individualized location.
  AND
- ☐ In this setting, there is a group transition area where schedules are displayed and the aim is to display the user's schedule there.

ADJUSTMENT BENEFITS

- Facilitates the schedule's management by the educator for the following:
  - Developing the user's schedule.
  - Observing the user as they use their schedule.
  - Planning several schedules.
- If the group transition area is centrally located in relation to where the user does their activities, it will facilitate the user's back and forth trips.

PRE-EVALUATION

Important: The pre-evaluation is not required if the user is handed a cue before each transition indicating to go consult their schedule *and* if this cue is personalized (e.g., related to the user's interests). In this case, use a cue to identify the user's schedule in the group transition area.

The pre-evaluation is required if:

- ☐ The user goes to consult their schedule on their own and does not bring the schedule cue with them.
  OR
- ☐ The user is handed a cue before each transition indicating to go consult their schedule, but this cue is not personalized (e.g., the word "schedule") and therefore does not distinguish their schedule from the others in the group transition area.

Required Materials

Section 4A in the Evaluation Protocol and in the SET Guide (i.e., from the beginning of Part 4 to the end of Section 4A).

Procedure

Fill in Section 4A in the Evaluation Protocol by following the instructions in the SET Guide.

However, for this adjustment, some of the instructions given in the SET Guide and the indications in the Evaluation Protocol will not apply:

- On p. B38 of the Evaluation Protocol, disregard the "Note: Only evaluate Section 4A if C was checked for 'Identification' (❺) when scoring Part 3 (Table 12)" instruction.
- On p. B38 of the Evaluation Protocol, the note "If C-2 was checked for 'Initiation' (❻) when scoring Part 3 (Table 12), it is important that the cue chosen is suitable, as it will need to be transportable and available in several copies" should read, "If the user is handed a cue indicating they should go consult their schedule, it is important that the cue chosen in Section 4A is suitable, as it will need to be transportable and available in several copies."
- Only evaluate Section 4A (do not evaluate 4B or 4C).

INTRODUCTION AND EVALUATION PHASES

Schedule Modifications

Make the required modifications, specifically:

- Move the schedule to the group transition area, make a schedule cue to identify it, and mount this cue on the schedule.

Introduction and Teaching

Provide the user with the support they need to learn their new schedule. Specifically, teach them how to recognize their schedule so that they are able to consult it.

Independence Evaluation

After five days of using this new schedule, evaluate the user's independence:

- Fill in the Independence Evaluation Grid four times per day for one day, making sure to evaluate different activities randomly.
    - If the user needed help in executing a step of the schedule, revert to the previous schedule and wait at least two months before attempting this adjustment again.
    - If the user is fully independent with their schedule, wait at least two weeks before attempting another adjustment if it makes using and managing the schedule easier.

  If desired, you can fill in the Recommendations Report with the new schedule characteristics.

ADJUSTMENT 5

Characteristics to adjust: Initiation.
Goal: At the end of the activity, to have the user take the schedule cue and walk back to consult their schedule on their own, bringing the cue with them.

PREREQUISITES FOR THIS ADJUSTMENT

- ☐ At the end of an activity, the user does not go to their schedule on their own. The educator must hand the user a cue letting them know it is time to go consult their schedule.

AND
☐ The aim is for the user to take the schedule cue and walk back to consult their schedule on their own, bringing the cue with them.

ADJUSTMENT BENEFITS

Makes managing the schedule easier for the educator as they will not need to be present at the end of each activity to hand the schedule cue to the user.

INTRODUCTION AND EVALUATION PHASES

Schedule Modifications

Make the required modifications; specifically ensure that it is clear for the user that the activity has ended:

- When the end of the activity is obvious (e.g., the task is done when there are no materials left), place the schedule cue somewhere the user can easily take it on their own when it is time to go consult their schedule. If the user uses a sequence of visual supports or a list of tasks, put the schedule cue at the end of this sequence.
- When the end of the activity is not obvious (e.g., break time), use a timer and put a schedule cue on the timer or next to it.

Introduction and Teaching

Provide the user with the support they need to learn their new schedule. Specifically, teach them how to take the schedule cue at the end of the activity, bring it with them to their schedule, and drop it in the schedule cue box or envelope.

Independence Evaluation

After two weeks of using this new schedule, evaluate the user's independence:

- Fill in the Independence Evaluation Grid four times per day for three days, making sure to evaluate different activities randomly.

- If the user needed help in executing a step of the schedule, revert to the previous schedule and wait at least six months before attempting this adjustment again.
- If the user is fully independent with their schedule but they needed help for more than a week to achieve this level of independence, keep this new schedule and wait at least six months before attempting a new adjustment.

If desired, you can fill in the Recommendations Report with the new schedule characteristics.

- If the user is fully independent with their schedule and they only needed help for less than a week to achieve this level of independence, you can try another adjustment, but only if it will make using and managing the schedule easier.

If desired, you can fill in the Recommendations Report with the new schedule characteristics.

ADJUSTMENT 6

Characteristics to adjust: Initiation.
Goal: At the end of the activity, to have the user use a schedule cue to let them know to go consult their schedule on their own without bringing the cue with them.

PREREQUISITES FOR THIS ADJUSTMENT

- ☐ At the end of an activity, the user takes the schedule cue and goes to consult their schedule, bringing the cue with them.
AND
- ☐ The aim is for the user to use a schedule cue to go consult their schedule on their own without bringing the cue with them.

ADJUSTMENT BENEFITS

- Facilitates the schedule's management by the educator.
- Requires less material.
- Makes it easier for the educator to manage a group.
- The user will no longer need to move around with a schedule cue at the end of activities.

INTRODUCTION AND EVALUATION PHASES

Schedule Modifications

Make the required modifications, specifically the following:
- Stick the schedule cues in appropriate locations where the activities take place (e.g., on the work desk, at the end of a work system, in the tasks, etc.) instead of leaving them as transportable cues.
- Remove the schedule cue box or envelope in which the user was dropping the schedule cues.

Introduction and Teaching

Provide the user with the support they need to learn their new schedule. Specifically, teach them how to go to consult their schedule on their own without bringing the schedule cue with them.

Independence Evaluation

After two weeks of using this new schedule, evaluate the user's independence:

- Fill in the Independence Evaluation Grid four times per day for three days, making sure to evaluate different activities randomly.
    - If the user needed help in executing a step of the schedule, revert to the previous schedule and wait at least six months before attempting this adjustment again.
    - If the user is fully independent with their schedule but they needed help for more than a week to achieve this level of independence, keep this new schedule and wait at least six months before attempting a new adjustment.
  If desired, you can fill in the Recommendations Report with the new schedule characteristics.
    - If the user is fully independent with their schedule and they only needed help for less than a week to achieve this level of independence, you can try another adjustment, but only if it makes using and managing the schedule easier.
  If desired, you can fill in the Recommendations Report with the new schedule characteristics.

ADJUSTMENT 7

Characteristics to adjust: Initiation.
Goal: At the end of the activity, to have the user go consult their schedule on their own without bringing the schedule cues. To have them rely on natural cues indicating the activity is finished.

PREREQUISITES FOR THIS ADJUSTMENT

- ☐ At the end of the activity, the user uses a schedule cue indicating to go consult their schedule and goes to consult their schedule on their own without bringing the cue with them.
AND
- ☐ The aim is for the user to go consult their schedule on their own without bringing a schedule cue with them and only relying on natural cues at the end of activities.

ADJUSTMENT BENEFITS

- Facilitates the schedule's management by the educators.
- Requires less material.
- Makes it easier for the educator to manage a group.

INTRODUCTION AND EVALUATION PHASES

Schedule Modifications

Make the required modifications, specifically:

- Natural cues are those we use to recognize that it is time to transition to another activity. Remove any cues that are not deemed natural and that allow the user to recognize that the activity is done (e.g., visual cues at the end of a sequence or list). It should be noted that the examiner should use their clinical judgment to decide whether a cue should be removed or not.

Introduction and Teaching

Provide the user with the support they need to learn their new schedule. Specifically, teach them how to go consult their schedule when required (e.g., when they are done with their work or at the end of a break).

Independence Evaluation

After two weeks of using this new schedule, evaluate the user's independence:

- Fill in the Independence Evaluation Grid four times per day for three days, making sure to evaluate different activities randomly.
    - If the user needed help in executing a step of the schedule, revert to the previous schedule and wait at least six months before attempting this adjustment again.
    - If the user is fully independent with their schedule but they needed help for more than a week to achieve this level of independence, keep this new schedule and wait at least six months before attempting a new adjustment.

  If desired, you can fill in the Recommendations Report with the new schedule characteristics.
    - If the user is fully independent with their schedule and they only needed help for less than a week to achieve this level of independence, you can try another adjustment, but only if it will make using and managing the schedule easier.

  If desired, you can fill in the Recommendations Report with the new schedule characteristics.

ADJUSTMENT 8

Characteristics to adjust: Manipulation.
Goal: At the end of the activity, to have the user remove the visual support representing the activity from their schedule and drop it into a container labelled "Finished" placed beside their schedule.

PREREQUISITES FOR THIS ADJUSTMENT

- ☐ The user moves from one activity to the next with visual cues and drops them into boxes or envelopes where the activities take place.
  AND
- ☐ At the end of the activity, the user goes back to consult their schedule on their own and without a schedule cue.

AND
- [ ] The aim is for the user to remove the visual support representing the activity from their schedule at the end of the activity and drop it into a container labelled "Finished" placed beside their schedule. This way the user would no longer move from activity to activity carrying visual supports.

ADJUSTMENT BENEFITS

- Facilitates the schedule's management by the educator as they will no longer need to collect the visual supports representing the activities in the different locations.
- Allows the educator to check if the user is in fact at the activity indicated on the schedule.
- The user no longer needs to carry the visual supports with them as they move from activity to activity.

INTRODUCTION AND EVALUATION PHASES

Schedule Modifications

Make the required modifications, specifically:

- Place a box or envelope labelled "Finished" next to the schedule (often placed at the bottom of the schedule).
- In the different locations, remove the matching boxes or envelopes in which the user was dropping the visual support if they are not being used by others.
- Identify the locations in another way (e.g., with a copy of the visual support used by the user).

Introduction and Teaching

Provide the user with the support they need to learn their new schedule. Specifically, teach them how to go from one activity location to the other without the visual supports representing those activities. Teach them to remove the visual support representing the activity when that activity is finished and drop it into the box or envelope labelled "Finished" placed beside their schedule.

Independence Evaluation

After two days of using this new schedule, evaluate the user's independence:

- Fill in the Independence Evaluation Grid four times per day for one day, making sure to evaluate different activities randomly.
  - If the user needed help in executing a step of the schedule, revert to the previous schedule and wait at least two months before attempting this adjustment again.
  - If the user is fully independent with their schedule, wait until they maintain this level of independence for at least two weeks before attempting another adjustment, and only if it will make using and managing the schedule easier.

If desired, you can fill in the Recommendations Report with the new schedule characteristics.

ADJUSTMENT 9

Characteristics to adjust: Manipulation.
Goal: At the end of the activity, to have the user flip over the visual support representing the completed activity on their schedule.

PREREQUISITES FOR THIS ADJUSTMENT

- ☐ At the end of the activity, the user removes the visual support representing the activity from their schedule and drops it into a container labelled "Finished" placed beside their schedule.
AND
- ☐ At the end of the activity, the aim is for the user to flip over the visual support representing the completed activity on their schedule.

ADJUSTMENT BENEFITS

- Facilitates the schedule's management by the educator, as certain daily routines are recurring and the educator will simply need to flip the visual supports back over.
- Allows the educator to check if the user is in fact at the activity indicated on the schedule.

- Allows the user to view the number of activities they have completed.
- Familiarizes the user with the fact that the visual supports can stay on the schedule.

INTRODUCTION AND EVALUATION PHASES

Schedule Modifications

Make the required modifications, specifically:

- Remove the box or envelope labelled "Finished" that was placed beside the schedule.
- Stick a strip of Velcro on both sides of the visual supports.

Introduction and Teaching

Provide the user with the support they need to learn their new schedule. Specifically, teach them how to take the visual supports on the schedule, flip them over, and stick them back on the schedule when an activity is finished, instead of dropping them into a box or envelope labelled "Finished."

Independence Evaluation

After two days of using this new schedule, evaluate the user's independence:

- Fill in the Independence Evaluation Grid four times per day for one day, making sure to evaluate different activities randomly.
  - If the user needed help in executing a step of the schedule, revert to the previous schedule and wait at least two months before attempting this adjustment again.
  - If the user is fully independent with their schedule, wait until they maintain this level of independence for at least two weeks before attempting another adjustment, and only if it will make using and managing the schedule easier.

  If desired, you can fill in the Recommendations Report with the new schedule characteristics.

> ## ADJUSTMENT 10
>
> **Characteristics to adjust:** Manipulation.
> **Goal:** At the end of the activity, to have the user write an X or a checkmark on their schedule or place a token next to the visual support representing the completed activity.

PREREQUISITES FOR THIS ADJUSTMENT

- ☐ At the end of the activity, the user goes back to their schedule without the schedule cue, removes the visual support representing the completed activity from their schedule, and drops it into a box or envelope labelled "Finished" placed beside their schedule or flips the visual support over.
  AND
- ☐ The user must use the words typed on the computer (WTC) or the words written by hand (WWH) visual support form, and their schedule must display at least six visual supports at a time.
  AND
- ☐ The aim is for the user to write an X or checkmark on their schedule at the end of the activity or place a token next to the visual support representing the completed activity.

ADJUSTMENT BENEFITS

- Facilitates the schedule's management by the educator.
- Allows the educator to check if the user is in fact at the activity indicated on the schedule.
- Allows the user to view the activities they have completed.

INTRODUCTION AND EVALUATION PHASES

Schedule Modifications

Make the required modifications, specifically:

- It is likely that you will need to make a new schedule. Specifically, this new schedule will need a space where the user can write an X or checkmark, or you will need to add a strip of Velcro where they will stick the tokens.
- Place a pencil or tokens beside the schedule.

Introduction and Teaching

Provide the user with the support they need to learn their new schedule. Specifically, teach them how to write an X or a checkmark or place a token next to the visual support representing the completed activity.

Independence Evaluation

After two days of using this new schedule, evaluate the user's independence:

- Fill in the Independence Evaluation Grid four times per day for one day, making sure to evaluate different activities randomly.
  - If the user needed help in executing a step of the schedule, revert to the previous schedule and wait at least two months before attempting this adjustment again.
  - If the user is fully independent with their schedule, wait until they maintain this level of independence for at least two weeks before attempting another adjustment, and only if it will make using and managing the schedule easier.

  If desired, you can fill in the Recommendations Report with the new schedule characteristics.

ADJUSTMENT 11

Characteristics to adjust: Visual support forms.
Goal: To have the user use a visual support with a simpler graphic representation or a smaller visual support (greater level of difficulty).

PREREQUISITES FOR THIS ADJUSTMENT

- ☐ The user has been using their schedule independently for at least six months and shows an ability to use a visual support with a simpler graphic representation (or a smaller visual support).
  AND
- ☐ The aim is for the user to use a visual support with a simpler graphic representation (or a smaller visual support).

AND
☐ The user does not use the WWH visual support form.

ADJUSTMENT BENEFITS

- Allows the user to use a visual support adapted to their ability.

PRE-EVALUATION

Important: The pre-evaluation is only required if the intended goal is to use a visual support form with a simpler graphic representation (and not a smaller visual support).

Required Materials

Parts 1 and 2 in the Evaluation Protocol and in the SET Guide (i.e., from the beginning of Part 1 to the end of Part 2) as well as the corresponding materials from the SET kit.

Procedure

Evaluate Parts 1 and 2 in the Evaluation Protocol following the instructions for those parts in the SET Guide.

However, for this adjustment, some instructions in the SET Guide or indications in the Evaluation Protocol do not apply:

- Do not evaluate or score Parts 3 and 4. Stop after scoring Part 2 (Table 6, p. B23, in the Evaluation Protocol). Consequently, follow the instructions and stop standards in the SET Guide and the Evaluation Protocol except for any that say to proceed with scoring or continue the evaluation beyond Part 2 (Table 6). As such, *disregard any instructions* in the stop standards that say to score Part 3 and continue the evaluation at Section 4C, Part 4.

Success Criteria

If the form of visual support selected (❶ in Table 6 of the Evaluation Protocol) corresponds to a simpler graphic representation than the one currently being used.

INTRODUCTION AND EVALUATION PHASES

Schedule Modifications

Make the required modifications, specifically the shape or size of the visual supports used in the schedule. If needed, also modify the shape or size of the visual supports used to identify the locations, the schedule, and the schedule cues.

Introduction and Teaching

Provide the user with the support they need to learn their new schedule. Specifically, teach them how to go to the locations where the activities take place on their own.

Independence Evaluation

After two days of using this new schedule, evaluate the user's independence:

- Fill in the Independence Evaluation Grid four times per day for one day, making sure to evaluate different activities randomly.
    - If the user needed help in executing a step of the schedule, revert to the previous schedule and wait at least six months before attempting to modify the visual support form and at least two months before attempting any other adjustment.
    - If the user is fully independent with their schedule, wait at least two months before attempting any sort of modification to the visual support form used in their schedule.
  If desired, you can fill in the Recommendations Report with the new schedule characteristics.
    - If the user is fully independent with their schedule, wait until they maintain this level of independence for at least two weeks before attempting another adjustment of a schedule characteristic, and only if it will make using and managing the schedule easier.
  If desired, you can fill in the Recommendations Report with the new schedule characteristics.

ADJUSTMENT 12

Characteristics to adjust: Schedule presentation mode.
Goal: To have the user move around with their schedule sheet (transportable schedule).

PREREQUISITES FOR THIS ADJUSTMENT

- ☐ At the end of the activity, the user writes an X or checkmark on their schedule, crosses out the completed activity, or simply consults their schedule on a wall or table without carrying out any action indicating the activity is completed.
AND
- ☐ The aim is for the user to move around with their schedule sheet.

ADJUSTMENT BENEFITS

- Familiarizes the user with a schedule that is similar to an agenda.
- The user can consult their schedule without having to move around.

INTRODUCTION AND EVALUATION PHASES

Schedule Modifications

Make the required modifications, specifically:

- Remove the schedule from the wall or table.
- Make a new transportable schedule.

Introduction and Teaching

Provide the user with the support they need to learn their new schedule. Specifically, teach them how to carry their schedule with them as they move from activity to activity. It is possible to include indications to let them know where to put down their schedule in the different activity locations. Ensure that the user has a pencil with them or that one is attached to their schedule.

Independence Evaluation

After two days of using this new schedule, evaluate the user's independence:

- Fill in the Independence Evaluation Grid four times per day for one day, making sure to evaluate different activities randomly.
  - If the user needed help in executing a step of the schedule, revert to the previous schedule and wait at least two months before attempting this adjustment again.
  - If the user is fully independent with their schedule, wait until they maintain this level of independence for at least two weeks before attempting another adjustment, and only if it will make using or managing the schedule easier.

If desired, you can fill in the Recommendations Report with the new schedule characteristics.

SCHEDULE EVALUATION TOOL

Johanne Mainville, Sonia Di Lillo,
Nathalie Poirier, and Nathalie Plante

INDEPENDENCE EVALUATION GRID

Instructions

- Fill in the user's name and evaluation date and check the day of the evaluation (first, second, or third).
- List the steps the user must currently perform to use their schedule.
- During the evaluation, specify the time and, using the legend at the bottom of the grid, specify the type of help provided during the different steps.
- Evaluate the user's independence in using their schedule over three days, four times per day. It is important to ensure that you randomly evaluate the schedule's use during different activities.
- If help was required to perform one of the steps, the user is not considered as fully independent.

Independence Evaluation Grid

User's name:				
Date: / / (DD/MM/YY)		Day: ☐ 1 ☐ 2 ☐ 3		
STEPS	**TIME**			

Legend: I = Independent, P = Physical prompt, G = Gestural prompt, V = Verbal prompt.

SCHEDULE EVALUATION TOOL

Johanne Mainville, Sonia Di Lillo,
Nathalie Poirier, and Nathalie Plante

APPENDIX 1
MATERIAL

Table of Contents

Full Description of a SET Kit B92
Purchase of Material B96
Material Preparation B98
    Make the Bottom and Back Panels and Assemble
    Matching Boxes B98
    Build the Schedule Strip B100
Material Assembly B101
    Label and Assemble the Object Bags B101
    Prepare Bag 1C B103
    Assemble the Filing Boxes B105
    Assemble the Examiner's Tray B111
    Assemble the 36 Schedule Sheets B112
    Identify and Assemble the Rest of the Material B112

List of Figures

Figure 1. White corrugated cardboard boxes B97
Figure 2. Bottom panel B98
Figure 3. Matching boxes mounted onto the bottom and back panels B98
Figure 4. Velcro on the matching boxes B99
Figure 5. Matching boxes assembled for the evaluation.... B100
Figure 6. Schedule sheet... B100
Figure 7. Labels on object bags B101
Figure 8. Velcro on objects, "Home" category B101
Figure 9. Velcro on objects, "Work/School" category B102
Figure 10. Velcro on objects, "Other" category.................... B102
Figure 11. "Bag 1C" basket, labelled and assembled B104
Figure 12. Use of objects from Bag 1C during the evaluation B104
Figure 13. Example of the back of a visual support B106
Figure 14. Assembled filing box.. B108
Figure 15. Assembled examiner's tray B111
Figure 16. Schedule cue box.. B112

Creating the SET kit is done in three stages. First, the required material must be obtained. This material can be purchased in big-box stores, apart from the toothbrushes, which must be purchased on the internet (this type of toothbrush cannot be found in stores). Second, some of the material needs to be cut out and assembled. And third, various components need to be sorted and labelled.

Full Description of a SET Kit

- A large 22 x 18 x 14 in. (21-litre) plastic bin to hold all the material
- One examiner's tray (16 x 12 x 4.5-inch plastic basket), in which to insert:
  - One plastic basket (10 x 3 x 2.5 in.), in which to insert:
    - One small square plastic basket (3 x 3 x 2 in.)
- One schedule strip (large yellow corrugated plastic sheet)
- Three baskets to hold the objects (10 x 6.5 x 2.5 in.), labelled "3B: Basket for Objects"
- Three bags of objects (11 x 10 in. medium-sized Ziploc-style bags):
  - One bag labelled "Home Bag: Order of Visual Supports on Matching Boxes: Toothbrush – Sock – Lego" and containing the following objects:
    - Six red toothbrushes
    - Six black socks
    - Six green Lego blocks
  - One bag labelled "Work/School Bag: Order of Visual Supports on Matching Boxes: Spoon – Pencil – Disc" and containing the following objects:
    - Six blue plastic spoons
    - Six orange HB pencils
    - Six silver discs
  - One bag labelled "Other: Order of Visual Supports on Matching Boxes: Ball – Marker – Sponge" and containing the following objects:
    - Six yellow tennis balls
    - Six yellow markers
    - Six yellow sponges
- One large bag labelled "Bag 1C" (17 x 13 in. large Ziploc-style bag), containing:

- One 16 x 12 x 4.5 in. plastic basket labelled "Bag 1C," containing:
  - One 10 x 3 x 2.5 in. plastic basket, containing:
    - One 3 x 3 x 2 in. small square plastic basket
- One 10 x 3 x 2.5 in. plastic basket, containing a 1 x 4 in. piece of corrugated plastic sheet labelled "Home: Order of Visual Supports on Matching Boxes: Toothbrush – Sock – Lego" and:
  - One red toothbrush
  - One black sock
  - One green Lego block
- One 10 x 3 x 2.5 in. plastic basket containing a 1 x 4 in. piece of corrugated plastic sheet labelled "Work/School: Order of Visual Supports on Matching Boxes: Spoon – Pencil – Disc" and:
  - One blue spoon
  - One orange HB pencil
  - One silver disc
- One 10 x 3 x 2.5 in. plastic basket containing a 1 x 4 in. piece of corrugated plastic sheet labelled "Other: Order of Visual Supports on Matching Boxes: Ball – Marker – Sponge" and:
  - One yellow tennis ball
  - One yellow marker
  - One yellow sponge
☐ Three filing boxes (10 x 4 x 4 in. large white corrugated cardboard boxes):
  - One large white box labelled "Home: 2–3 + 3H; 2–3 (2–3.001 to 2–3.075); 3H (3H.001 to 3H.052)," containing visual supports Home 2–3.001 to 2–3.075 and 3H.001 to 3H.052 filed behind nine dividers (five blue dividers beginning with 2–3 and four yellow dividers beginning with 3H) and a 10 x 4 in. corrugated plastic sheet used to assemble the dividers
  - One large white box labelled "Work/School: 2–3 + 3H; 2–3 (2–3.076 to 2–3.150); 3H (3H.001 to 3H.052)," containing visual supports Work/School 2–3.076 to 2–3.150 and 3H.001 to 3H.052 filed behind nine dividers (five blue dividers beginning with 2–3 and four yellow dividers beginning with 3H) and a 10 x 4 in. corrugated plastic sheet used to assemble the dividers
  - One large white box labelled "Other: 2–3 + 3H; 2–3 (2–3.151 to 2–3.225); 3H (3H.001 to 3H.052)," containing visual supports

Other 2–3.151 to 2–3.225 and 3H.001 to 3H.052 filed behind nine dividers (five blue dividers beginning with 2–3 and four yellow dividers beginning with 3H) and a 10 x 4 in. corrugated plastic sheet used to assemble the dividers
- ☐ One filing box (8 x 4 x 4 in. white corrugated cardboard box):
  - One white box labelled "1B + 1C; 1B (1B.001 to 1B.090); 1C (1C.001 to 1C.045)," containing visual supports 1B.001 to 1B.090 and 1C.001 to 1C.045 filed behind ten dividers (five blue dividers beginning with 1B and five yellow dividers beginning with 1C) and a 8 x 4 in. corrugated plastic sheet used to assemble the dividers
- ☐ Three matching boxes (8 x 4 x 4 in. white corrugated cardboard boxes) labelled "Matching box"
  - Two white corrugated plastic sheets:
    - ➢ One 27 x 5.5 in. sheet labelled "Bottom panel"
    - ➢ One 27 x 8 in. sheet labelled "Back panel"
- ☐ One schedule cue box (8 x 4 x 4 in. white corrugated cardboard box) labelled "Schedule cue box"
- ☐ One token box (Glad-type plastic container with lid with a capacity of one fluid cup), containing 12 cardboard tokens or bingo chips
- ☐ One piggy bank with 12 tokens; or, if a piggy bank is not available, one small plastic container with 12 poker chips
- ☐ One non-permanent marker
- ☐ Blue mounting putty
- ☐ 36 "token schedule" and "checkmark schedule" sheets to be laminated and placed in a 16 x 20 in. plastic envelope labelled "Token and checkmark schedules." Each laminated sheet is respectively identified as follows:
  - 3B.1: Demos; Home Category; Token Schedule; WTC
  - 3B.1: 3 Attempts; Home Category; Token Schedule; WTC
  - 3B.2: 6 Attempts; Home Category; Token Schedule; WTC
  - 3B.1: Demos; Home Category; Token Schedule; WWH
  - 3B.1: 3 Attempts; Home Category; Token Schedule; WWH
  - 3B.2: 6 Attempts; Home Category; Token Schedule; WWH
  - 3B.1: Demos; Work/School Category; Token Schedule; WTC
  - 3B.1: 3 Attempts; Work/School Category; Token Schedule; WTC
  - 3B.2: 6 Attempts; Work/School Category; Token Schedule; WTC

- 3B.1: Demos; Work/School Category; Token Schedule; WWH
- 3B.1: 3 Attempts; Work/School Category; Token Schedule; WWH
- 3B.2: 6 Attempts; Work/School Category; Token Schedule; WWH
- 3B.1: Demos; Other Category; Token Schedule; WTC
- 3B.1: 3 Attempts; Other Category; Token Schedule; WTC
- 3B.2: 6 Attempts; Other Category; Token Schedule; WTC
- 3B.1: Demos; Other Category; Token Schedule; WWH
- 3B.1: 3 Attempts; Other Category; Token Schedule; WWH
- 3B.2: 6 Attempts; Other Category; Token Schedule; WWH
- 3B.1: Demos; Home Category; Checkmark Schedule; WTC
- 3B.1: 3 Attempts; Home Category; Checkmark Schedule; WTC
- 3B.2: 6 Attempts; Home Category; Checkmark Schedule; WTC
- 3B.1: Demos; Home Category; Checkmark Schedule; WWH
- 3B.1: 3 Attempts; Home Category; Checkmark Schedule; WWH
- 3B.2: 6 Attempts; Home Category; Checkmark Schedule; WWH
- 3B.1: Demos; Work/School Category; Checkmark Schedule; WTC
- 3B.1: 3 Attempts; Work/School Category; Checkmark Schedule; WTC
- 3B.2: 6 Attempts; Work/School Category; Checkmark Schedule; WTC
- 3B.1: Demos; Work/School Category; Checkmark Schedule; WWH
- 3B.1: 3 Attempts; Work/School Category; Checkmark Schedule; WWH
- 3B.2: 6 Attempts; Work/School Category; Checkmark Schedule; WWH
- 3B.1: Demos; Other Category; Checkmark Schedule; WTC
- 3B.1: 3 Attempts; Other Category; Checkmark Schedule; WTC
- 3B.2: 6 Attempts; Other Category; Checkmark Schedule; WTC
- 3B.1: Demos; Other Category; Checkmark Schedule; WWH
- 3B.1: 3 Attempts; Other Category; Checkmark Schedule; WWH
- 3B.2: 6 Attempts; Other Category; Checkmark Schedule; WWH

Purchase of Material

The two-dimensional visual supports (photos, pictograms, word cards), as well as the dividers and labels used to identify all the material can be obtained by writing to trousse.ouest@gmail.com. Since visual supports in object form will be matched with visual supports in photo form, we strongly recommend that you obtain the two-dimensional visual supports first to ensure you buy items that match the photos. The nine objects in question (you will need seven copies of each object) are listed below in bold.

The items in the kit can be purchased at multiple stores, including office supply stores. They are thus easy to replace if broken or lost.

The plastic baskets, piggy banks, coins, token boxes, and tokens/chips can usually be found in dollar stores.

The white corrugated cardboard boxes can be purchased at Staples (see product details below). Corrugated plastic sheets can be found in art supply stores (e.g., DeSerres) or large retail chains (e.g., Rona).

All the following items are essential. The nine visual supports in object form are listed in bold.

- ☐ **Seven small red children's toothbrushes**
- ☐ **Seven small black children's socks (size: 2 to 3 years)**
- ☐ **Seven green 8-stud 1 x 2 in. Lego bricks**
- ☐ **Seven blue plastic spoons**
- ☐ **Seven orange HB pencils**
- ☐ **Seven silver discs**
- ☐ **Seven yellow tennis balls**
- ☐ **Seven yellow markers**
- ☐ **Seven yellow sponges (usually sold with a green scouring pad that can be easily removed)**
- ☐ One non-permanent marker
- ☐ Blue mounting putty
- ☐ Velcro
- ☐ Three medium-sized Ziploc-style bags (11 x 10 in.)
- ☐ One large-sized Ziploc-style bag (at least 17 x 13 in.)
- ☐ One piggy bank or one small plastic container if you cannot find a piggy bank
- ☐ 12 tokens (to go with a piggy bank) or 12 poker chips (to go with a small plastic container)
- ☐ One Glad-style plastic container with lid (one fluid cup capacity)

Appendix 1: Material B97

- ☐ 12 cardboard tokens or bingo chips
- ☐ Two plastic baskets measuring 16 x 12 x 4.5 in.
- ☐ Five plastic baskets measuring 10 x 3 x 2.5 in.
- ☐ Two small square plastic baskets measuring 3 x 3 x 2 in.
- ☐ Three plastic baskets measuring 10 x 6.5 x 2.5 in.
- ☐ One 22 x 28 in. white corrugated plastic sheet
- ☐ One 22 x 28 in. yellow corrugated plastic sheet
- ☐ One 16 x 20 in. large plastic envelope to hold the schedule sheets used in Section 3B
- ☐ One large 22 x 18 x 14 in. (21-litre) plastic bin to hold all the material
- ☐ Five white corrugated cardboard boxes measuring 8 x 4 x 4 in. – product number 427852*
- ☐ Three white corrugated cardboard boxes measuring 10 x 4 x 4 in. – product number 427854*

Figure 1. White corrugated cardboard boxes.

Source: Artimage 2015.

*These specific cardboard box sizes are harder to find. However, if the box dimensions are not the exact size, the evaluation may be more difficult as the visual supports could get mixed up or not fit easily into the boxes. We therefore recommend buying them directly at Staples (or on their website). The product numbers provided were valid in September 2022. Boxes are sold in packs of five.

Material Preparation

Make the Bottom and Back Panels and Assemble Matching Boxes

First, cut out a white corrugated plastic sheet to 27 in. x 5.5 in. and another to 27 x 8 in. Then, make a fold in the centre of each panel so they can be folded in half and stored easily (see Figure 2). Last, stick the "Bottom panel" label on the 27 x 5.5 sheet and the "Back panel" label on the 27 x 8 in. sheet.

Figure 2. Bottom panel.

Source: Artimage 2015.

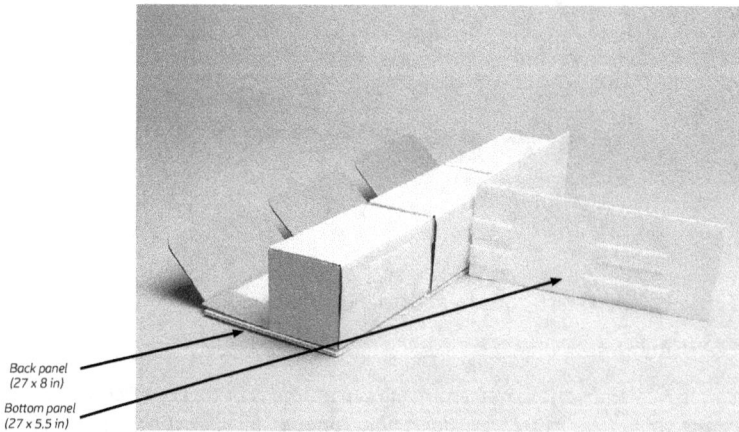

Figure 3. Matching boxes mounted onto the bottom and back panels.

Source: Artimage 2015.

Stick two strips of Velcro (hook) about 4 in. long on the bottom of the three white 8 x 4 x 4 in. corrugated cardboard boxes (see Figure 4a). On the back of the boxes, stick a strip of Velcro (hook) towards the bottom of the box and at the top of the centre panel. In addition, stick a strip of Velcro (loop) on the top of the box as shown in Figure 4B. Last, stick the "Matching box" label on the back of the three boxes as shown in Figure 4C. Figures 5 and 12 (pp. 100 and 104) show how the matching boxes are used.

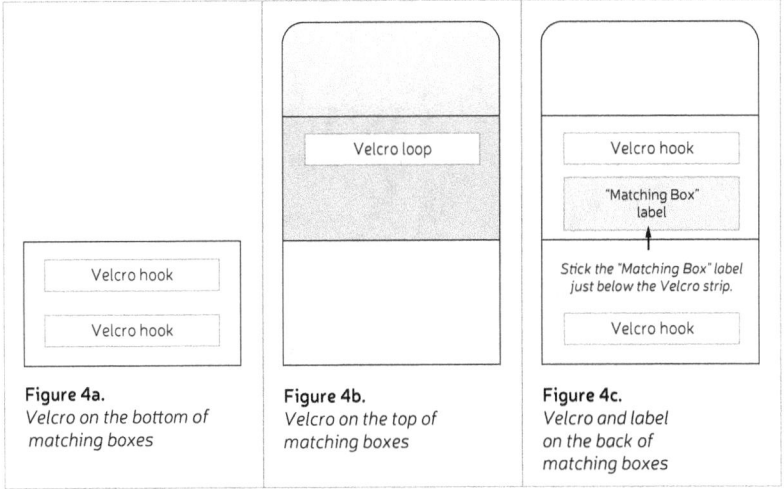

Figure 4. Velcro on the matching boxes.

Source: Artimage 2015.

Then stick Velcro strips (loop) on the corrugated plastic sheet, ensuring the strips line up with the ones on the matching boxes when the boxes are mounted on the panels, as shown in Figure 3.

Before the evaluation, assemble the back and bottom panels and the matching boxes. To do this, unfold the two panels and mount the three boxes as shown in Figure 3.

During the evaluation, stick the first three visual supports from left to right at the centre of the matching boxes according to the order in which they were filed and then turn the panels and boxes so they face the user (see Figure 5).

Figure 5. Matching boxes assembled for the evaluation.
Source: Artimage 2015.

Build the Schedule Strip

Cut the yellow corrugated plastic sheet down to size and stick a strip of Velcro (loop) as shown in Figure 6. Then, stick the "Schedule Sheet" label on the back.

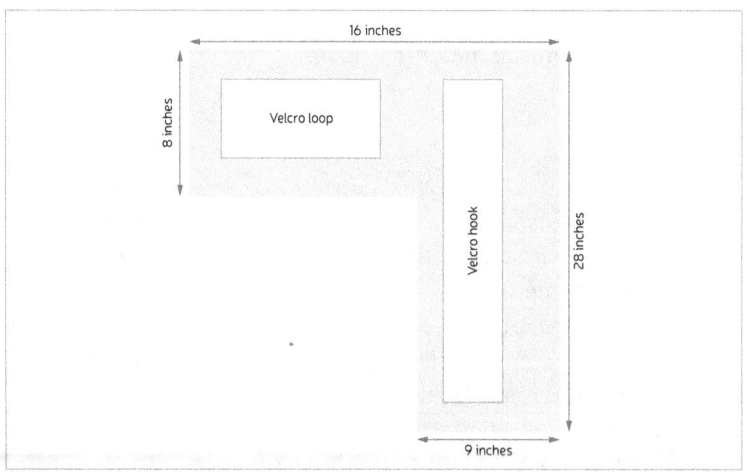

Figure 6. Schedule sheet.
Source: Artimage 2015.

Material Assembly

Label and Assemble the Object Bags

Stick the "Home Bag: Order of Visual Supports on Matching Boxes: Toothbrush – Sock – Lego," "Work/School Bag: Order of Visual Supports on Matching Boxes: Spoon – Pencil – Disc," and "Other Bag: Order of Visual Supports on Matching Boxes: Ball – Marker – Sponge" labels on the medium-sized Ziploc-style bags (11 x 10 in.) as shown in Figure 7. Then stick a strip of Velcro (hook) onto the objects as shown in Figures 8, 9, and 10, and arrange the objects in the bags as described below.

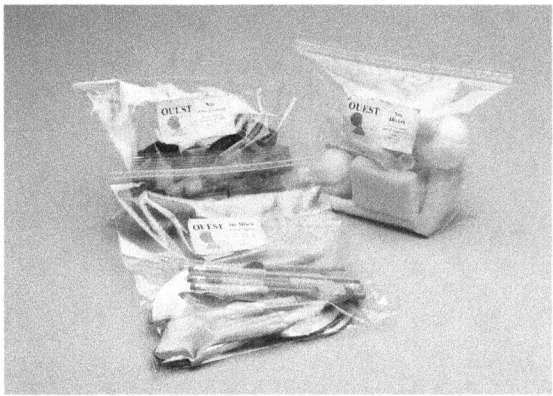

Figure 7. Labels on object bags.

Source: Artimage 2015.

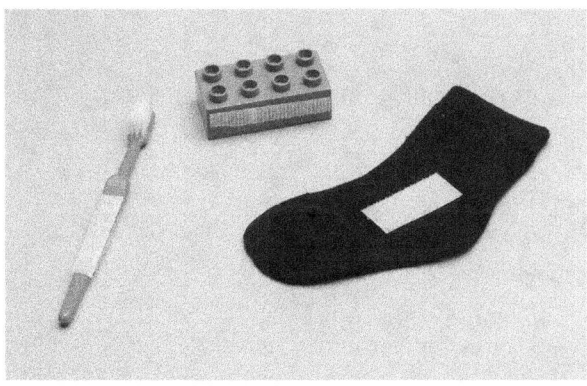

Figure 8. Velcro on objects, "Home" category.

Source: Artimage 2015.

Figure 9. Velcro on objects, "Work/School" category.
Source: Artimage 2015.

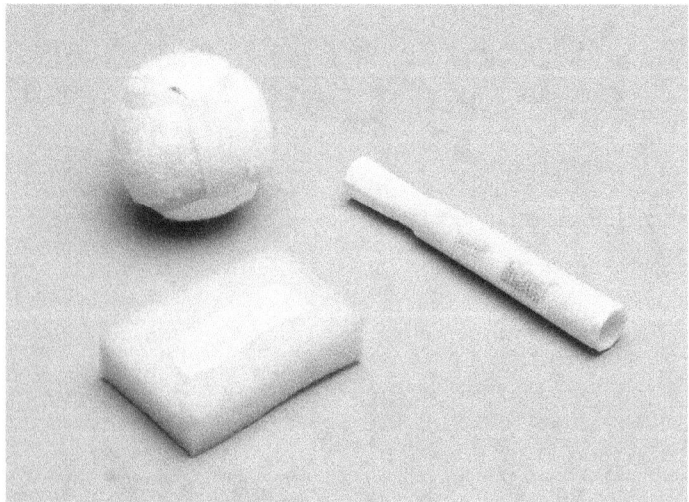

Figure 10. Velcro on objects, "Other" category.
Source: Artimage 2015.

- The Home Bag includes six red toothbrushes, six black socks, and six green Lego bricks
- The Work/School Bag contains six blue plastic spoons, six HB pencils, and six silver discs
- The Other Bag contains six yellow tennis balls, six yellow markers, and six yellow sponges

After sorting the objects into the three bags, you should have one copy of each object left. These will be used in Bag 1C.

Prepare Bag 1C

Bag 1C will be used at the end of Part 1 of the evaluation. This bag is useful for the evaluation to run smoothly. To assemble Bag 1C, stick the "Bag 1C" label on a Ziploc-style bag measuring at least 17 x 13 in.

Then, cut out three pieces of white corrugated plastic sheet to 1 x 4 in. On one of the pieces, stick the vertical "Home Bag: Order of Visual Supports on Matching Boxes: Toothbrush – Sock – Lego" label. Do the same thing with the vertical "Work/School Bag: Order of Visual Supports on Matching Boxes: Spoon – Pencil – Disc" and "Other Bag: Order of Visual Supports on Matching Boxes: Ball – Marker – Sponge" labels on the two other pieces. Then, using a strip of Velcro, stick each labelled corrugated plastic piece to the edge of a 10 x 3 x 2.5 basket. Each basket will therefore be dedicated to one category and can be used to hold one copy of each object.

To be able to mount the objects to the matching boxes during the evaluation, stick a strip of Velcro to each object.

The Home Basket will hold one red toothbrush, one black sock, and one green Lego brick. The Work/School Basket will hold one blue plastic spoon, one orange HB pencil, and one silver disc. The Other Basket will hold one yellow tennis ball, one yellow marker, and one yellow sponge.

To ensure better stability of the set-up during the evaluation, insert the three baskets into a large 16 x 12 x 4.5 in. basket identified with the "Bag 1C" label. The examiner can also add another small basket (the same size as the other three) and insert the square 3 x 3 x 2 in. basket to complete the examiner's tray. This small square basket can hold the reinforcers, which will be used to keep the user motivated throughout the evaluation. Figure 11 illustrates the "Bag 1C" assembled and labelled. All of this material will be stored in the large Ziploc-style bag also labelled "Bag 1C."

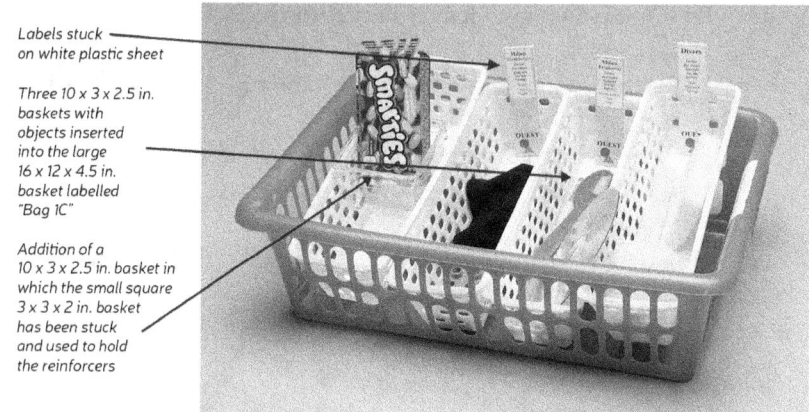

Figure 11. "Bag 1C" basket, labelled and assembled.

Source: Artimage 2015

During the evaluation, the objects from Bag 1C will be placed on the matching boxes, and the user will need to match the corresponding visual supports from filing box 1B + 1C or from the object bags. Figure 12 shows the material prepared for evaluating the Other category.

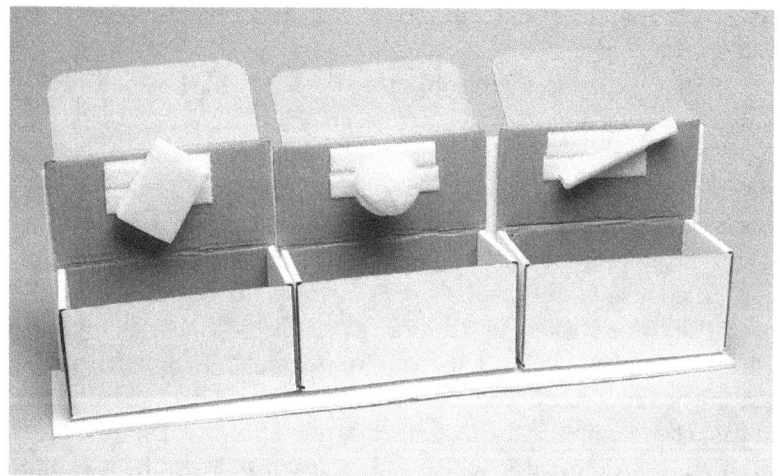

Figure 12. Use of objects from Bag 1C during the evaluation.

Source: Artimage 2015 .

After the evaluation, the examiner may need to dismantle the different components of Bag 1C by stacking the baskets one into the other if there is not enough storage space in the SET kit bin.

Assemble the Filing Boxes

Stick the labels on the white corrugated cardboard boxes as follows (see Figure 1):

- One 8 x 4 x 4 in. box: green "1B + 1C; 1B (1B.001 to 1B.090); 1C (1C.001 to 1C.045)" label
- One 10 x 4 x 4 in. box: orange "Home Category; 2–3 + 3H; 2–3 (2–3.001 to 2–3.075); 3H (3H.001 to 3H.052)" label
- One 10 x 4 x 4 in. box: beige "Work/School Category; 2–3 + 3H; 2–3 (2–3.076 to 2–3.150); 3H (3H.001 to 3H.052)" label
- One 10 x 4 x 4 in. box: pink "Other Category; 2–3 + 3H; 2–3 (2–3.151 to 2–3.225); 3H (3H.001 to 3H.052)" label

Then, cut out three 10 x 4 in. pieces of white corrugated plastic sheet, which will be inserted into the Home, Work/School, and Other filing boxes. Cut out another 8 x 4 in. piece of corrugated plastic sheet and insert it on the bottom of filing box 1B + 1C. As the boxes are deep, this piece will make it easier to handle the visual supports. Moreover, once the dividers have been folded to form three sides, the dividers from one file can be stuck together and then everything can be stuck to the corrugated plastic sheet instead of to the bottom of the box (which is an uneven surface).

To reduce the time spent separating the visual supports, we recommend sorting them:

- Divide the visual supports by category (e.g., "1B.XXX and 1C.XXX", "2–3.XXX Home", "2–3.XXX Work/School" or "2–3.XXX Other"). Then, referring to the number on the bottom of each visual support, make the following stacks:
  - Two stacks containing the visual supports with the following numbers organized in ascending order:
    - 1B.002 to 1B.090
    - 1C.001 to 1C.045
  - Two stacks containing the visual supports with the following numbers organized in ascending order:

- 2–3.001 to 2–3.075
- 3H.001 to 3H.052 Home
◦ Two stacks containing the visual supports with the following numbers organized in ascending order:
  - 2–3.076 to 2–3.150
  - 3H.001 to 3H.052 Work/School;
◦ Two stacks containing the visual supports with the following numbers organized in ascending order:
  - 2–3.151 to 2–3.225
  - 3H.001 to 3H.052 Other

As illustrated in Figure 13, the visual supports are numbered according to the order in which they will be used in the evaluation. Some visual supports have a lowercase "v" at the end of the number: this indicates that a strip of Velcro must be stuck on the square at the centre of the visual support (see Figure 13). In filing box 1B + 1C, there are 45 visual supports requiring a strip of Velcro (hook). In the files with 2–3 + 3H in their name, 75 visual supports require a Velcro strip (hook).

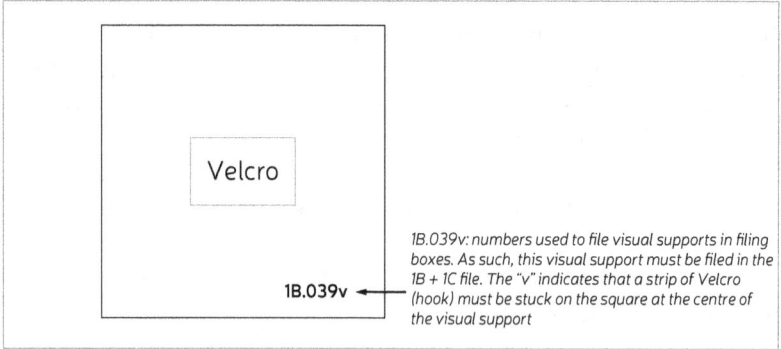

Figure 13. Example of the back of a visual support.

Source: Artimage 2015.

Then separate the dividers according to the information found on the upper right corner and put them in the order specific to each file.

- Filing box 1B + 1C consists of the following dividers in this order:
  - 1B.PHO

    - 1B.PIC
    - 1B.BWP
    - 1B.WTC
    - 1B.WWH
    - 1C.PHO
    - 1C.PIC
    - 1C.BWP
    - 1C.WTC
    - 1C.WWH
  - The Home file consists of the following dividers in this order:
    - 2–3.PHO Home
    - 2–3.PIC Home
    - 2–3.BWP Home
    - 2–3.WTC Home
    - 2–3.WWH Home
    - 3H.PHO/3H.PIC Home
    - 3H.BWP Home
    - 3H.WTC Home
    - 3H.WWH Home
  - The dividers for the Work/School file should also be placed in the same order (i.e., 2–3.PHO Work/School, 2–3.PIC Work/School, 2–3.BWP Work/School, 2–3.WTC Work/School, 2–3.WWH Work/School, 3H.PHO/3H.PIC Work/School, 3H.BWP Work/School, 3H.WTC Work/School, and 3H.WWH Work/School).
  - The schedule cues filed behind the yellow 3H.XXX dividers will be used in Part 3 of the evaluation to encourage the user to go consult the proposed schedule.

Figure 14 illustrates an assembled filing box for the Home category. The label has been stuck on the front of the box to identify it. The dividers on the inside are used to file the visual supports.

Here is the detailed order of the visual supports found in each filing box.

Filing Box 1B + 1C; 1B (1B.001 to 1B. 090); **1C** (1C.001 to 1C.045)

This box includes the visual supports used in Part 1 of the evaluation. The material should be filed as follows:

- Five blue dividers identified as follows and used to file the visual supports in this order:

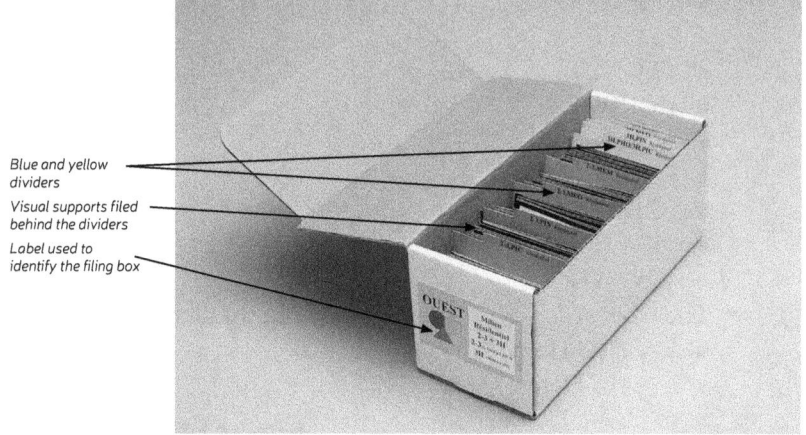

Figure 14. Assembled filing box.

Source: Artimage 2015.

- "1B.PHO," behind which to file the 18 photos numbered 1B.001v to 1B.018
- "1B.PIC," behind which to file the 18 colour pictograms numbered 1B.019v to 1B.036
- "1B.BWP," behind which to file the 18 black-and-white pictograms numbered 1B.037v to 1B.054
- "1B.WTC," behind which to file the 18 words typed on the computer numbered 1B.055v to 1B.072
- "1B.WWH," behind which to file the words written by hand numbered 1B.073v to 1B.090
- Five yellow dividers identified as follows and used to file the visual supports in this order:
  - "1C.PHO," behind which to file the nine photos numbered 1C.001 to 1C.009
  - "1C.PIC," behind which to file the nine colour pictograms numbered 1C.010 to 1C.018
  - "1C.BWP," behind which to file the nine black-and-white pictograms numbered 1C.019 to 1C.027
  - "1C.WTC," behind which to file the nine words typed on the computer numbered 1C.028 to 1C.036
  - "1C.WWH," behind which to file the nine words written by hand numbered 1C.037 to 1C.045

Home Filing Box; 2–3 + 3H; 2–3 (2–3.001 to 2–3.075); **3H** (3H.001 to 3H.052)

This file is used in Parts 2 and 3 of the evaluation if the "Home" category is selected. The material should be filed as follows:

- Five blue dividers identified as follows and used to file the visual supports in this order:
  - "2–3.PHO Home," behind which to file the 15 photos numbered 2–3.001v to 2–3.015v
  - "2–3.PIC Home," behind which to file the 15 colour pictograms numbered 2–3.016v to 2–3.030v
  - "2–3.BWP Home," behind which to file the 15 black-and-white pictograms numbered 2–3.031v to 2–3.045v
  - "2–3.WTC Home," behind which to file the 15 words typed on the computer numbered 2–3.046v to 2–3.060v
  - "2–3.WWH Home," behind which to file the 15 words written by hand numbered 2–3.061v to 2–3.075v
- Four yellow dividers identified as follows and used to file the visual supports in this order:
  - "3H.PHO/3H.PIC Home," behind which to file the 13 colour pictograms numbered 3H.001v to 3H.013
  - "3H.BWP Home," behind which to file the 13 black-and-white pictograms numbered 3H.014v to 3H.026
  - "3H.WTC Home" behind which to file the 13 words typed on the computer numbered 3H.027v to 3H.039
  - "3H.WWH Home," behind which to file the 13 words written by hand numbered 3H.040v to 3H.052

Work/School Filing Box; 2–3 + 3H; 2–3 (2–3.076 to 2–3.150); **3H** (3H.001 to 3H.052)

As with the previous filing box, this filing box may be used in Parts 2 and 3 of the evaluation if the "Work/School" category is selected. The material should be filed as follows:

- Five blue dividers identified as follows and used to file the visual supports in this order:
  - "2–3.PHO Work/School," behind which to file the 15 photos numbered 2–3.076v to 2–3.090v
  - "2–3.PIC Work/School," behind which to file the 15 colour pictograms numbered 2–3.091v to 2–3.105v

- "2–3.BWP Work/School," behind which to file the 15 black-and-white pictograms numbered 2–3.106v to 2–3.120v
- "2–3.WTC Work/School," behind which to file the 15 words typed on the computer numbered 2–3.121v to 2–3.135v
- "2–3.WWH Work/School," behind which to file the 15 words written by hand numbered 2–3.136v to 2–3.150v
- Four yellow dividers identified as follows and used to file the visual supports in this order:
  - "3H.PHO/3H.PIC Work/School," behind which to file the 13 colour pictograms numbered 3H.001v to 3H.013
  - "3H.BWP Work/School," behind which to file the 13 black-and-white pictograms numbered 3H.014v to 3H.026
  - "3H.WTC Work/School," behind which to file the 13 words typed on the computer numbered 3H.027v to 3H.039
  - "3H.WWH Work/School," behind which to file the 13 words written by hand numbered 3H.040v to 3H.052

Other Filing Box; 2–3 + 3H; 2–3 (2–3.151 to 2–3.225); 3H (3H.001 to 3H.052)

As with the previous filing box, this filing box may be used in Parts 2 and 3 of the evaluation if the "Other" category is selected. The material should be filed as follows:

- Five blue dividers identified as follows and used to file the visual supports in this order:
  - "2–3.PHO Other," behind which to file the 15 photos numbered 2–3.151v to 2–3.165v
  - "2–3.PIC Other," behind which to file the 15 colour pictograms numbered 2–3.166v to 2–3.180v
  - "2–3.BWP Other," behind which to file the 15 black-and-white pictograms numbered 2–3.181v to 2–3.195v
  - "2–3.WTC Other," behind which to file the 15 words typed on the computer numbered 2–3.196v to 2–3.210v
  - "2–3.WWH Other" behind which to file the 15 words written by hand numbered 2–3.211v to 2–3.225v
- Four yellow dividers identified as follows and used to file the visual supports in this order:
  - "3H.PHO/3H.PIC Other," behind which to file the 13 colour pictograms numbered 3H.001v to 3H.013
  - "3H.BWP Other," behind which to file the 13 black-and-white pictograms numbered 3H.014v to 3H.026

- "3H.WTC Other," behind which to file the 13 words typed on the computer numbered 3H.027v to 3H.039
- "3H.WWH Other," behind which to file the 13 words written by hand numbered 3H.040v to 3H.052

Assemble the Examiner's Tray

During Parts 2 and 3 of the evaluation, the user moves around in a chosen setting matching the different visual supports. Using the examiner's tray is recommended as it will facilitate scoring. The tray can be assembled using a 16 x 12 x 4.5 in. basket identified with the "Examiner's tray" label. Insert the small 10 x 3.25 x 2.5 in. basket into the large basket. Then insert the small square 3 x 3 x 2 in. basket into the latter and secure it in place using the Velcro. The Schedule Evaluation Protocol should be placed into the basket.

The examiner's tray is used to hold the Schedule Evaluation Protocol, the reinforcers, and the visual supports and schedule cues needed for the part, section, or subsection being evaluated (see Figure 15).

After the evaluation, the examiner may need to dismantle the examiner's tray as there may not be enough storage room in the SET kit plastic bin.

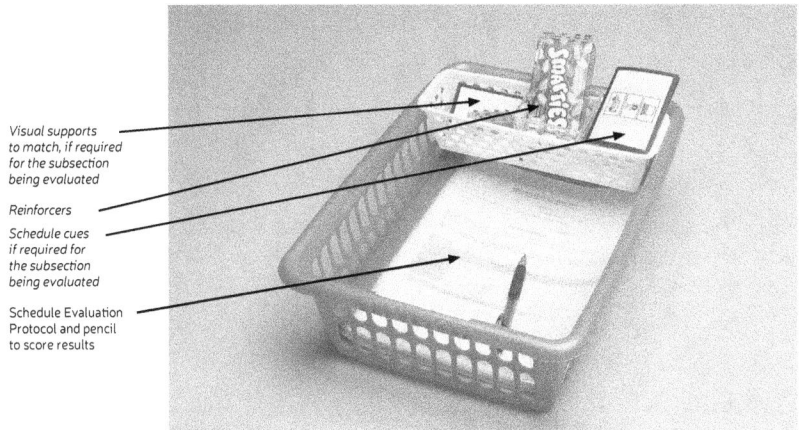

Figure 15. Assembled examiner's tray.

Source: Artimage 2015.

Assemble the 36 Schedule Sheets

Photocopy the Token Schedule and Checkmark Schedule sheets found in Appendix 2. To properly identify them, make two-sided copies on a letter-size paper (8.5 x 11 in.). Then laminate each sheet and stick a small strip of Velcro (loop) on the small rectangle where indicated. These sheets will be used in Part 3 of the evaluation. They should be kept in a large plastic 16 x 20 in. sleeve identified with the "Token and Checkmark Schedule Sheets" label.

Identify and Assemble the Rest of the Material

Stick the "Schedule Cue Box" label on the last corrugated white 8 x 4 x 4 in. cardboard box (see Figure 1). Stick a strip of Velcro (loop) on the top front of the box so that a visual support can be mounted there during Part 3A of the evaluation (see Figure 16a). Also stick a strip of Velcro (hook) of about 4 in. on the central panel on the back of the box so that you can stick the box to the yellow schedule strip during Part 2 of the evaluation (see Figure 16b).

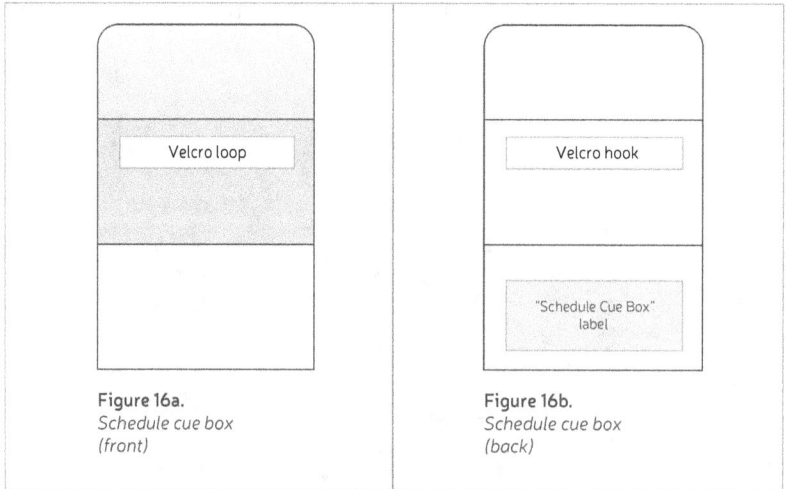

Figure 16a.
Schedule cue box (front)

Figure 16b.
Schedule cue box (back)

Figure 16. Schedule cue box.

Source: Artimage 2015

Stick the "3B: Basket for Objects" labels on the three plastic 10 x 6.5 x 2.5 in. baskets.

Stick the "Token Box" label on the Glad-style container with plastic lid (with a one fluid cup capacity); this container will be used to store the 12 cardboard tokens or bingo chips.

Stick a strip of Velcro (hook) on the piggy bank (or on the back of the small plastic container, so that the opening is at the top when it is mounted on the schedule strip), and on the back of the 12 poker chips.

Last, stick the remaining "SET Kit" label on the large 22 x 18 x 14 in. (21-litre) plastic bin. This bin will be used to store all the material in the SET kit once the evaluation is finished.

SCHEDULE EVALUATION TOOL

Johanne Mainville, Sonia Di Lillo,
Nathalie Poirier, and Nathalie Plante

APPENDIX 2
TOKEN SCHEDULE AND CHECKMARK SCHEDULE SHEETS

Instructions

Photocopy all schedule sheets on both sides of a letter-size (8.5 × 11 in.) sheet of paper.

Appendix 2: Token Schedule and Checkmark Schedule Sheets   B117

3B.1: DEMOS

HOME CATEGORY

TYPE OF SCHEDULE EVALUATED
TOKEN SCHEDULE

VISUAL SUPPORT FORM EVALUATED
WTC

THIS SCHEDULE BELONGS TO:

Toothbrush [VELCRO]

Sock [VELCRO]

Lego [VELCRO]

Appendix 2: Token Schedule and Checkmark Schedule Sheets   B119

3B.1: 3 ATTEMPTS

HOME CATEGORY

TYPE OF SCHEDULE EVALUATED
TOKEN SCHEDULE

VISUAL SUPPORT FORM EVALUATED
WTC

THIS SCHEDULE BELONGS TO:

Lego

[VELCRO]

Sock

[VELCRO]

Toothbrush

[VELCRO]

3B.2: 6 ATTEMPTS

HOME CATEGORY

TYPE OF SCHEDULE EVALUATED
TOKEN SCHEDULE

VISUAL SUPPORT FORM EVALUATED
WTC

THIS SCHEDULE BELONGS TO:

Sock   `VELCRO`

Lego   `VELCRO`

Toothbrush   `VELCRO`

Lego   `VELCRO`

Toothbrush   `VELCRO`

Sock   `VELCRO`

3B.1: DEMOS

HOME CATEGORY

TYPE OF SCHEDULE EVALUATED
TOKEN SCHEDULE

VISUAL SUPPORT FORM EVALUATED
WWH

THIS SCHEDULE BELONGS TO:

Toothbrush　　　　　　　VELCRO

Sock　　　　　　　VELCRO

Lego　　　　　　　VELCRO

3B.1: 3 ATTEMPTS

HOME CATEGORY

TYPE OF SCHEDULE EVALUATED
TOKEN SCHEDULE

VISUAL SUPPORT FORM EVALUATED
WWH

THIS SCHEDULE BELONGS TO:

Lego   [VELCRO]

Sock   [VELCRO]

Toothbrush   [VELCRO]

3B.2: 6 ATTEMPTS

HOME CATEGORY

TYPE OF SCHEDULE EVALUATED
TOKEN SCHEDULE

VISUAL SUPPORT FORM EVALUATED
WWH

THIS SCHEDULE BELONGS TO:

Sock   [VELCRO]

Lego   [VELCRO]

Toothbrush   [VELCRO]

Lego   [VELCRO]

Toothbrush   [VELCRO]

Sock   [VELCRO]

3B.1: DEMOS

WORK/SCHOOL CATEGORY

TYPE OF SCHEDULE EVALUATED
TOKEN SCHEDULE

VISUAL SUPPORT FORM EVALUATED
WTC

THIS SCHEDULE BELONGS TO:

Spoon `VELCRO`

Pencil `VELCRO`

Disc `VELCRO`

3B.1: 3 ATTEMPTS

WORK/SCHOOL CATEGORY

TYPE OF SCHEDULE EVALUATED
TOKEN SCHEDULE

VISUAL SUPPORT FORM EVALUATED
WTC

THIS SCHEDULE BELONGS TO:

Disc   [VELCRO]

Pencil   [VELCRO]

Spoon   [VELCRO]

3B.2: 6 ATTEMPTS

WORK/SCHOOL CATEGORY

TYPE OF SCHEDULE EVALUATED
TOKEN SCHEDULE

VISUAL SUPPORT FORM EVALUATED
WTC

THIS SCHEDULE BELONGS TO:

# Pencil	`VELCRO`

# Disc	`VELCRO`

# Spoon	`VELCRO`

# Disc	`VELCRO`

# Spoon	`VELCRO`

# Pencil	`VELCRO`

3B.1: DEMOS

WORK/SCHOOL CATEGORY

TYPE OF SCHEDULE EVALUATED
TOKEN SCHEDULE

VISUAL SUPPORT FORM EVALUATED
WWH

THIS SCHEDULE BELONGS TO:

Spoon   [VELCRO]

Pencil   [VELCRO]

Disc   [VELCRO]

3B.1: 3 ATTEMPTS

WORK/SCHOOL CATEGORY

TYPE OF SCHEDULE EVALUATED
TOKEN SCHEDULE

VISUAL SUPPORT FORM EVALUATED
WWH

THIS SCHEDULE BELONGS TO:

Disc   [VELCRO]

Pencil   [VELCRO]

Spoon   [VELCRO]

3B.2: 6 ATTEMPTS

WORK/SCHOOL CATEGORY

TYPE OF SCHEDULE EVALUATED
TOKEN SCHEDULE

VISUAL SUPPORT FORM EVALUATED
WWH

THIS SCHEDULE BELONGS TO:

Pencil · VELCRO

Disc · VELCRO

Spoon · VELCRO

Disc · VELCRO

Spoon · VELCRO

Pencil · VELCRO

3B.1: DEMOS

OTHER CATEGORY

TYPE OF SCHEDULE EVALUATED
TOKEN SCHEDULE

VISUAL SUPPORT FORM EVALUATED
WTC

THIS SCHEDULE BELONGS TO:

Ball
`VELCRO`

Marker
`VELCRO`

Sponge
`VELCRO`

3B.1: 3 ATTEMPTS

OTHER CATEGORY

TYPE OF SCHEDULE EVALUATED
TOKEN SCHEDULE

VISUAL SUPPORT FORM EVALUATED
WTC

THIS SCHEDULE BELONGS TO:

Sponge   [VELCRO]

Marker   [VELCRO]

Ball   [VELCRO]

3B.2: 6 ATTEMPTS

OTHER CATEGORY

TYPE OF SCHEDULE EVALUATED
TOKEN SCHEDULE

VISUAL SUPPORT FORM EVALUATED
WTC

THIS SCHEDULE BELONGS TO:

Marker [VELCRO]

Sponge [VELCRO]

Ball [VELCRO]

Sponge [VELCRO]

Ball [VELCRO]

Marker [VELCRO]

3B.1: DEMOS

OTHER CATEGORY

TYPE OF SCHEDULE EVALUATED
TOKEN SCHEDULE

VISUAL SUPPORT FORM EVALUATED
WWH

THIS SCHEDULE BELONGS TO:

Ball [VELCRO]

Marker [VELCRO]

Sponge [VELCRO]

3B.1: 3 ATTEMPTS

OTHER CATEGORY

TYPE OF SCHEDULE EVALUATED
TOKEN SCHEDULE

VISUAL SUPPORT FORM EVALUATED
WWH

THIS SCHEDULE BELONGS TO:

Sponge   [VELCRO]

Marker   [VELCRO]

Ball   [VELCRO]

3B.2: 6 ATTEMPTS

OTHER CATEGORY

TYPE OF SCHEDULE EVALUATED
TOKEN SCHEDULE

VISUAL SUPPORT FORM EVALUATED
WWH

THIS SCHEDULE BELONGS TO:

Marker — VELCRO

Sponge — VELCRO

Ball — VELCRO

Sponge — VELCRO

Ball — VELCRO

Marker — VELCRO

3B.1: DEMOS

HOME CATEGORY

TYPE OF SCHEDULE EVALUATED
CHECKMARK SCHEDULE

VISUAL SUPPORT FORM EVALUATED
WTC

THIS SCHEDULE BELONGS TO:

Toothbrush ◯

Sock ◯

Lego ◯

Appendix 2: Token Schedule and Checkmark Schedule Sheets   B155

3B.1: 3 ATTEMPTS

HOME CATEGORY

TYPE OF SCHEDULE EVALUATED
CHECKMARK SCHEDULE

VISUAL SUPPORT FORM EVALUATED
WTC

THIS SCHEDULE BELONGS TO:

Lego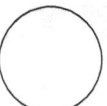

Sock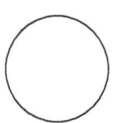

Toothbrush   ◯

Appendix 2: Token Schedule and Checkmark Schedule Sheets   B157

3B.2: 6 ATTEMPTS

HOME CATEGORY

TYPE OF SCHEDULE EVALUATED

CHECKMARK SCHEDULE

VISUAL SUPPORT FORM EVALUATED

WTC

THIS SCHEDULE BELONGS TO:

Sock ◯

Lego ◯

Toothbrush ◯

Lego ◯

Toothbrush ◯

Sock ◯

3B.1: DEMOS

HOME CATEGORY

TYPE OF SCHEDULE EVALUATED
CHECKMARK SCHEDULE

VISUAL SUPPORT FORM EVALUATED
WWH

THIS SCHEDULE BELONGS TO:

Toothbrush ○

Sock ○

Lego ○

3B.1: 3 ATTEMPTS

HOME CATEGORY

TYPE OF SCHEDULE EVALUATED
CHECKMARK SCHEDULE

VISUAL SUPPORT FORM EVALUATED
WWH

THIS SCHEDULE BELONGS TO:

Lego ○

Sock ○

Toothbrush ○

3B.2: 6 ATTEMPTS

HOME CATEGORY

TYPE OF SCHEDULE EVALUATED
CHECKMARK SCHEDULE

VISUAL SUPPORT FORM EVALUATED
WWH

THIS SCHEDULE BELONGS TO:

Sock ○

Lego ○

Toothbrush ○

Lego ○

Toothbrush ○

Sock ○

3B.1: DEMOS

WORK/SCHOOL CATEGORY

TYPE OF SCHEDULE EVALUATED

CHECKMARK SCHEDULE

VISUAL SUPPORT FORM EVALUATED

WTC

THIS SCHEDULE BELONGS TO:

Spoon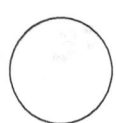

Pencil

Disc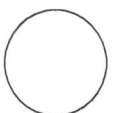

3B.1: 3 ATTEMPTS

WORK/SCHOOL CATEGORY

TYPE OF SCHEDULE EVALUATED

CHECKMARK SCHEDULE

VISUAL SUPPORT FORM EVALUATED

WTC

THIS SCHEDULE BELONGS TO:

Disc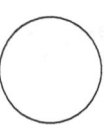

Pencil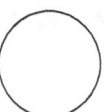

Spoon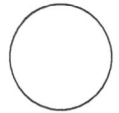

3B.2: 6 ATTEMPTS

WORK/SCHOOL CATEGORY

TYPE OF SCHEDULE EVALUATED
CHECKMARK SCHEDULE

VISUAL SUPPORT FORM EVALUATED
WTC

THIS SCHEDULE BELONGS TO:

Pencil ○

Disc ○

Spoon ○

Disc ○

Spoon ○

Pencil ○

3B.1: DEMOS

WORK/SCHOOL CATEGORY

TYPE OF SCHEDULE EVALUATED
CHECKMARK SCHEDULE

VISUAL SUPPORT FORM EVALUATED
WWH

THIS SCHEDULE BELONGS TO:

Spoon ◯

Pencil ◯

Disc ◯

3B.1: 3 ATTEMPTS

WORK/SCHOOL CATEGORY

TYPE OF SCHEDULE EVALUATED
CHECKMARK SCHEDULE

VISUAL SUPPORT FORM EVALUATED
WWH

THIS SCHEDULE BELONGS TO:

Disc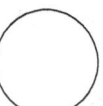

Pencil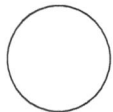

Spoon ◯

3B.2: 6 ATTEMPTS

WORK/SCHOOL CATEGORY

TYPE OF SCHEDULE EVALUATED
CHECKMARK SCHEDULE

VISUAL SUPPORT FORM EVALUATED
WWH

THIS SCHEDULE BELONGS TO:

Pencil ○

Disc ○

Spoon ○

Disc ○

Spoon ○

Pencil ○

3B.1: DEMOS

OTHER CATEGORY

TYPE OF SCHEDULE EVALUATED
CHECKMARK SCHEDULE

VISUAL SUPPORT FORM EVALUATED
WTC

THIS SCHEDULE BELONGS TO:

Ball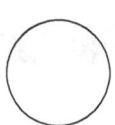

Marker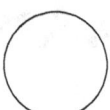

Sponge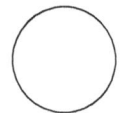

3B.1: 3 ATTEMPTS

OTHER CATEGORY

TYPE OF SCHEDULE EVALUATED
CHECKMARK SCHEDULE

VISUAL SUPPORT FORM EVALUATED
WTC

THIS SCHEDULE BELONGS TO:

Sponge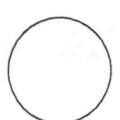

Marker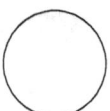

Ball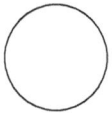

3B.2: 6 ATTEMPTS

OTHER CATEGORY

TYPE OF SCHEDULE EVALUATED
CHECKMARK SCHEDULE

VISUAL SUPPORT FORM EVALUATED
WTC

THIS SCHEDULE BELONGS TO:

Marker ○

Sponge ○

Ball ○

Sponge ○

Ball ○

Marker ○

3B.1: DEMOS

OTHER CATEGORY

TYPE OF SCHEDULE EVALUATED
CHECKMARK SCHEDULE

VISUAL SUPPORT FORM EVALUATED
WWH

THIS SCHEDULE BELONGS TO:

Ball ◯

Marker ◯

Sponge ◯

Appendix 2: Token Schedule and Checkmark Schedule Sheets   B185

3B.1: 3 ATTEMPTS

OTHER CATEGORY

TYPE OF SCHEDULE EVALUATED
CHECKMARK SCHEDULE

VISUAL SUPPORT FORM EVALUATED
WWH

THIS SCHEDULE BELONGS TO:

Sponge ○

Marker ○

Ball ○

3B.2: 6 ATTEMPTS

OTHER CATEGORY

TYPE OF SCHEDULE EVALUATED
CHECKMARK SCHEDULE

VISUAL SUPPORT FORM EVALUATED
WWH

THIS SCHEDULE BELONGS TO:

Marker ○

Sponge ○

Ball ○

Sponge ○

Ball ○

Marker ○

Education

Series Editors: Nicholas Ng-A-Fook and Carole Fleuret

Our *Education* series seeks to advance thought-provoking research within the broader field of education. Scholarly works in this series examine educational research from a multidisciplinary perspective and address a variety of issues in the field, including curriculum studies, arts-based education, educational philosophy, life writing, foundations in education, teacher education, evaluation, and counselling.

Previous titles in the *Education* Series

Robert K. Crocker, *Religion and Schooling in Canada: The Long Road to Separation of Church and State*, 2022.

Timothy M. Sibbald and Victoria Handford, eds., *The Academic Sabbatical: A Voyage of Discovery*, 2022.

Joël Thibeault and Carole Fleuret, eds., *Didactique du français en contextes minoritaires : entre normes scolaires et plurilinguismes*, 2020.

Timothy M. Sibbald and Victoria Handford, eds., *Beyond the Academic Gateway: Looking Back on the Tenure-Track Journey*, 2020.

Anne M. Phelan, William F. Pinar, Nicholas Ng-A-Fook, and Ruth Kane, eds., *Reconceptualizing Teacher Education: A Canadian Contribution to a Global Challenge*, 2020.

Michelle Forrest and Linda Wheeldon, *Scripting Feminist Ethics in Teacher Education*, 2019.

William F. Pinar, *Moving Images of Eternity: George Grant's Critique of Time, Teaching, and Technology*, 2019.

Pierre Jean, *Planification de formations en santé : guide des bonnes pratiques*, 2019.

Thomas R. Klassen and John A. Dwyer, *Décrocher son diplôme (et l'emploi de ses rêves !) : comment maîtriser les compétences essentielles menant au succès à l'école, au travail et dans la vie*, 2018.

Timothy M. Sibbald and Victoria Handford, eds., *The Academic Gateway: Understanding the Journey to Tenure*, 2017.

Lise Gremion, Serge Ramel, Valérie Angelucci, and Jean-Claude Kalubi, eds., *Vers une école inclusive : regards croisés sur les défis actuels*, 2017.

For a complete list of the University of Ottawa Press titles, please visit:
www.press.uOttawa.ca

www.ingramcontent.com/pod-product-compliance
Lightning Source LLC
Chambersburg PA
CBHW052012290426
44112CB00014B/2207